W9-BAH-792

The Big Book of
SMALL HOUSE DESIGNS

The Big Book of
SMALL HOUSE DESIGNS

75 Award-Winning Plans for Houses 1,250 Square Feet or Less

From the Editors of Black Dog & Leventhal

BLACK DOG
& LEVENTHAL
PUBLISHERS
NEW YORK

Published by
Black Dog & Leventhal Publishers, Inc.
151 West 19th Street
New York, NY 10011

Distributed by
Workman Publishing Company
708 Broadway
New York, NY 10003

Portions of the material contained in this work were originally published by Storey Publishing LLC as:

Small House Designs edited by Kenneth R. Tremblay, Jr. , & Lawrence Von Bamford.
Copyright © 1997 by Kenneth R. Tremblay, Jr., and Lawrence Von Bamford

The Compact House Book edited by Don Metz.
Copyright © 1983 by Storey Communications, Inc. Second Edition 1988.

New Compact House Design edited by Don Metz. Copyright © 1991 by Storey Communications, Inc.

Dream Cottages by Catherine Tredway. Copyright © 2001 by Catherine Tredway.

Manufactured in The United States of America

Cover design by Sheila Hart Design
Interior design by Cindy Joy

Cover photograph courtesy Getty Images

ISBN: 1-57912-365-1

h g f e d c b a

Library of Congress Cataloging-in-Publication Data available on file.

Contents

Modern Scottish Manor House

English Suburb
1,050 gross square feet

The objective of this design is to create a strong house that incorporates both modern and traditional elements, and that introduces novelties where possible to maximize aesthetics and utility. The ideal occupants would desire an imaginative spatial layout, despite modest means.

The central design concept is a wall that spirals, evolving like a seashell forming an organic sequence of three spaces that repeats on the two upper levels.

Kitchen and bathroom services occupy the central core, which opens to form the dining room (ground floor), bedrooms (first and second floors), and finally the primary space—a double-height living room. The living room opens onto the garden terrace and is oriented for passive solar gain, with a curtain wall facing south. An insulated solid wall to the north minimizes heat loss.

Nigel A. Holloway

Perspective

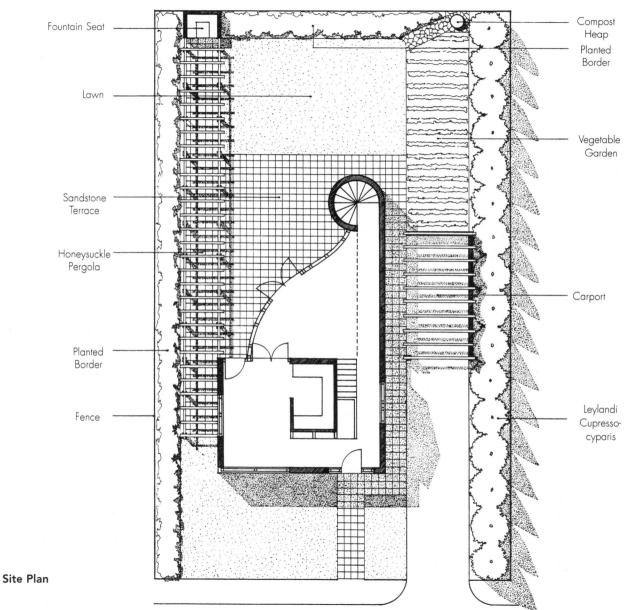

Fountain Seat

Lawn

Sandstone Terrace

Honeysuckle Pergola

Planted Border

Fence

Compost Heap

Planted Border

Vegetable Garden

Carport

Leylandi Cupresso-cyparis

Site Plan

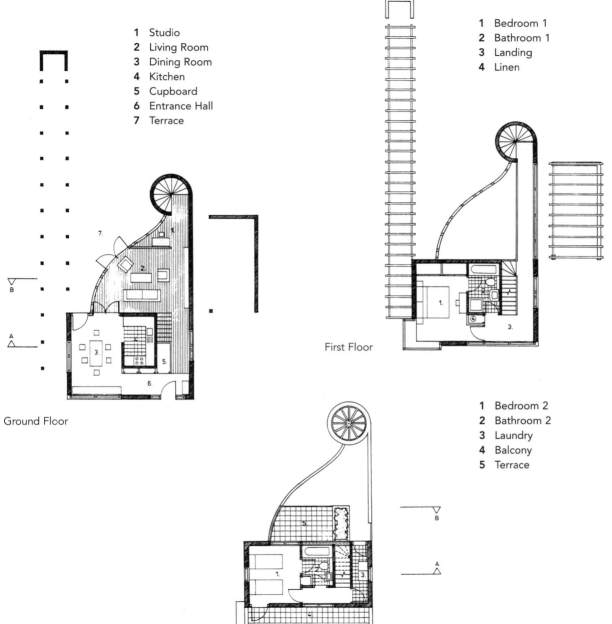

1 Studio
2 Living Room
3 Dining Room
4 Kitchen
5 Cupboard
6 Entrance Hall
7 Terrace

Ground Floor

1 Bedroom 1
2 Bathroom 1
3 Landing
4 Linen

First Floor

1 Bedroom 2
2 Bathroom 2
3 Laundry
4 Balcony
5 Terrace

Second Floor

Floor Plans

Modern Scottish Manor House

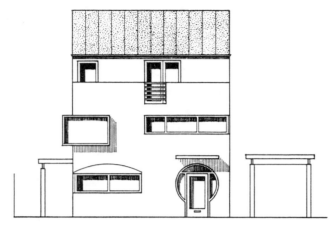

North

East

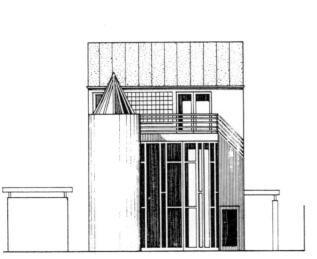

South

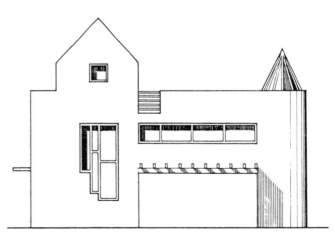

West

Elevations

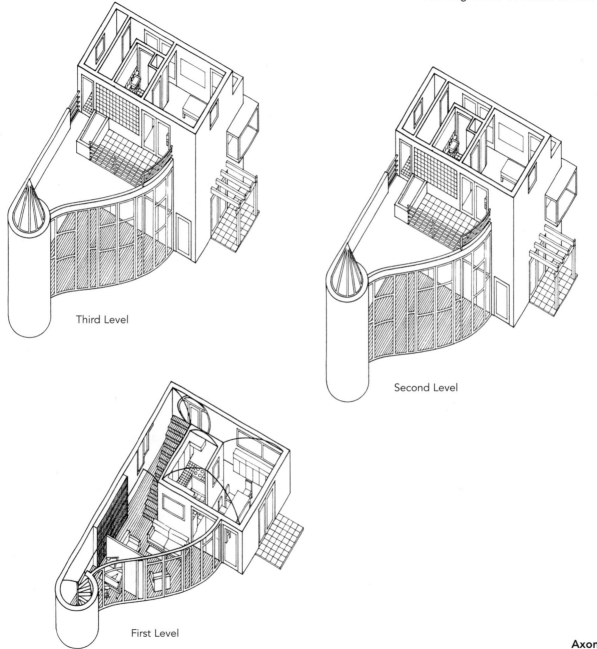

Third Level

Second Level

First Level

Axonometrics

Solar-Efficient Saltbox

Northampton, Massachusetts

1,230 gross square feet

Located in a Massachusetts college town, this two-story home nestles among old lilacs, maple and black walnut trees, and evergreens. The design effectively uses passive solar heating and cooling. To achieve maximum efficiency it features a southern orientation with a minimum fenestration on the north. In the winter, solar energy is collected directly through the two-story solarium and south windows. In the summer, deciduous trees on the south side interrupt the flow of solar energy before it strikes the ground, windows, and wall surfaces.

The first floor consists of public or shared areas. The second includes a master bedroom that enjoys a private deck, another bedroom that opens below to the solarium, and a full bathroom connected to laundry space. All living areas downstairs and the bedrooms upstairs share the south view.

Hasan Akkurt and Cigdem T. Akkurt

Perspective

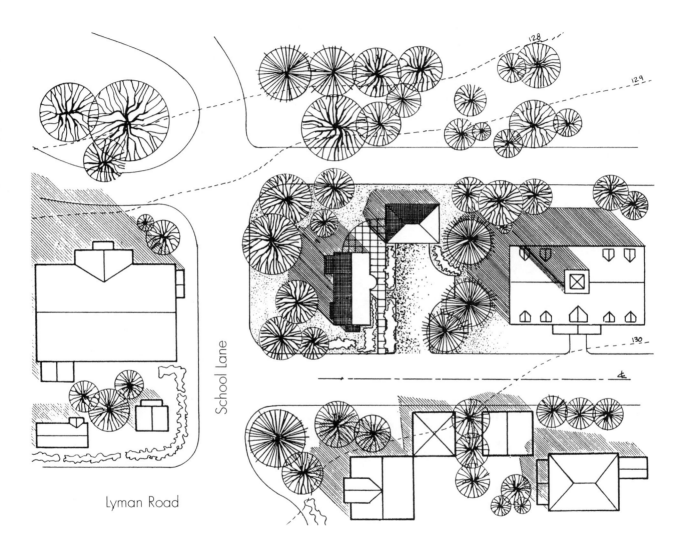

128

129

School Lane

130

Lyman Road

Site Plan

Solar-Efficient Saltbox

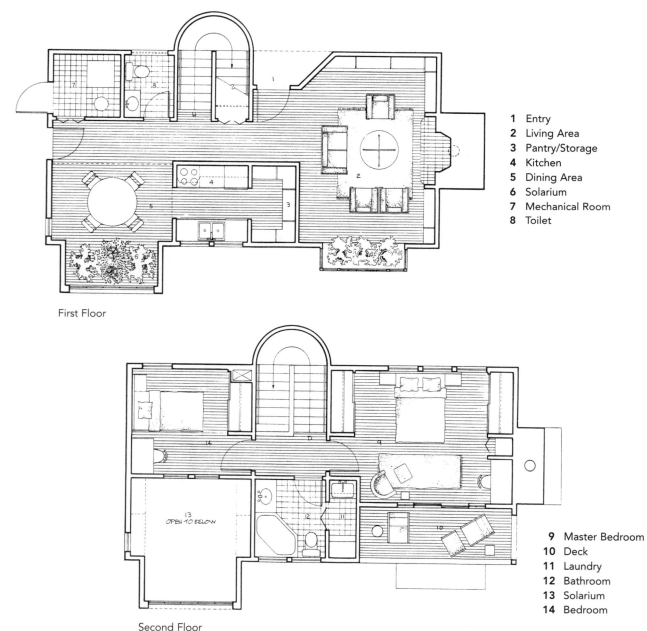

First Floor

1 Entry
2 Living Area
3 Pantry/Storage
4 Kitchen
5 Dining Area
6 Solarium
7 Mechanical Room
8 Toilet

Second Floor

9 Master Bedroom
10 Deck
11 Laundry
12 Bathroom
13 Solarium
14 Bedroom

Floor Plans

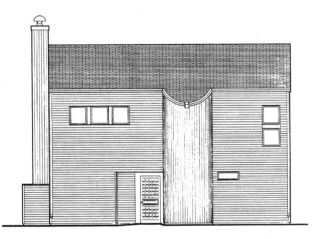

North

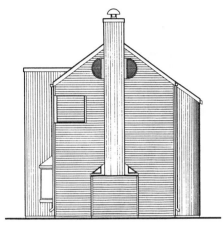

East

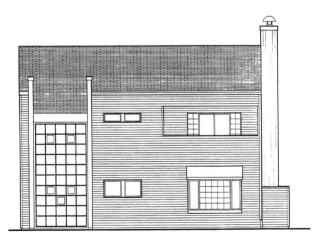

South

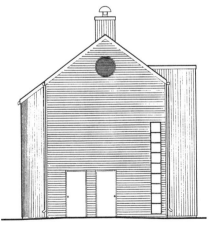

West

Elevations

Solar-Efficient Saltbox

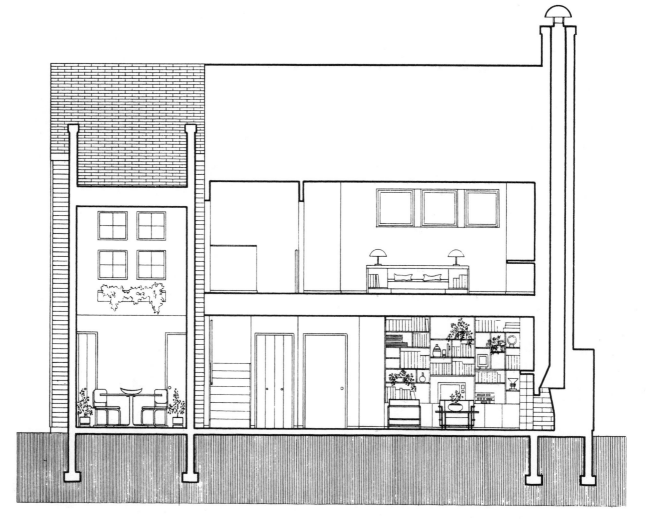

Cutaway

Friendly Neighborhood Home

Winston-Salem, North Carolina
1,230 gross square feet

We designed this affordable home as a prototype for the Northeast Winston Redevelopment Area in Winston-Salem, North Carolina. The area features small frame bungalows and clapboard farmhouse-style duplexes ranging from forty to seventy years old. The house and garage form components of an extended L-shaped plan. Depending on site conditions, the pieces can be rotated or reflected to provide different arrangements.

By balancing public and private zones, sun and shade, curb appeal, outdoor spaces that expand the rooms, and indoor-outdoor

circulation sequences, this design constitutes a thoughtful addition to the neighborhood fabric. Styled in a manner that appeals to prospective first-time home buyers, it relates well to neighboring houses and is conventionally constructed.

Reed M. Axelrod

Perspective

Locust Avenue

Twentieth Street

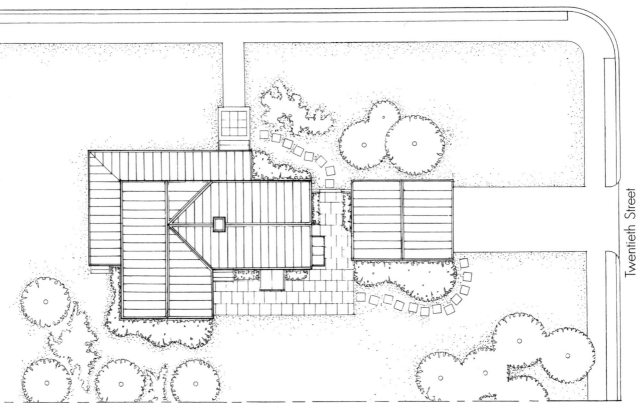

Site Plan

First Floor

1 Living Room
2 Dining Room
3 Stair to 2nd Floor
4 Stair to Basement
5 Kitchen
6 Bathroom
7 Covered Porch
8 Garage
9 Outdoor Terrace
   at Rear Yard

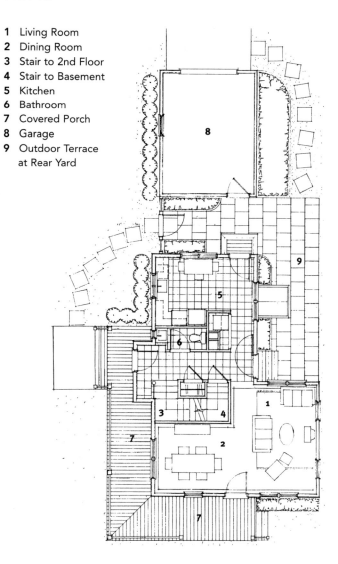

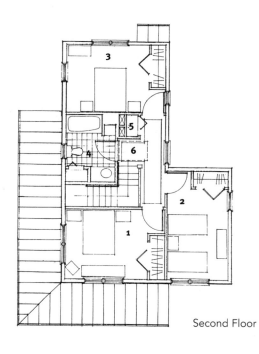

Second Floor

1 Master Bedroom
2 Bedroom 1
3 Bedroom 2 or Office
4 Bathroom
5 Linen Closet
6 Hallway

Floor Plans

West

South

North

East

Elevations

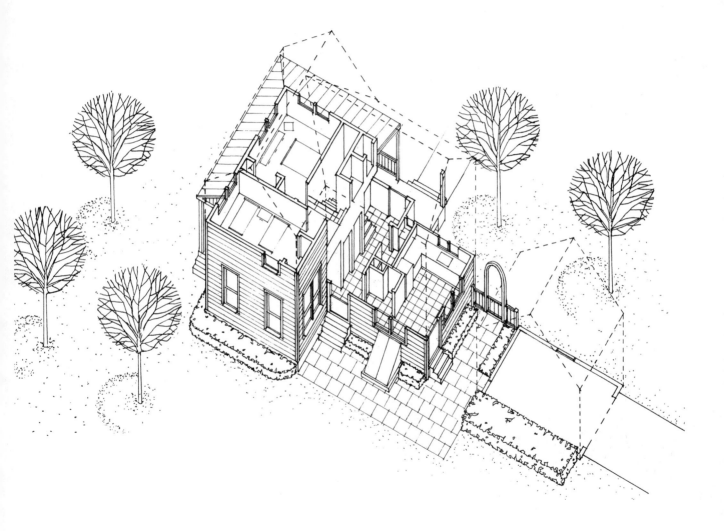

Axonometric

Cottage in the Woods

Snowy Regions of the U.S.
1,250 gross square feet

The cottage nestled deep in the woods recalls childhood fairy tales. This winter residence alludes to these images through the use of the steeply pitched roof, the wrap-around porch, and the projected bays.

The walls dematerialize in the main living space, allowing residents to feel as if they are sitting under a light canopy in the midst of the forest. The layering of the columns provides a constructed forest, as a foreground to the natural one beyond.

Employing the most efficient principles of mechanical systems, bathroom plumbing is stacked, the heating system is forced air, and the main duct runs in a plenum under the stairs to service each floor.

Christopher Blake

Perspective

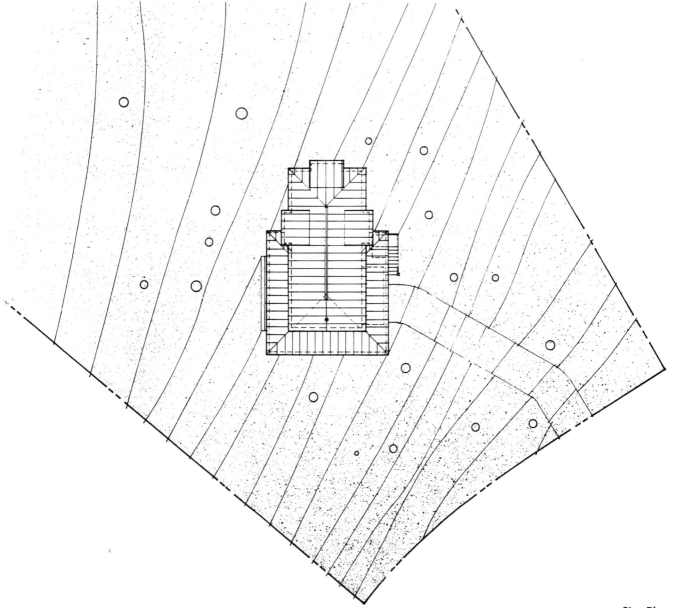

Site Plan

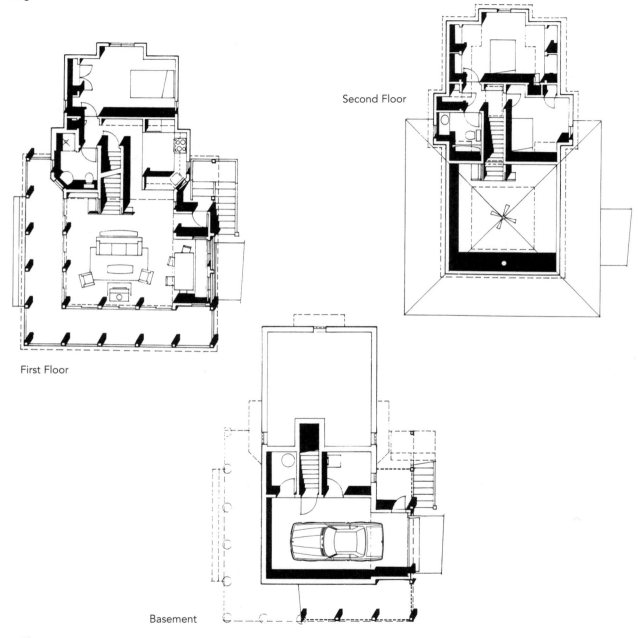

Second Floor

First Floor

Basement

Floor Plans

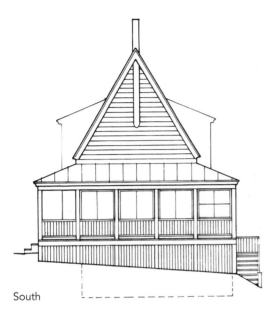

South

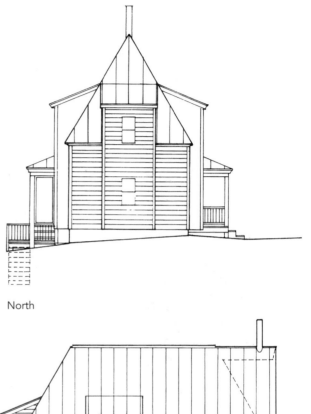

North

East

West

Elevations

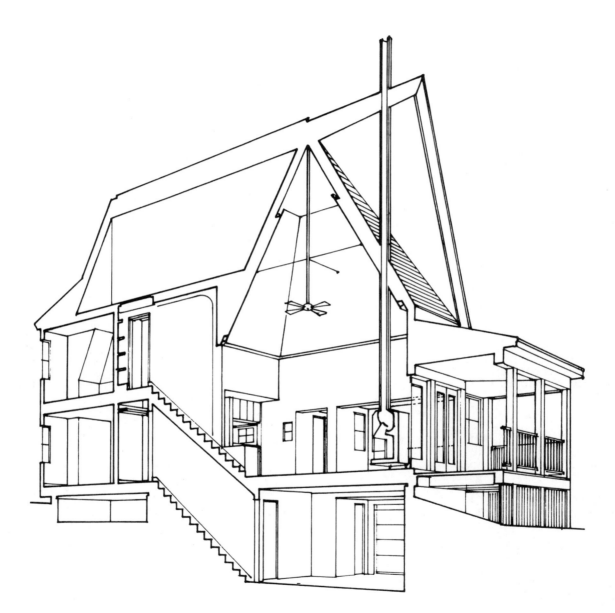

Section

Private Lakeside Retreat

Mascoma Lake, New Hampshire
995 gross square feet

The rectangular configuration and mostly blind side wall (west) allow for sitting on small lots (rural, suburban, or urban) while still maintaining privacy. The primary living space is barnlike (20 feet high), with a loft over the back portion, giving occupants both light and openness plus protection and shelter. The space can be occupied in many different ways, depending upon the season and the lifestyle of the occupants. The stairs perform a number of roles: bringing high, filtered light into the entry; acting as the hallway to the bathroom, separating it from both the private and public areas; and providing a pantry/washroom at the half-level below, near the kitchen.

William H. Boehm

Perspective

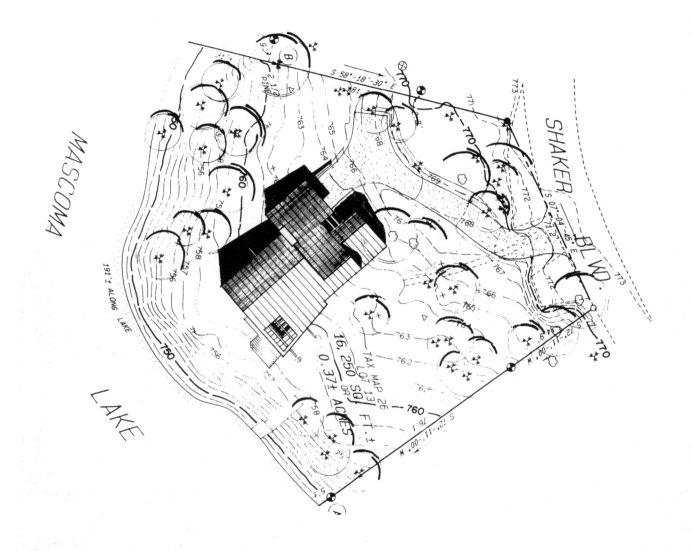

Site Plan

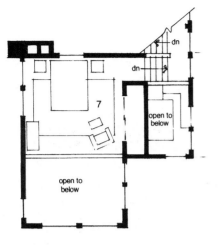

Loft

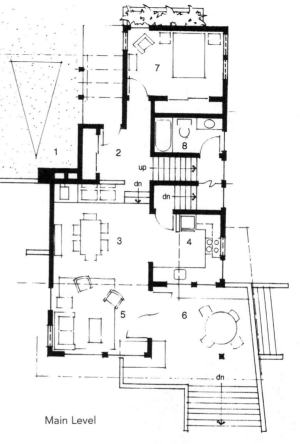

Main Level

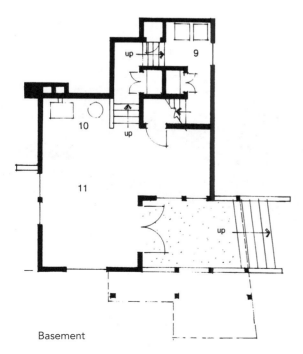

Basement

1 Carport
2 Entry
3 Dining
4 Kitchen
5 Living
6 Deck
7 Bedroom
8 Bathroom
9 Laundry
10 Mechanical
11 Basement

Floor Plans

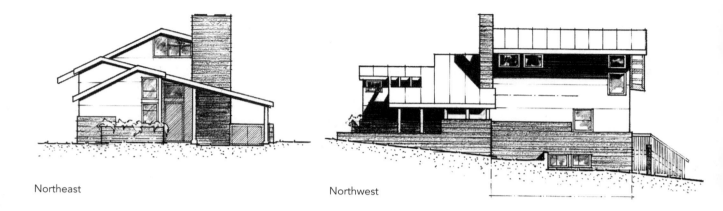

Northeast

Northwest

Southwest

Southeast

Elevations

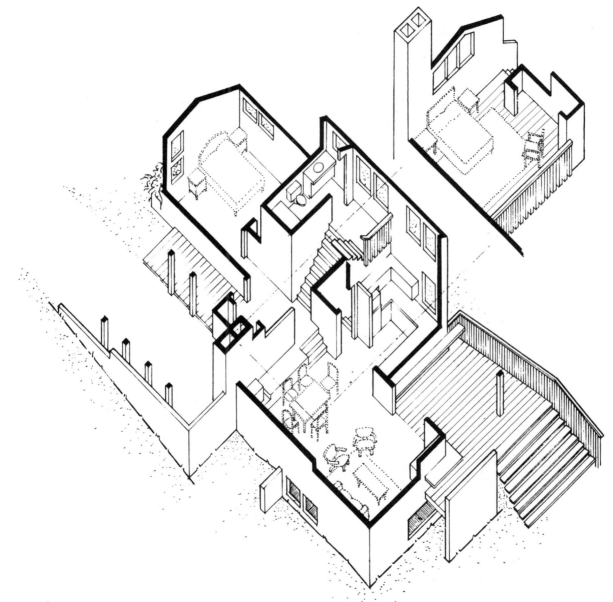

Axonometric

Evergreen Hide-Away

Wisconsin Dells, Wisconsin
1,200 gross square feet

The design concept for this home evolved after seeing a lakeside property, secluded and surrounded by rolling hills covered with tall evergreen trees, in Wisconsin.

A small entryway expands into a large open interior space. The home features a very open kitchen, dining room, and family room. Vaulted ceilings in the main area provide inhabitants a feeling of greater space.

The family room opens onto a deck area that overlooks the lake to the north. Windows on the south side have been limited to reduce solar heating of the interior.

A geothermal water pump provides heating and cooling as well as hot water. All rooms have ceiling fans and operable windows that allow for natural cooling at night. All appliances and fixtures are water efficient.

James M. Corkill

Perspective

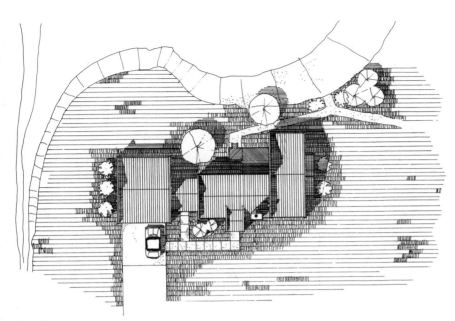

Site Plan

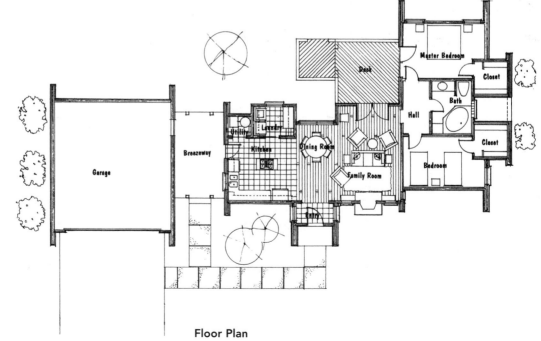

Floor Plan

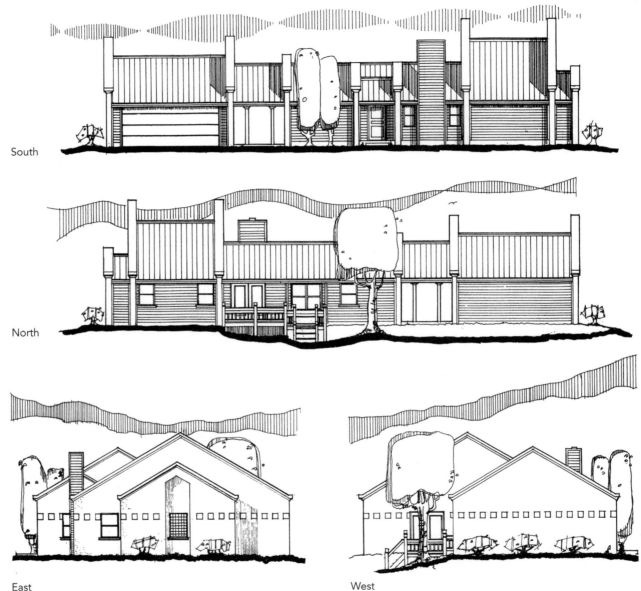

South

North

East

West

Elevations

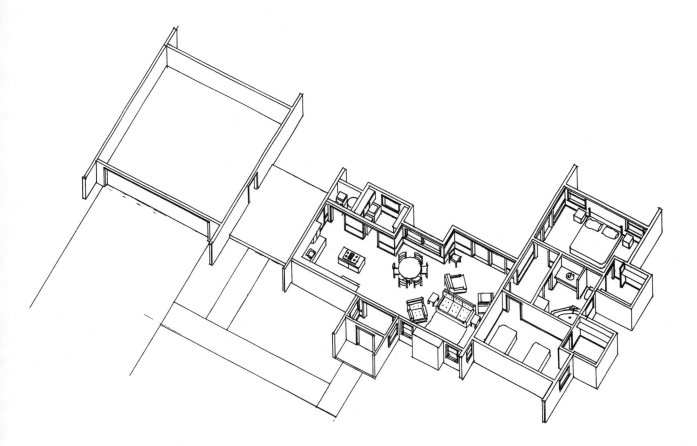

Axonometric

Solar Ranch

Northeast U.S.
1,000 gross square feet

The "Solar Ranch" brings relatively unobtrusive, high-performance, active solar heating and passive cooling to conventional suburban neighborhoods in an elevation-flexible, fundamental box. The design arises from an arrangement and rescaling of five 10-foot by 20-foot function-labeled modules. The resulting fundamental envelope configuration allows flexible solar positioning and a variety of floor plans and elevations.

Primary solar features include a Mylar "Space Blanket" vapor barrier (80 percent thermally reflective), a cooling tower, and a semiautomatic, active, liquid-convection solar heating system intended for areas with 4,000 to 8,000 heating degree days. This system is capable of building up a charge in excess of 10 million Btus.

Ten 320-square-foot wall-mounted collector boxes, containing approximately 2,000 feet of 1-inch low-emissivity/high-absorption coated copper tubing, are covered with single-pane low-E glass and use antifreeze as the medium. Heat storage employs a pressurized, insulated, 2,500-gallon coated concrete storage tank, installed vertically in the cellar below floor grade. Where a cellar is not feasible, a coated steel tank may be located horizontally in the garage.

Other solar heating components include (1) the delivery system: two-zone, thermostatically controlled, radiant floor coils, with a backup electric furnace and temperature-activated storage tank bypass; (2) the collector night shield: storage-tank-to-storage-tank collector bypass and one-way directional valves; and (3) domestic hot water heating: preheating of the cold water supply via a coil looped through a thermal storage tank, with a backup electric water heater.

James F. Finigan

Perspective

30

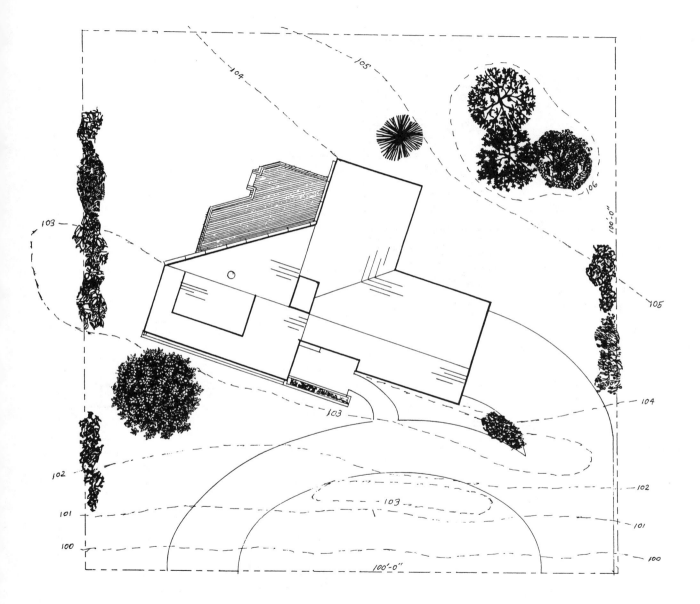

Site Plan

Solar Ranch

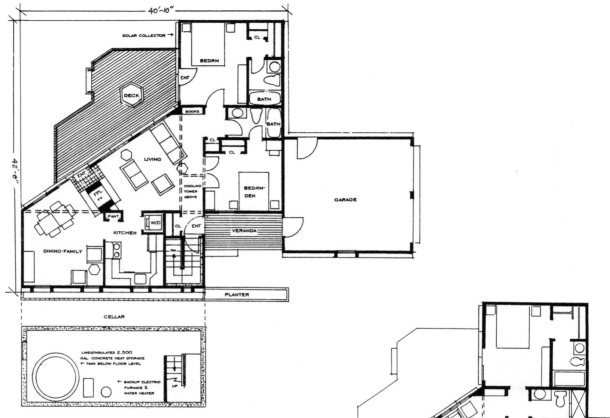

SOLAR COLLECTOR →

BEDRM

CL

ENT

BATH

BOOKS

BATH

DECK

CL

LIVING

CL

COOLING
TOWER
ABOVE

BEDRM-
DEN

GARAGE

FPL

EN

PANT

W/D

CL

ENT

KITCHEN

DN

VERANDA

DINING-FAMILY

UP

PLANTER

40'-10"

42'-0"

CELLAR

LINED/INSULATED 2,500
GAL. CONCRETE HEAT STORAGE
← TANK BELOW FLOOR LEVEL

← BACKUP ELECTRIC
FURNACE &
WATER HEATER

UP

Floor Plans

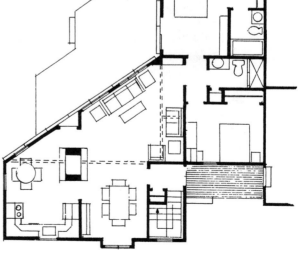

Alternate

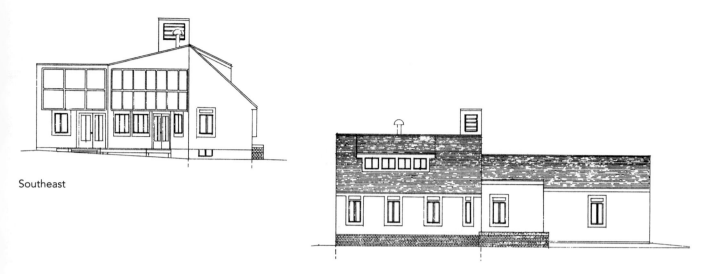

Southeast

Northeast

Southwest

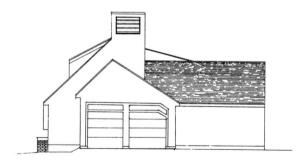

Northwest

Elevations

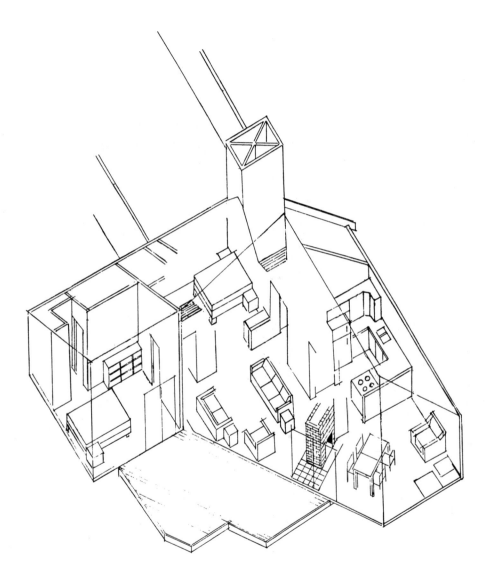

Axonometric

Abstract Farmhouse

Midwestern, U.S.
1,237 gross square feet

This is a Midwestern home in every sense, abstractly based on simple farmhouse plans of earlier times. The house is compact and efficient. Outdoor spaces are modest in size but integral to the overall scheme. The sloping site allows the basement level to provide additional living space, as a walk-out.

The primary design focus is a two-story volume, around which the remainder of the plan is organized. From an interior standpoint this creates a sense of spaciousness. From a practical standpoint it provides excellent natural ventilation with the use of an attic fan. The interior bal-cony also serves a dual role. It allows for spatial communication between the master bedroom and the living room, enhancing the natural ventilation, but also provides a needed sense of scale to the upper portion of the two-story space — scale that is conspicuously absent from most vaulted rooms in homes today.

Jeffrey Fleming

Perspective

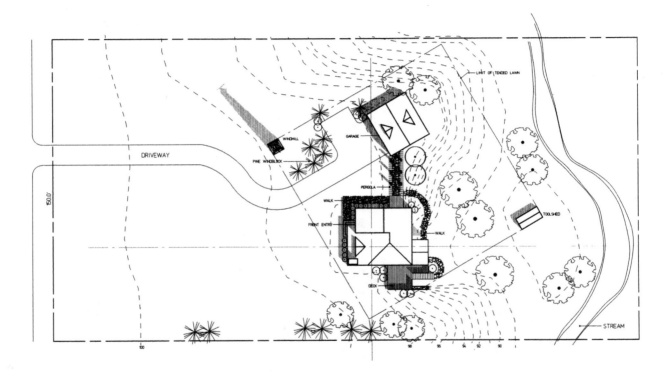

Site Plan

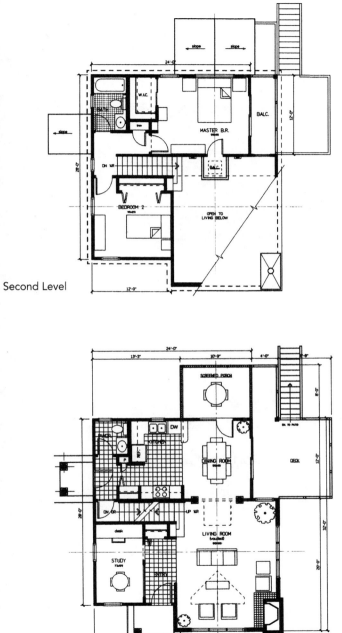

Second Level

First Level

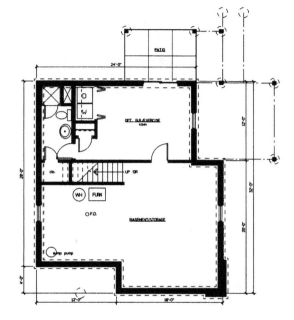

Foundation/Basement

Abstract Farmhouse

North

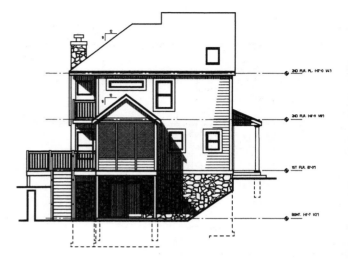

East

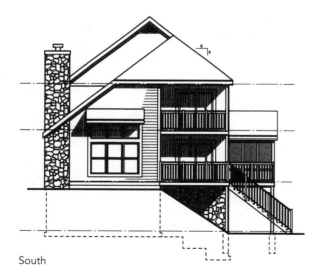

South

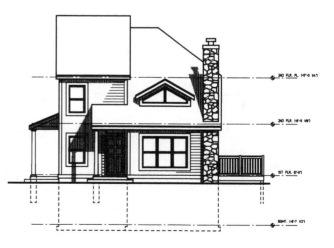

West

Elevations

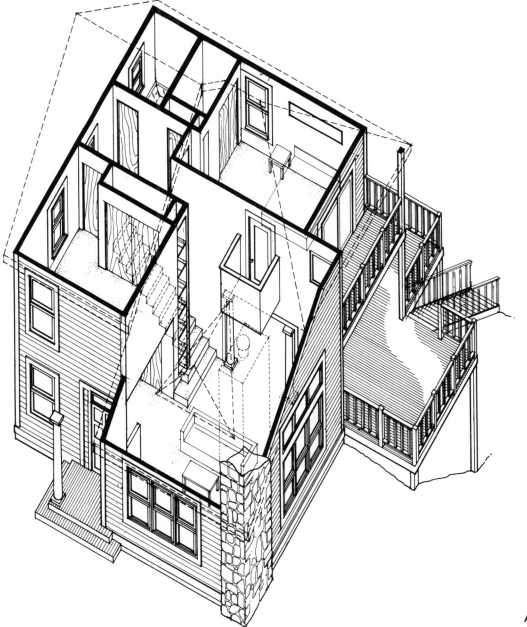

Axonometric

Rustic Retreat

British Columbia, Canada

1,250 gross square feet

This two-story design reflects the owners' desire for informal comfort, privacy, views, and a rusticity that blends with the natural environment.

A raised wooden deck wraps around the base of the house; a wide overhang on the south side protects it from sun and wind. Reached via covered stairway, the functionally compact entry expands immediately into a large two-and-a-half-story living space illuminated by a large east-facing window. The window adds visual dimension and view space as well as a feeling of integration with the forest.

Smaller dining and kitchen areas with adjacent service/storage space complete the simple, rectangular ground-floor plan. Accessible by stairway, a second-story bedroom wing and hallway overlook the informal living space, where an overhead fan aids air circulation.

Kenneth E. King

Perspective

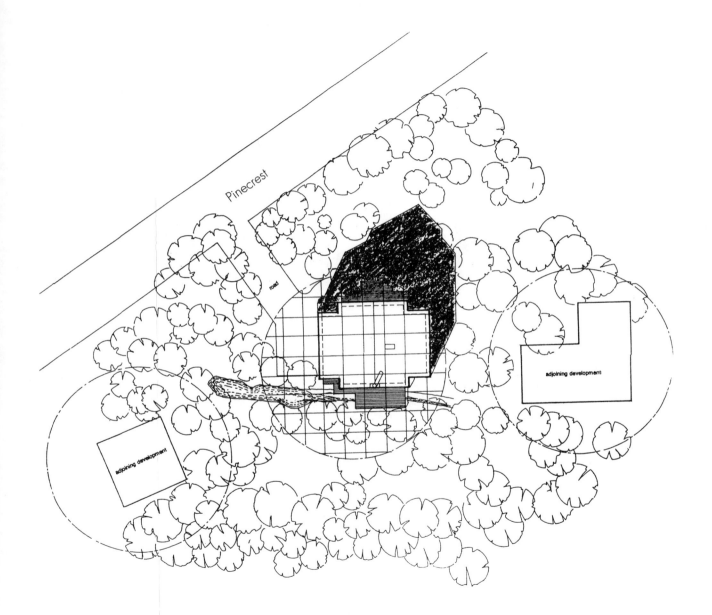

Pinecrest

road

adjoining development

adjoining development

Site Plan

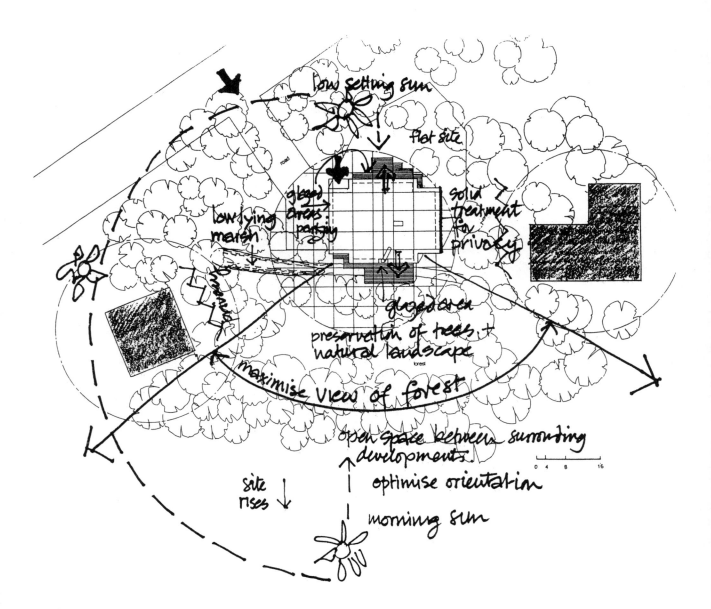

Site Influence Plan

1 Deck
2 Master Bedroom
3 Bathroom
4 Bedroom
5 Upper Volume of Living Room

Second Floor

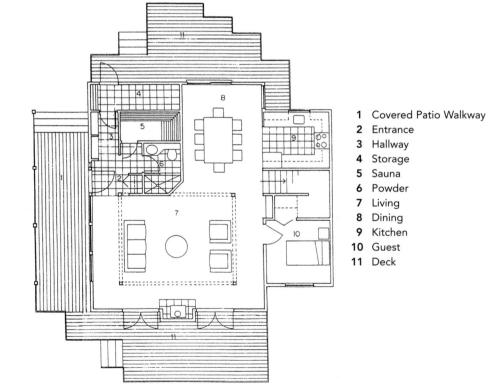

1 Covered Patio Walkway
2 Entrance
3 Hallway
4 Storage
5 Sauna
6 Powder
7 Living
8 Dining
9 Kitchen
10 Guest
11 Deck

Ground Floor

Floor Plans

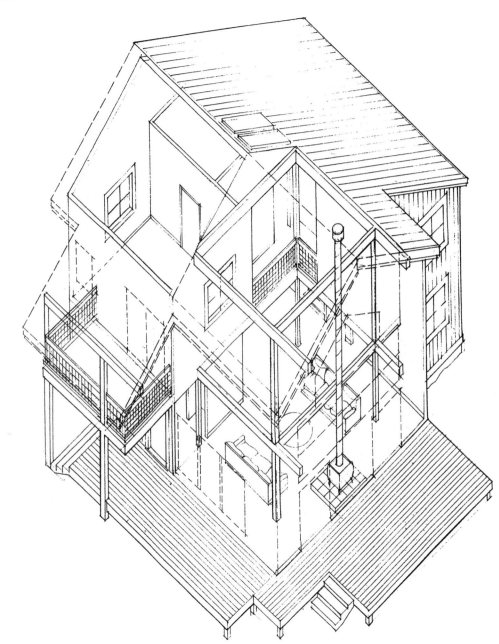

Axonometric

Sunshine Home

Southern Ontario, Canada
1,025 gross square feet

Located in southern Ontario and economical to construct, the house efficiently uses both space and energy. To provide richness in spatial expression and experience, the design lets the inhabitants wake up to, and perform most major activities with, the sun. Window seats, covered porch, open balconies, and decks offer variety.

The greenhouse/patio provides for indoor gardening and outdoor living space. With its 8-foot ceiling, the basement may be turned into a den/office or a bedroom (especially desirable if raised) or a walk-out basement. Landscaping on site promotes a variety of outdoor activities and experiences.

The design realizes energy savings through the southern orientation, the landscaping, the use of environmentally friendly and recyclable materials, and energy-efficient systems. Materials and components, including a combination natural gas furnace and heat-recovery ventilator, were chosen to achieve the lowest energy impact and costs. Energy-saving plumbing and electric fixtures further reduce waste. Thus the house is designed to reduce, reuse, and recycle.

Remus S. L. Tsang

Perspective

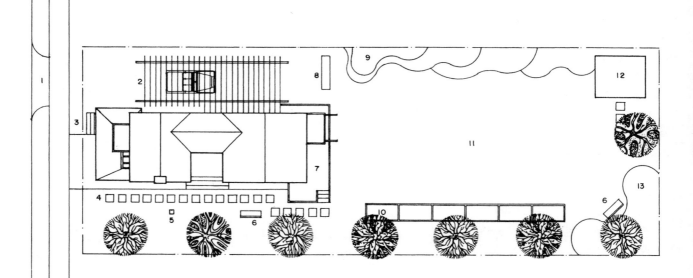

1 Driveway
2 Carport
3 Entry
4 Walkway
5 Sculpture
6 Bench
7 Deck
8 Storage
9 Rock Formation/Garden
10 Trellis Walk
11 Play Area
12 Hot Tub/Sauna
13 Landscaped Area

Site Plan

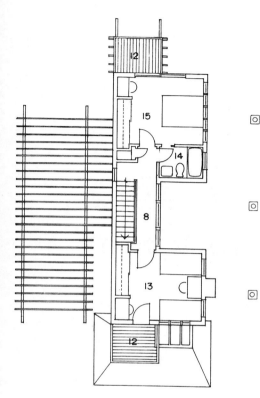

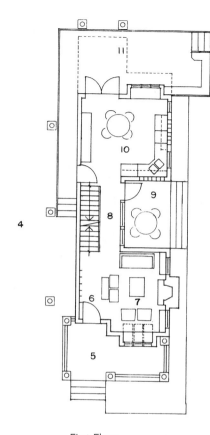

1 Future Washroom
2 Furnace
3 Recreation
4 Carport
5 Porch
6 Entry
7 Living
8 Passage
9 Greenhouse/Patio
10 Kitchen/Dining
11 Deck
12 Balcony
13 Bedroom
14 Washroom
15 Master Bedroom

Second Floor

First Floor

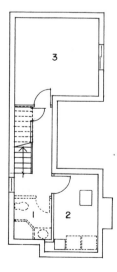

Basement

Floor Plans

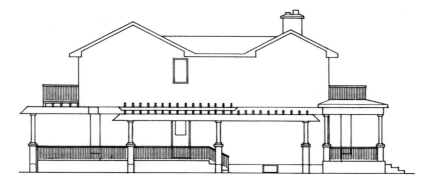

North

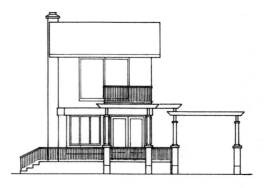

East

South

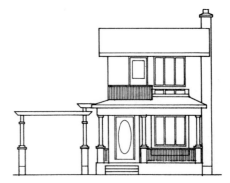

West

Elevations

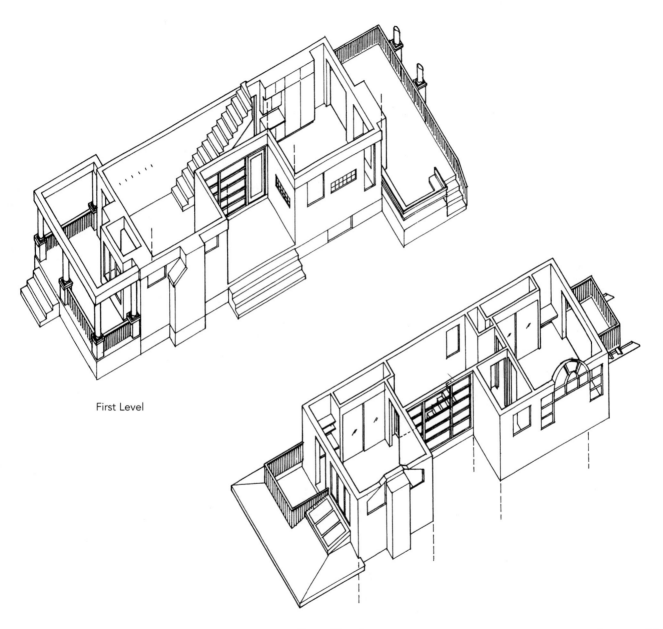

First Level

Second Level

Axonometrics

Metaphoric Ark

Vancouver, British Columbia, Canada
1,150 gross square feet

Built on a wooden deck (raft), this small house's clapboard/wood-panel walls contain a free-flowing open plan for the public space. A spiral staircase leads to the private rooms, which push up through the roof form, almost like a ship's bridge.

One enters the site through a pergola that accommodates vines and flowers. From this semi-interior space that leads through the forest and meadow, one steps onto the edge of the deck and enters the deep porch. This gradual transition between exterior and interior attempts to blur the distinction between the two.

The entryway, articulated as a glazed box with built-in window seat, reveals the four main views in varying degrees. Bay windows help to extend the spaces into the landscape. Built-in furniture pieces guide activities within the structure.

Clerestory windows provide ambient light as well as induce air convection. The fireplace and stack stand central in the plan and, with appropriate venting and the aid of a natural gas furnace, heat the entire house. The south wall with its large overhang not only frames the site's best view, but also exposes the house to natural breezes and the sun's radiant heating in winter months.

Andy Verhiel

Perspective

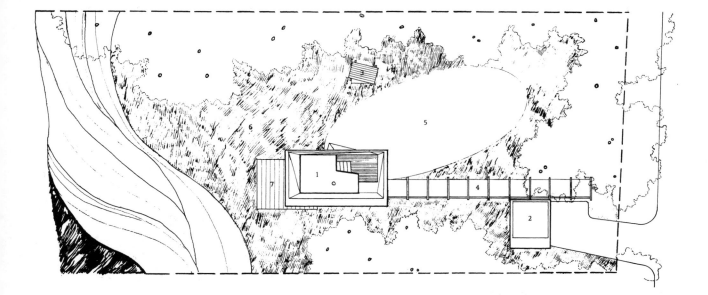

1 House
2 Garage
3 Gazebo
4 Pergola
5 Oval Green
6 Meadow Green
7 Wood Deck

Site Plan

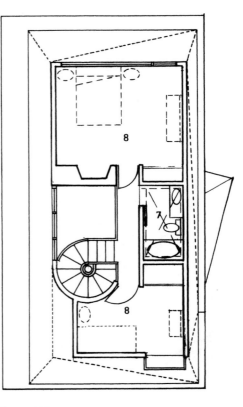

Second Floor

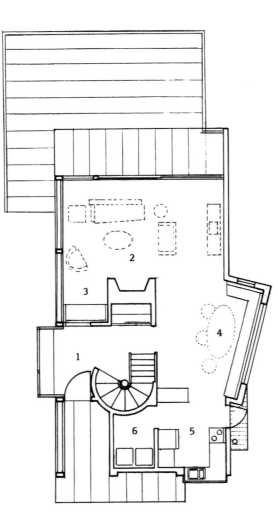

First Floor

1 Entry
2 Living Room
3 Reading Alcove
4 Dining Room
5 Kitchen
6 Laundry/Storage
7 Bathroom
8 Bedroom

Floor Plans

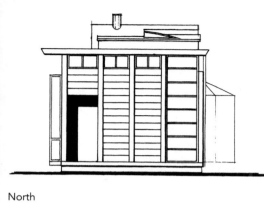

North

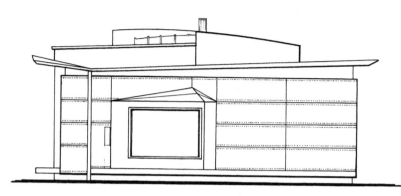

West

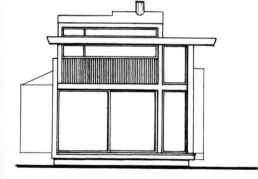

South

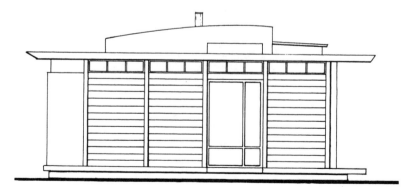

East

Elevations

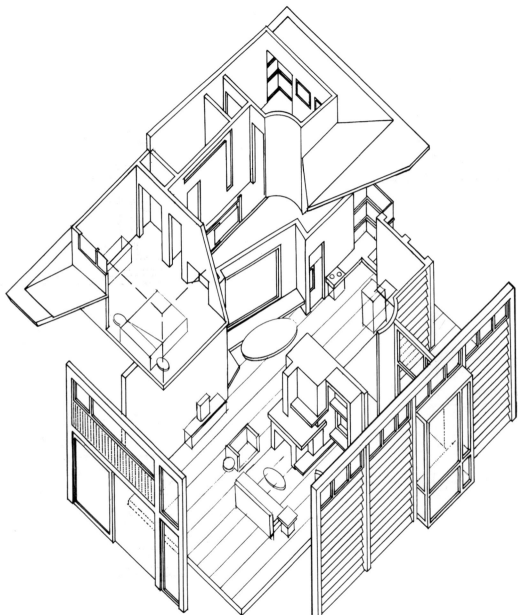

Axonometric

Simple, Adaptable Two Story

Vermont
1,152 gross square feet

The "Cape" house form described here is simple to build and very efficient. The design incorporates double use of spaces—both visually and physically. For example, the porch in summer is used as the carport in winter.

Energy-efficient design features include the airlock vestibule, passive solar in the central hall, and wood heat, which offers lower dependence on nonrenewable energy resources. A masonry stove with glass doors has switchbacks built into the flues, which turn the mass of chimney into a radiant heat storage system in the central hall (backup with gas burner in firebox). An optional decorative stove or fireplace can be added to the master bedroom.

Expanded spaces include the two-story living room and the kitchen counter area with pass-through to the dining area. A stacked washer/dryer located in the second-floor bath is close to the source of laundry. The plan maximizes closet space. A basement can be added for storage.

Tom Leytham

Perspective

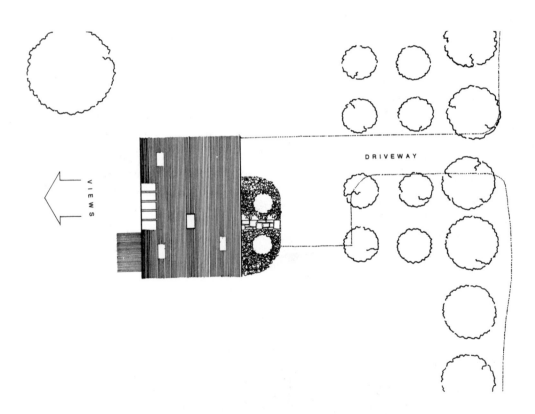

DRIVEWAY

VIEWS

Site Plan

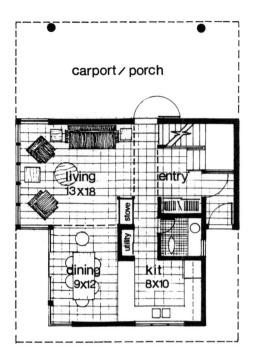

First Floor

carport / porch

living
13x18

entry

stove

utility

dining
9x12

kit
8x10

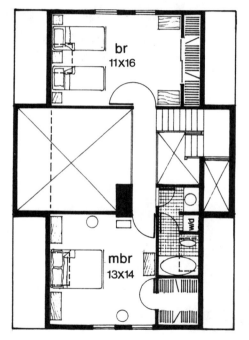

Second Floor

br
11x16

mbr
13x14

wd

Floor Plans

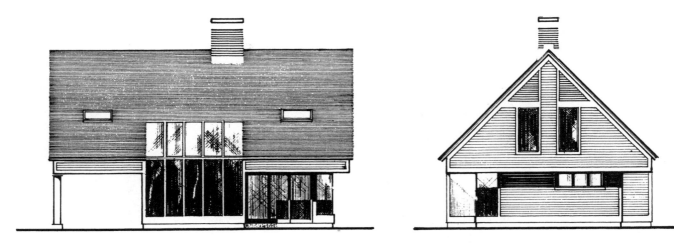

South

East

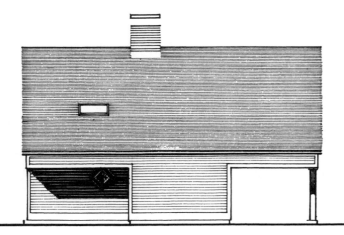

North

West

Elevations

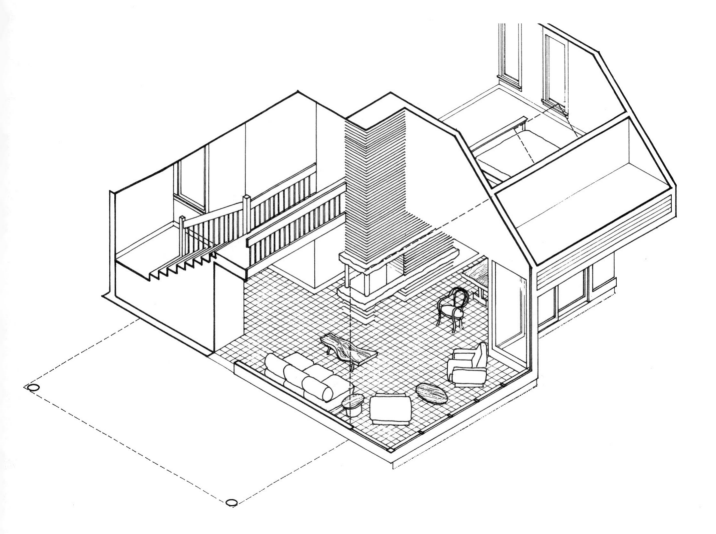

Axonometric

All-Weather Rustic

Alberta, Canada
1,115 gross square feet

The house is designed to capture sun for both heat and light. Since the south side faces a neighboring house that will shade the lower level, a garage is placed on that side. This gesture accommodates a two-story scheme, which is set back from the neighboring property line to allow light to enter. Light from the upper level illuminates the living area via the open stairwell, with long overhangs to shade the hot summer sun. Overhangs are used extensively to mediate both light and heat.

In response to cold winters, the highly insulated and tightly sealed house has front and back porches, which act as airlock entries. In other seasons, the back exterior enclosed veranda (unheated) accommodates evening outdoor living, with operable vents and ample insect screening. During the day the veranda can be opened with overhead garage-type doors.

Active solar collectors on the roof supplement the heating of domestic hot water and the in-floor hydronic space-heating system. Zoned for the living area and sleeping area, the heating system also includes a supplementary energy-efficient gas fireplace.

A storage tank holds graywater from bathing, which pipes then convey to a storage tank that provides water for the toilet. Water collected from the roof flows either to the graywater tank or to the long masonry wall, where it is channeled to a cistern. Small amounts of rainwater from the roof are scuppered to the surrounding landscape.

Lillian Mei Ngan Mah

Perspective

60

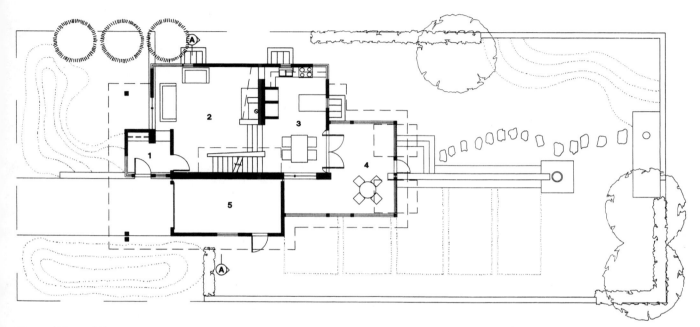

Site and Ground Floor

1 Entry Porch
2 Living Room
3 Kitchen/Dining
4 Unheated Veranda
5 Garage
6 Bedroom
7 Bathroom
8 Roof Deck
9 Basement/Laundry/Mechanical

Site and Floor Plans

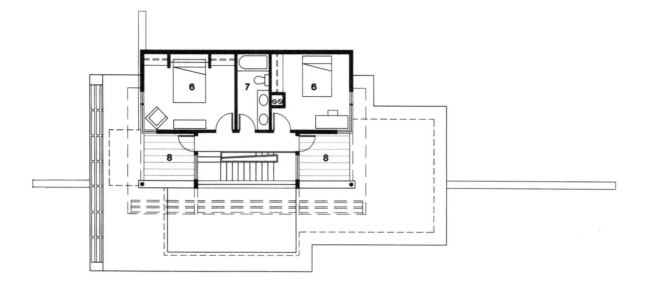

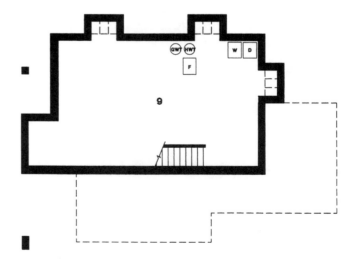

Basement

West

East

Elevations

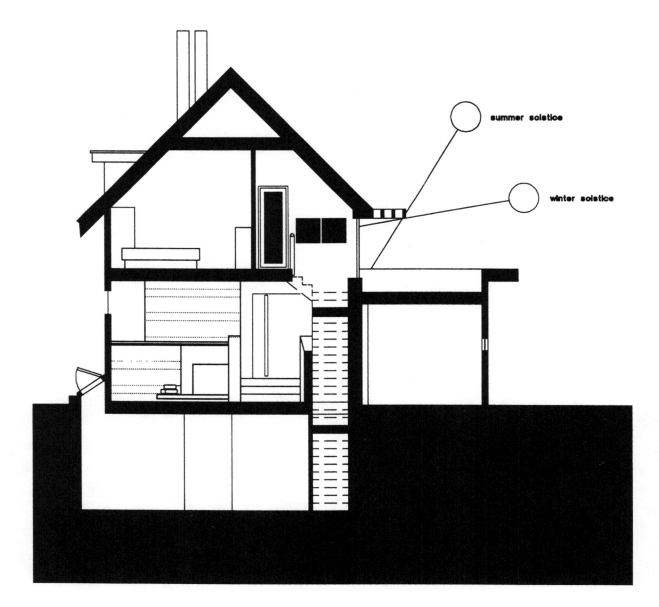

summer solstice

winter solstice

Section

West Coast Wood Frame

Pacific Northwest, U.S.
1,240 square feet

Set in a natural clearing surrounded by coniferous and deciduous trees, this house takes advantage of spectacular views of the Pacific Ocean.

The double-height element at the east end anchors the house and connects to a skylit gallery that doubles as circulation and library. The latter acts as a datum connecting sleeping, service, and living areas. Circulation is concentrated along the north wall to serve as a buffer from the heavily used road. The living spaces open up to the south to capture the spectacular ocean views.

The Pacific Northwest climate features mild, wet winters and warm summers. Local materials—wood for framing, cedar siding, and metal roofing—are used because of their availability and durability. Cellulose insulation made of recycled newsprint is blown into the wall cavities. A natural gas furnace assisted by a wood-burning fireplace provides winter warmth. Summer cooling relies on ocean-tempered natural air currents, enhanced by the stack effect of the open loft. The trellis extending over the south terrace provides summer shading.

Eleanor Lee and Michael Noble

Perspective

Site Plan

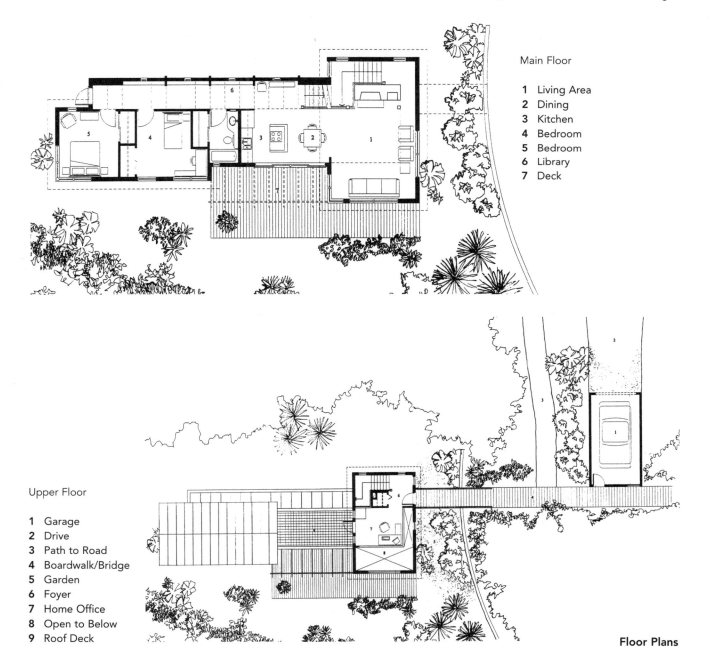

Main Floor

1 Living Area
2 Dining
3 Kitchen
4 Bedroom
5 Bedroom
6 Library
7 Deck

Upper Floor

1 Garage
2 Drive
3 Path to Road
4 Boardwalk/Bridge
5 Garden
6 Foyer
7 Home Office
8 Open to Below
9 Roof Deck

Floor Plans

West Coast Wood Frame

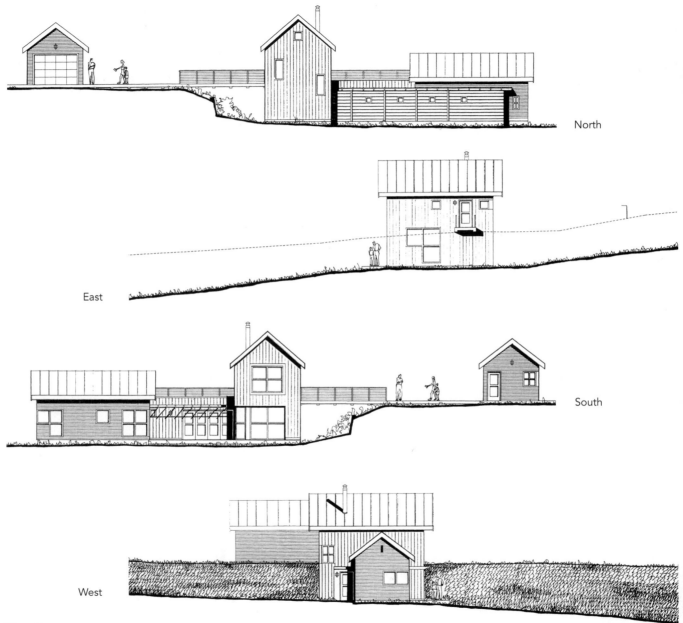

North

East

South

West

Elevations

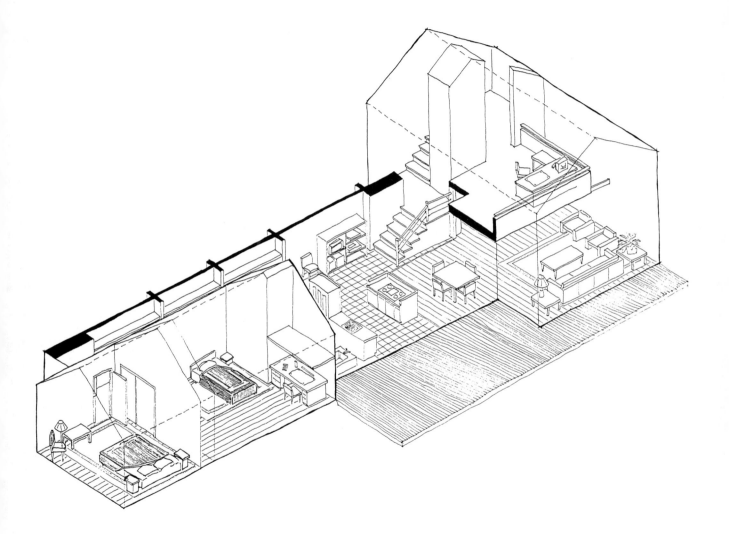

Axonometric

Modified A-Frame

Poland
1,092 gross square feet

Arising from nature and landscape, good architecture features simplicity and clarity, combined with environmentally friendly materials.

This design is heavily influenced by cost, both to build it and to live in it. Other design considerations include size, compactness, simplicity in construction and function, durability, technological potential, and energy efficiency (for example, well-insulated floors, walls,

windows, and roofs). Within these elements we look for a space that gives worthy conditions for living and a feeling of safety. We effectively use the cubic content of the house to maximize space in the day area, where family life concentrates, expanding outward to the exterior space.

Olgierd Miloszewicz

Perspective

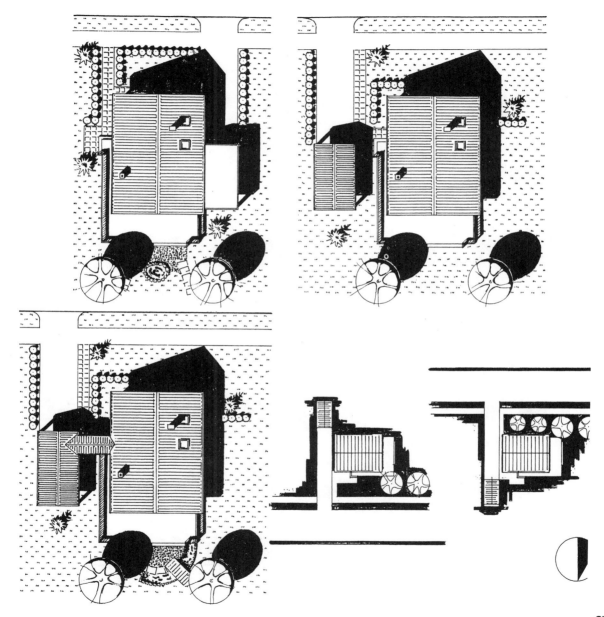

Site Plans

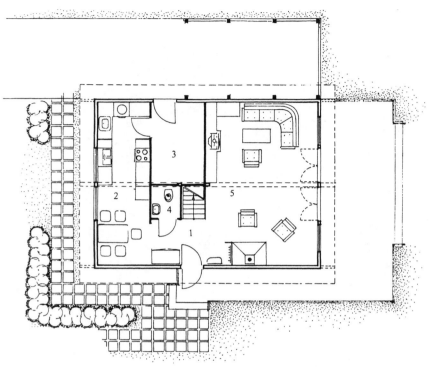

First Floor

1 Entry and Stairway
2 Kitchen with Dining Area
3 Laundry, Storage, Mechanical
4 Water Closet
5 Living Room
6 Hall and Stairway
7 Bedroom
8 Bathroom
9 Bedroom
10 Bedroom

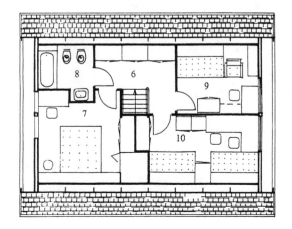

Second Floor

Floor Plans

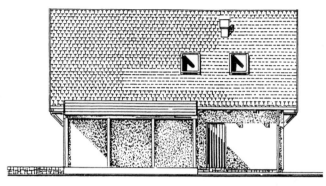

East

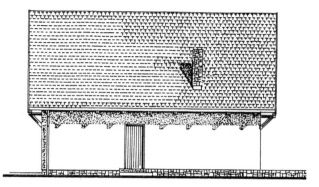

West

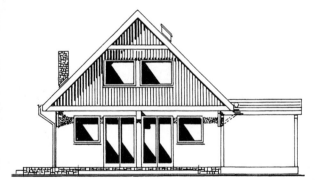

South

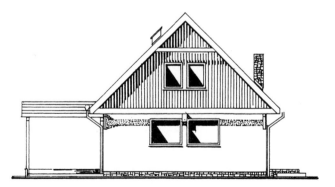

North

Elevations

Modified A-frame

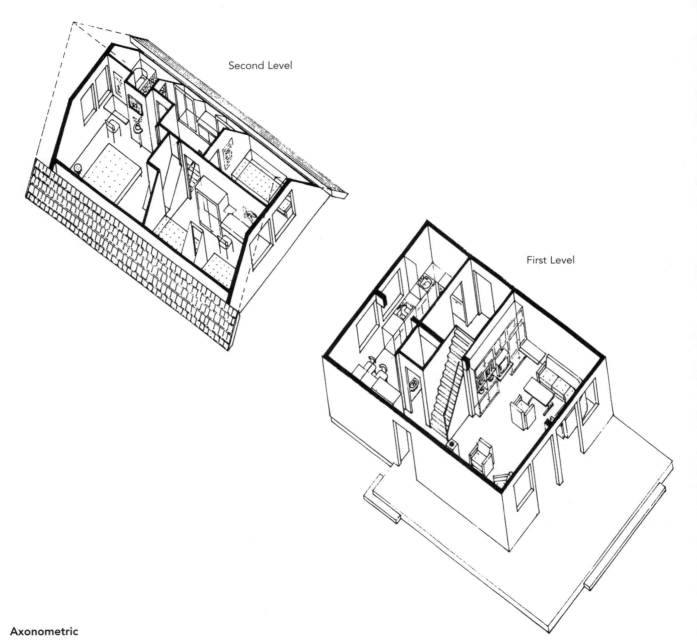

Second Level

First Level

Axonometric

74

Sheep Farm Ranch

Australia
1,200 gross square feet

The setting is a large sheep farm in Western Australia. The region enjoys an abundance of sunshine with a fairly consistent prevailing wind.

The design criteria are (1) to harness the natural elements by positioning solar collectors on the north-facing roof and by installing a wind generator; (2) to provide a cool house in the summer and a warm house in the winter, which in the Southern Hemisphere requires a north-facing orientation; and (3) to create a feeling of space within the limits of a small house.

I set out to achieve a spacious feeling by allowing the attic floor to extend into a mezzanine, with access via a pullout ladder. The attic space can provide both convenient storage and a recreation area for children during the winter months. The cross-section also allows cross-ventilation during the summer.

Agricultural buildings in Western Australia inspired and influenced this design.

W. I. Shipley

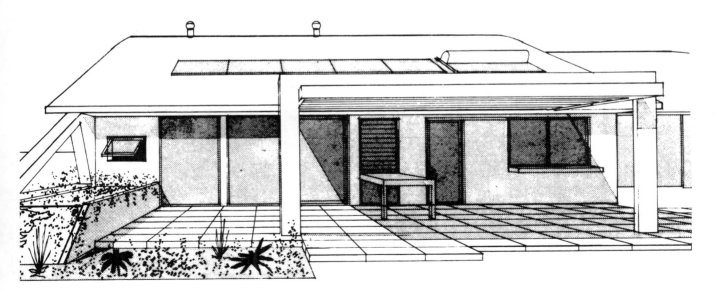

Perspective

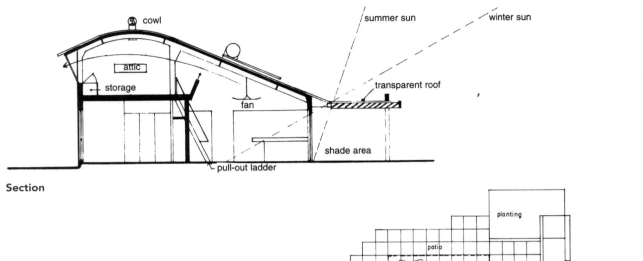

Section

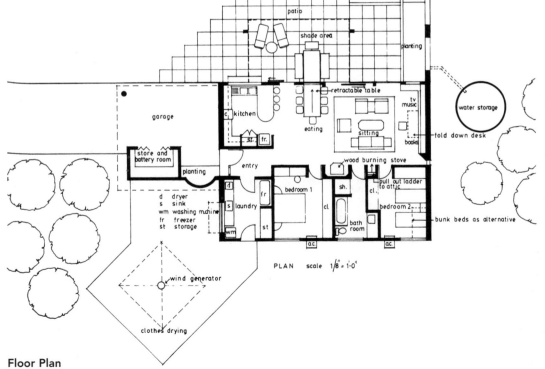

Floor Plan

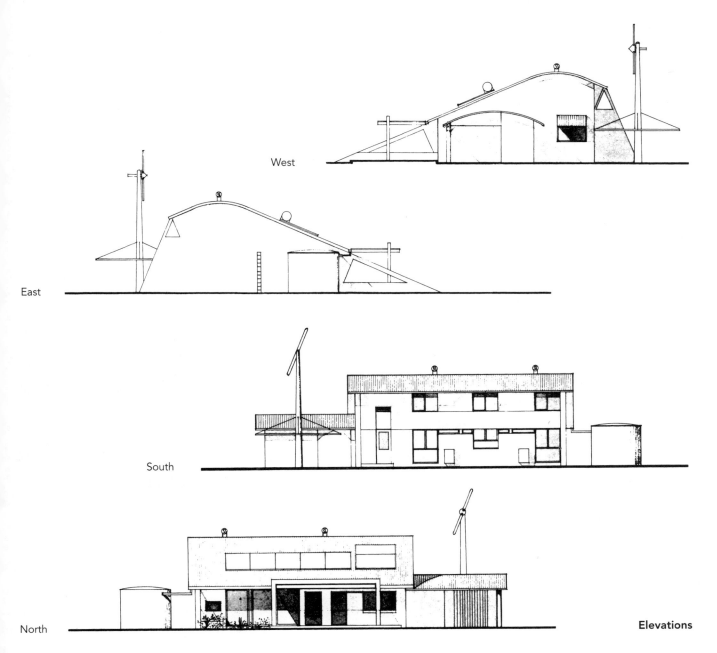

West

East

South

North

Elevations

Subtropical Solar Home

Brisbane, Queensland, Australia
1,022 gross square feet

The compact footprint of this plan enables placement on small lots. With the home sited to take maximum advantage of solar access, the focus of outdoor activity is to the north and east (appropriate to the Southern Hemisphere). Likewise, all living spaces and bedrooms face north and east. Daylight to all spaces eliminates the need for electric lighting during the day. A sloping roof minimizes overshadowing on neighbors and assists smooth airflow over the building to reduce heat loss.

The design groups together all service areas to minimize hot water pipe runs. The house is insulated to higher-than-usual levels. Appropriately sized and shaded windows achieve maximum solar efficiency using timber rather than aluminum window frames. A south-north air path cross-ventilates all spaces. Other energy-efficient and environmentally friendly features include a gas-boosted solar hot water system, compact fluorescent lights, small cisterns for toilets, aerators on water taps, nontoxic termite barriers, and acrylic paints. Collection of rainwater and pressurized pumping using solar power are key energy features. A covered area outside allows laundry to dry even in wet weather.

Robert Takken and Matthew Cooper

Perspective

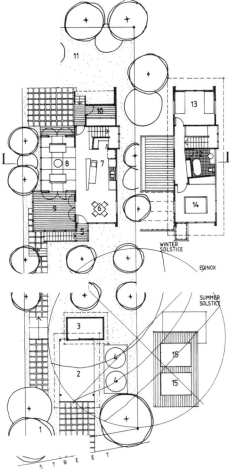

1 Gatehouse
2 Carpet
3 Storage
4 Rainwater Tanks
5 Entry
6 Dining
7 Kitchen
8 Living Room
9 Deck
10 Laundry
11 Courtyard
12 Bathroom
13 Bedroom 2
14 Bedroom 1
15 Solar Collectors

West Elevation

Site and Floor Plans

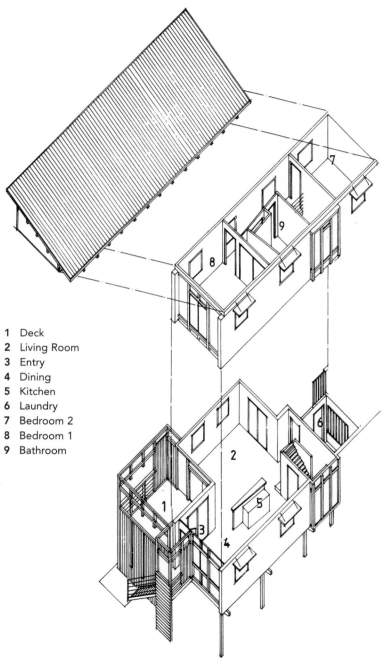

1 Deck
2 Living Room
3 Entry
4 Dining
5 Kitchen
6 Laundry
7 Bedroom 2
8 Bedroom 1
9 Bathroom

Axonometric

European Splendor

Italian Countryside
1,180 gross square feet

This home consists of two different blocks: a low, long, linear element and, opposite, the massive element of the tower. In the linear part, the day area—an open space only interrupted by the chimney—separates the living room from the dining area.

The main axis of the plan goes through the sheet of water in front of the house, passes through the home, and stops at the semicircular fountain fed by a little brook. That solution extends the perception of interior space, which directly communicates with the exterior, as encouraged by the glass doors that face the porticos.

As far as energy savings are concerned, the house has solar panels on the tower roof, which consists of lamellate (layered) wood; a chimney with boiler system connected to the heating system; a serpentine solar hot water heater under the grass; and a cooling system that takes advantage of the sheet of water in front of the house.

The design is conceived for a flat site. The home stands out in an ornate landscape inspired by the geometry of Renaissance gardens.

Giulio Fabbri

Perspective

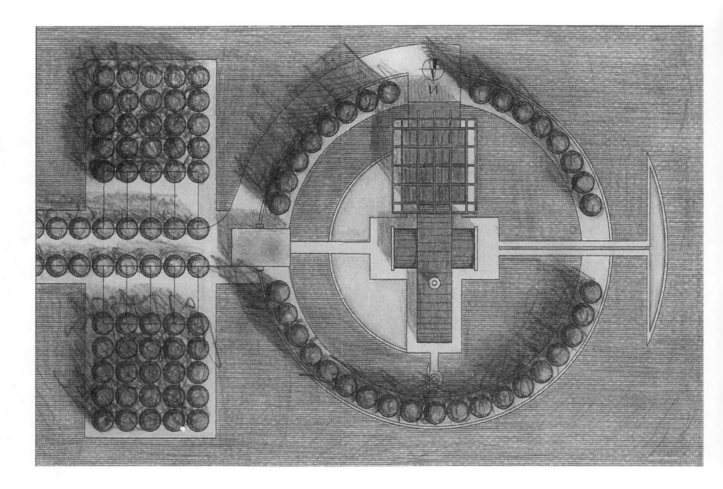

Site Plan

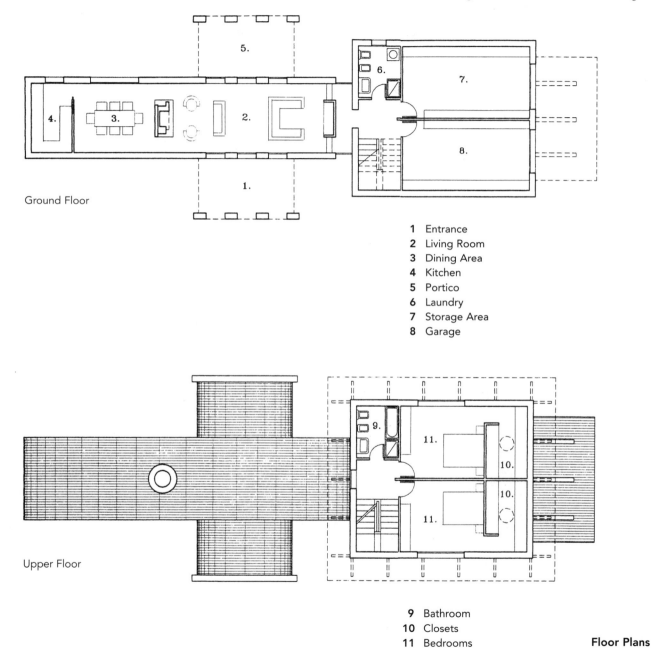

Ground Floor

1 Entrance
2 Living Room
3 Dining Area
4 Kitchen
5 Portico
6 Laundry
7 Storage Area
8 Garage

Upper Floor

9 Bathroom
10 Closets
11 Bedrooms

Floor Plans

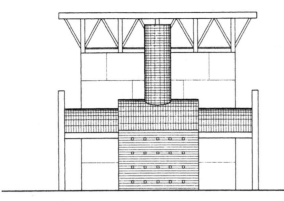

North

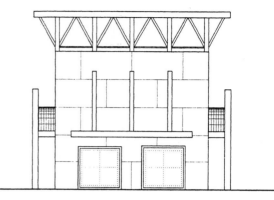

South

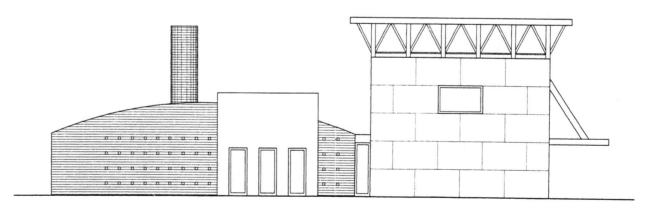

West

Elevations

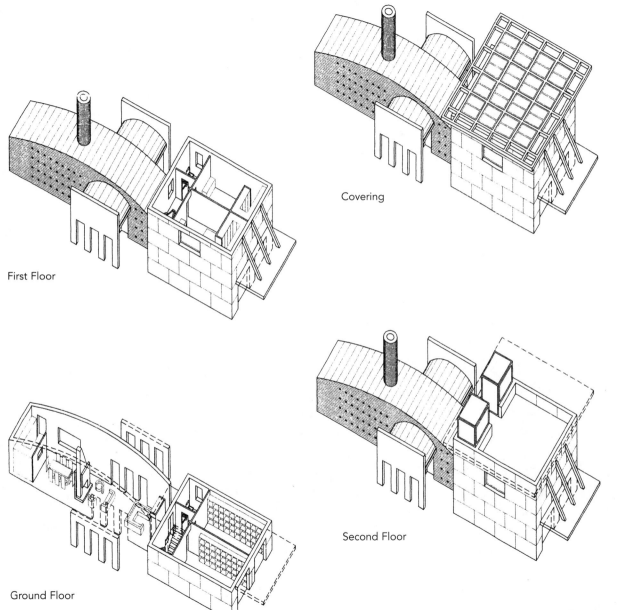

First Floor

Covering

Ground Floor

Second Floor

Axonometrics

Geometric Contemporary

Italy
1,250 gross square feet

This house has two functional floors: one for the living areas and the other for resting and studying. The ground floor includes the dining and lounge areas with adjacent kitchen and conservatory, as well as a laundry and a storeroom that contains the main plant and systems. The double volume of the entrance lounge incorporates a circular wooden staircase that connects the two levels. At ground level is a box garage.

On the upper floor are the spaces for study and work, and a separate night area—two bedroms with half baths. This level also has a full bathroom as well as a stairway leading to the terrace.

The construction technique employs reinforced concrete frame and curtain walls. Inside, gypsum walls and an insulation layer create a heat-cold barrier. The flooring consists of polished lime and fired terracotta powder. The external window and door frames are in copper and zinc alloy. Lime plaster and marble sawdust cover the outside walls, while copper sheets cover the roof.

Carlo Giuliani

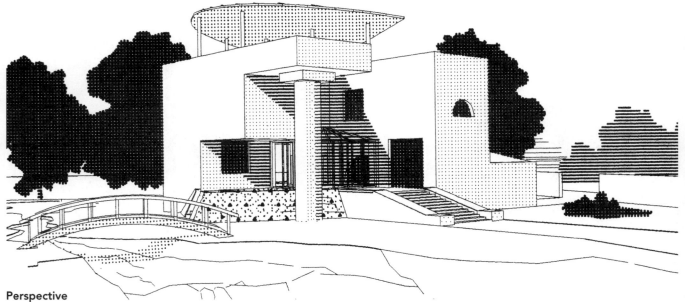

Perspective

Site Plan

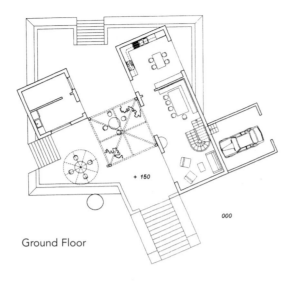

Ground Floor

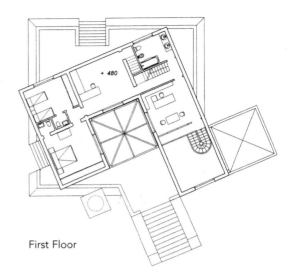

First Floor

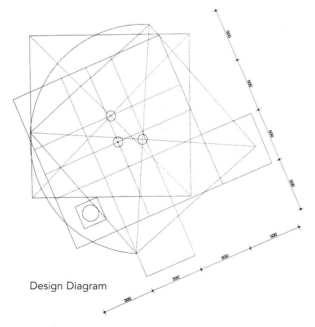

Design Diagram

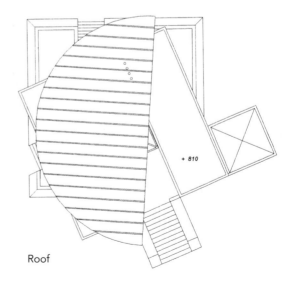

Roof

Floor Plans

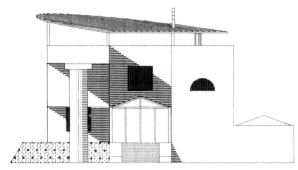

Northeast

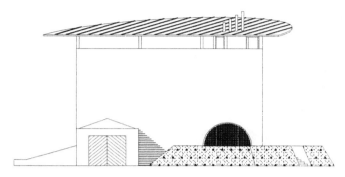

Northwest

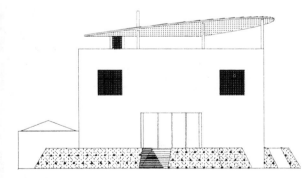

Southwest

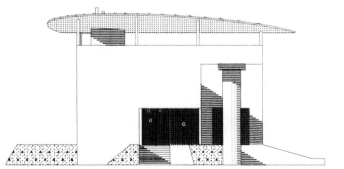

Southeast

Elevations

Garden Paradise

Norway
1,008 gross square feet

The design focuses on providing a clean indoor environment for the occupants of this house. A living indoor garden produces oxygen and helps to filter indoor air pollutants. Mechanically operated blinds between the glass in the garden walls regulate heat transmission. A tank in the ground or under the house stores fresh water for occupants and plants.

A heat exchanger in the loft replaces used air with outside air. Air intake from the roof is distributed to the garden area, partly through soil ventilation. In this way the garden serves as a fresh-air filter. When designing the garden, it is important to select plants that are resistant to low temperatures and to choose plant nutrients that do not adversely affect human living conditions.

The house design provides for privacy, a view outdoors from the kitchen, controlled traffic areas inside and outside, and direct access from the living area to the garden. The possibility exists for future expansion.

Ulrik Hellum

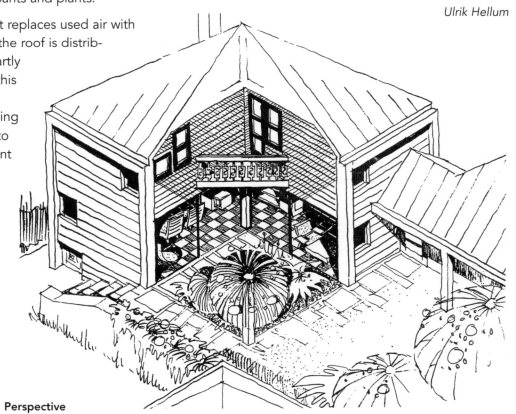

Perspective

90

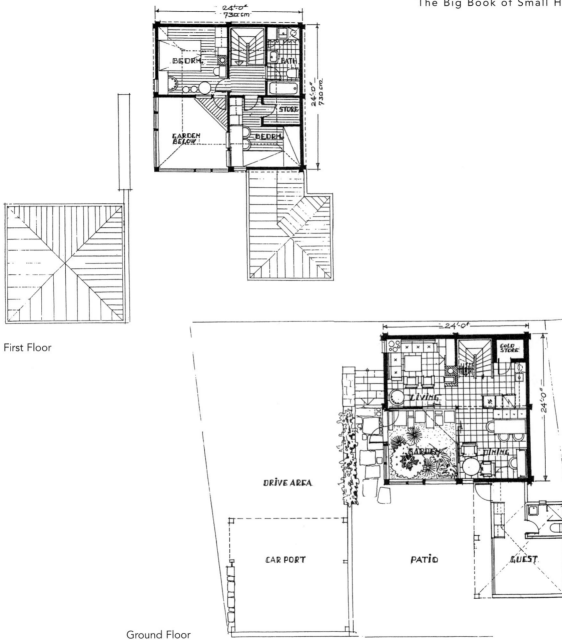

24'-0"
730 cm

BEDRM.

BATH

STORE

24'-0"
730 cm

GARDEN
BELOW

BEDRM.

First Floor

24'-0"

COLD
STORE

LIVING

24'-0"

GARDEN

DINING

DRIVE AREA

CAR PORT

PATIO

GUEST

Ground Floor

Floor Plans

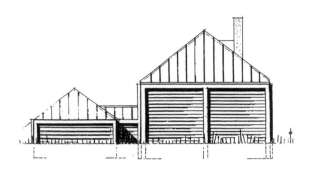

East

West

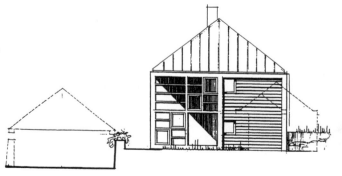

North

South

Elevations

Sustainable Living

Melbourne, Australia
1,080 gross square feet

The objective of this design is to promote a sustainable living environment within the requirements of a small house. These requirements include passive solar design, efficient and economical use of building materials, and a garden for produce and compost. Such features strengthen and become an integral part of a small house design. Flexible and adaptable space echoes the concept of sustainability.

This design incorporates a hybrid mechanical system. Passive solar heating and cooling combine with the radiant-hydronic floor system and conventional ceiling ventilation fans. Solar hot water integrates with the hydronic heating system. The central stairwell produces negative air pressure at the cupola, enhancing natural ventilation.

An innovative structural system employs highly insulated stress-skin panels. These panels not only reduce by about 60 percent the consumption of timber when compared to conventional housing, but conserve energy as well. A lightweight, ventilated metal roof, insulated at the ceiling, helps reduce summer cooling loads. The assembly of this modular system allows for easy future additions.

Mark B. Luther

Perspective

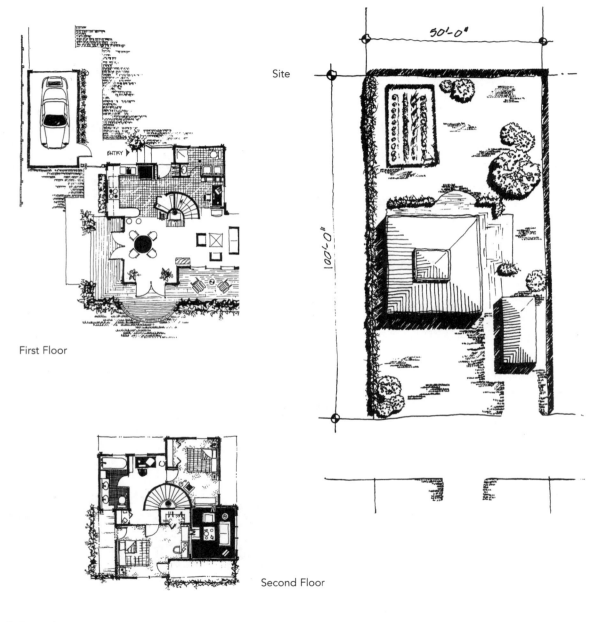

First Floor

Site

50'-0"

100'-0"

Second Floor

Site and Floor Plans

East

North

South

West

Elevations

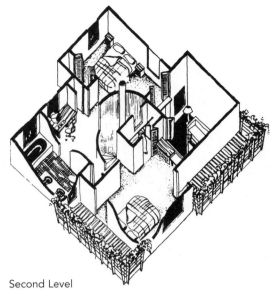

Second Level

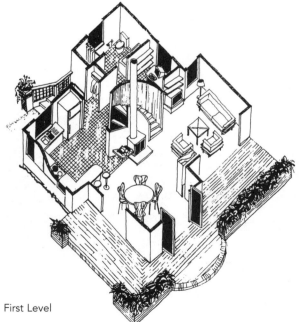

First Level

Axonometrics

Spacious, Compact Ranch

Oklahoma
1,248 gross square feet

My proposal is a design that will fit into existing neighborhoods while providing a comfortable, compact, and efficient environment. A gracious entry disperses traffic to the various living spaces, obviating any need to pass through other areas of the house. The exterior not only accommodates outdoor activities, but also offers views from the interior, making the small house appear larger. On the street side of the property, a front porch allows for relaxed viewing.

Energy efficiency is a primary concern in the design, from the orientation of the plan to the use of appropriate construction materials. The design specifies masonry walls with a 6-inch superinsulation system and large roof overhangs with extensive insulation in the attic. The air-conditioning and heating system consists of a closed-loop, ground-source heat pump, using a deep-well concept for the heat exchanger. This prevents equipment damage due to exposure to the elements, eliminates the need to hide the equipment with landscaping, and reduces noise pollution.

Don Buoen

Perspective

Spacious, Compact Ranch

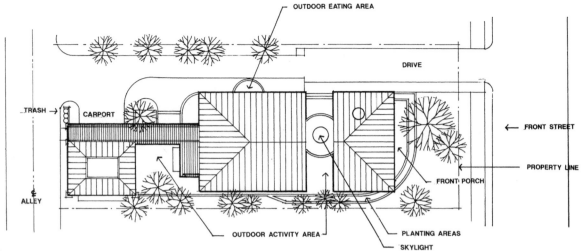

Site Plan

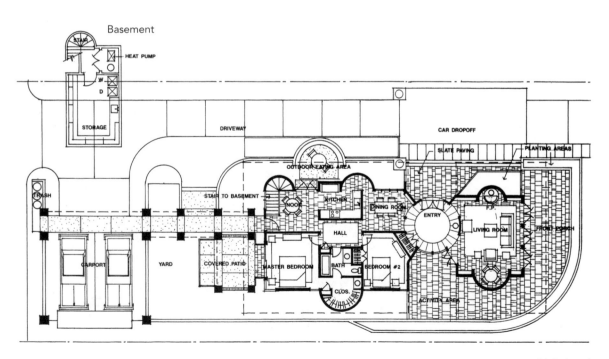

Floor Plans

Basement

Main Level

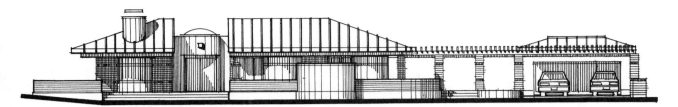

North

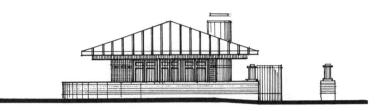

East

South

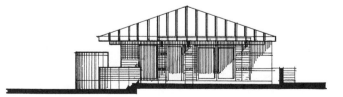

West

Elevations

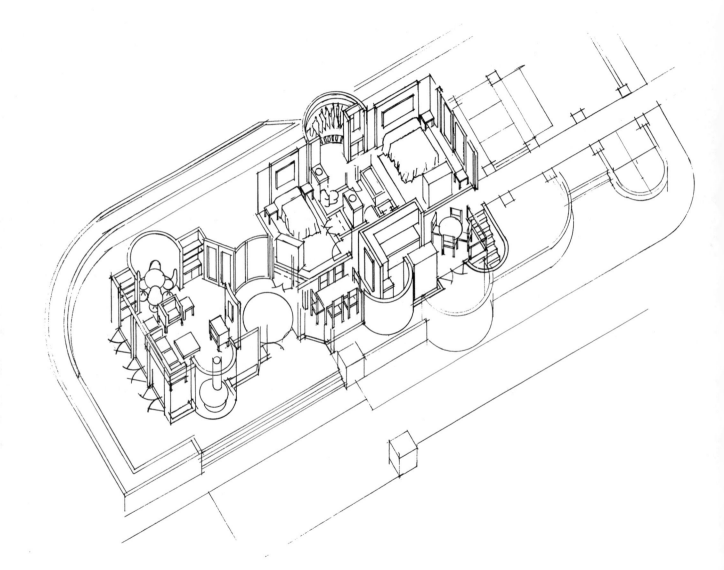

Axonometric

Versatile Split Level

North Dakota
1,250 gross square feet

This small residence includes features for changing lifestyles: a home office with a private entry (which can be used as a third bedroom), and a lower-level interior atrium space for a family theater. The design incorporates privacy gradients and a half-hidden garden, bedrooms with east light, and sheltering roofs. The split-level layout stresses integration with the landscape through the use of a courtyard, focused views, and transitional spaces. A front porch places emphasis on the public realm of the street and encourages neighborhood supervision.

The design visually enhances the exterior dimensions by using saddlebags and dormers and by repeating building forms as outbuildings in the landscape. Placing the garage in profile, as seen from the street, minimizes its visual impact and adds to the frontal aspect of the house. Open planning in the living/dining/kitchen, combined with raised ceiling areas, increases the sense of interior space. A central entry and stairway minimize unnecessary circulation.

Daniel L. Faoro

Perspective

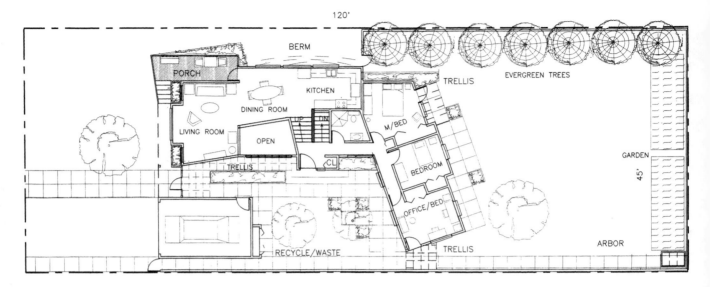

120'

BERM

PORCH

KITCHEN

DINING ROOM

LIVING ROOM

UP   DN

OPEN

CL

TRELLIS

RECYCLE/WASTE

TRELLIS

M/BED

BEDROOM

OFFICE/BED

TRELLIS

EVERGREEN TREES

GARDEN

45'

ARBOR

Site and Ground Floor

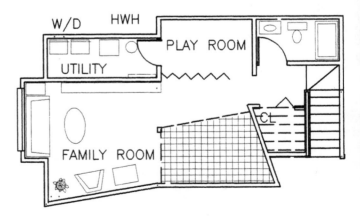

W/D   HWH

UTILITY

PLAY ROOM

CL

FAMILY ROOM

Lower Level

Site and Floor Plans

North

East

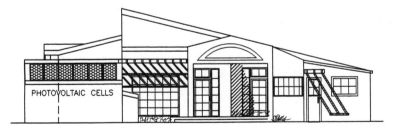

South

West

Elevations

103

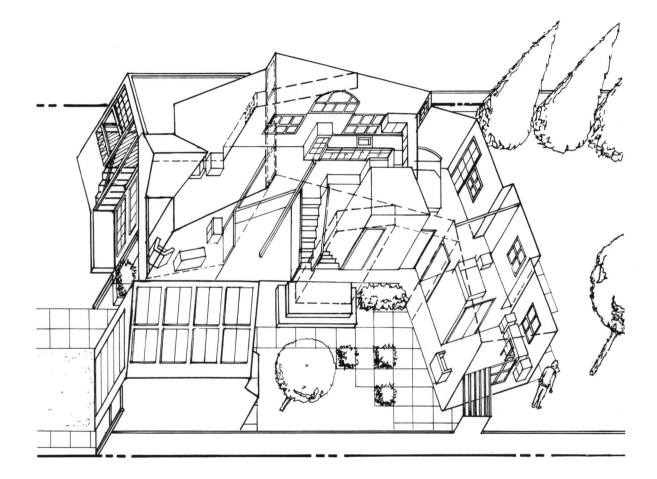

Axonometric

Family-Oriented Split Level

Central Pennsylvania
1,250 gross square feet

The vertical spatial hierarchy of the open plan is easy to modify with minimal architectural intervention. The living, dining, and kitchen areas and the spaces around the central staircase collectively form one large continuum that permits multiple uses. The covered deck and the walk-up attic also provide additional living space for the future. The articulated spaces create a visually connected and dramatic interior environment—both horizontally and vertically—especially for children.

The design addresses energy savings and environmental concerns primarily through orientation, with the majority of the windows facing southeast or southwest. Insulation and proper ventilation devices help to create an energy-efficient home.

Jawaid Haider and Talat Azhar

This particular design takes advantage of a 5-foot drop toward the middle of the site, but can be easily modified to effectively accommote a half-raised or walkout basement on a flat site. The covered deck or terrace, which overlooks a picturesque park across the street, provides a safe play area for children and can be either screened or left open.

Perspective

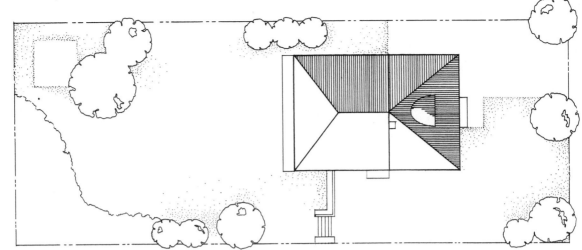

Site Plan

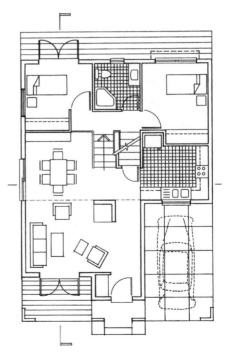

Floor Plans

Levels 1 and 2   Levels 3 and 4

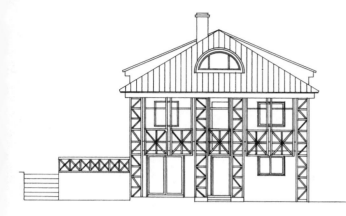

Northeast

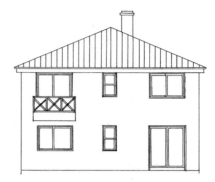

Southwest

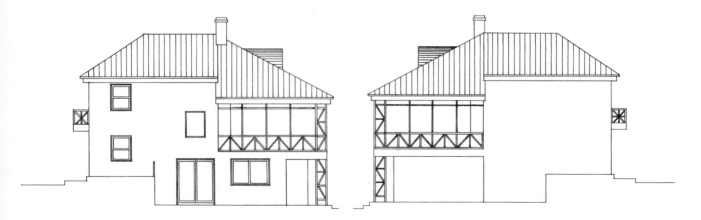

Southeast

Northwest

Elevations

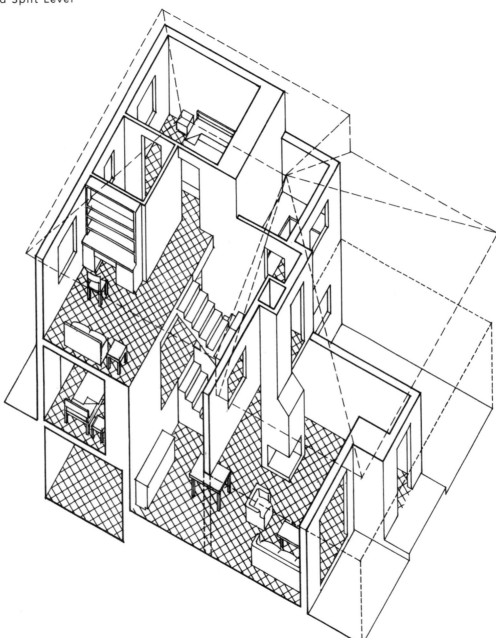

Axonometric

Solar, Modular Prefab

Anywhere, U.S.A.
1,248 gross square feet

This design consists of a small prefab modular house with integrated passive solar heating, solar power, and solar hot water, thereby allowing homeowners to reduce the amount of income spent on basic shelter. The prefab house is versatile, offering the owners and builders elevation, material, and plan variations to produce a "custom" house.

The concept arranges four modules, each 13 x 24 feet, so as to capture a basement (12 x 23 feet) and a passive solar sunroom (13 x 18 feet), the latter featuring a prefab greenhouse that closes the southernmost wall. Metal module trusses (floor joist, studs, and roof rafters screwed together) slide into and bolt into two 24-foot-long metal channel beams with sleeves at 24 inches on center. The builders add metal blocking, plate straps, and so on, before attaching

plywood sheeting, windows, and exterior materials.

The finished modules, set by crane and sealed, anchor the site-built garage and patio covers. The insulated thermal-mass slab, combined with built-in sliding window insulation work, delays temperature fluctuation and reduces the need for air conditioning.

Bruce Shindelus

Perspective

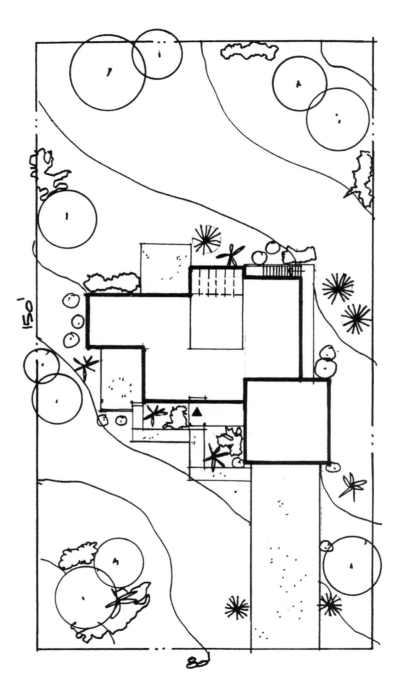

150'

80'

Site Plan

Floor Plans

Second Floor

First Floor

Basement

Elevations

West

South

East

North

Underground Earth Home

Adirondack Park, New York
1,250 gross square feet

The architects' ideas translated into an exposed concrete facade with rusticated joints, rough wood-grain patterns, and exposed form-ties. An accent band of earth-toned ceramic tiles above and below the windows and a custom redwood sunscreen add color and depth to the facade. Natural Adirondack bluestone, available on site, is incorporated in the design facade, at the retaining wing walls, in the monitor projections through the earth roof, and as an accent at the vestibule wall with the circular door opening.

The southern exposure of this facade illuminates the interior through large expanses of glass. The windows allow light to enter deep within the building, eliminating the impression of an uninviting hole and creating a warm, sunlit home. The sunscreen is designed to shade the harsh summer sun while welcoming the winter's rays.

Another design feature is a central chimney structure that contains the flue for the Russian fireplace as well as plumbing, kitchen, and mechanical penetrations. We also incorporated the intake and exhaust air from the air-to-air heat exchanger that was required for improved indoor air quality. Conceived in an effort to reduce roof penetrations, this chimney and its symbolic heat source, and the adjacent skylight monitors, illuminate the darker areas of the "underground den" while punctuating the unsuspecting south-facing slope in the Adirondack Mountains.

Synthesis Architects

Perspective

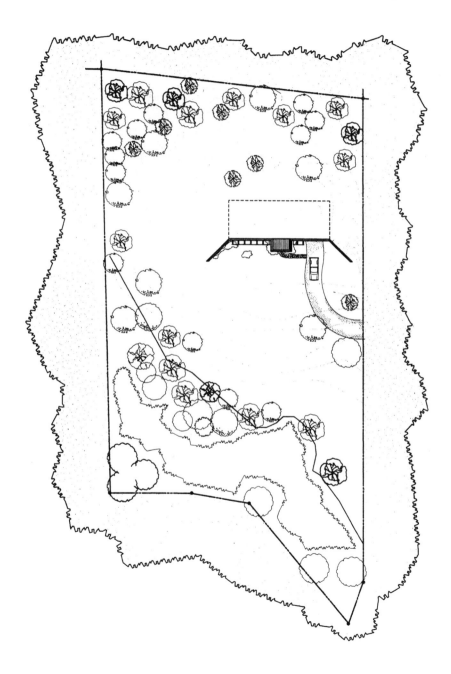

Site Plan

South Elevation

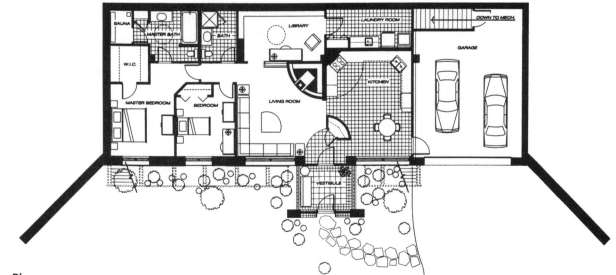

Floor Plan

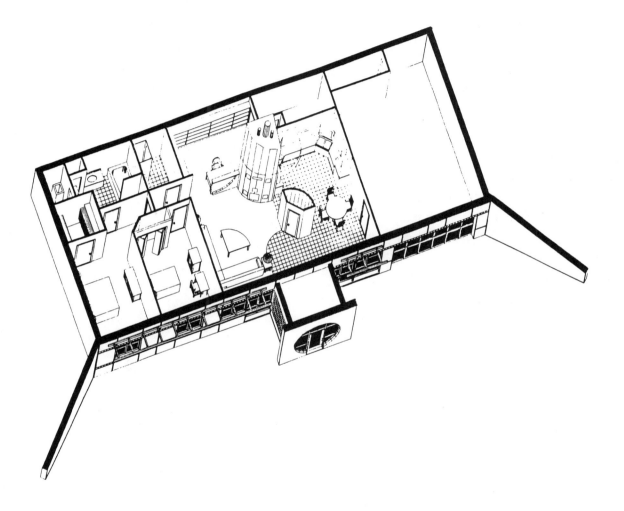

Axonometric

Cozy Vermont Cabin

Vermont
1,124 gross square feet

Given a hypothetical site in Vermont, the most energy- and cost-saving design strategy is to build a highly insulating shell. A continuous air/vapor barrier increases heat retention, prevents drafts, and creates an environment where air quality can be controlled. A fan draws fresh air into second-floor closets, where it interflows with ambient air to reduce cold drafts before being ducted into bedrooms and living spaces. Fans in kitchen and bathroom provide air exhaust. The system maintains slight positive air pressure, which helps keep external toxins out of the home environment.

The plan of the home provides optimum solar gain and generous daylight. Low-occupancy spaces, such as the stair, mudroom, and bathroom, are to the north. All living spaces and bedrooms have southern exposure.

The living room, with its concrete slab floor, angles slightly to the east, to benefit from early-morning solar gain and to reduce overheating in the afternoons.

Firewood is a readily available, inexpensive, local, renewable source of fuel in Vermont. Superinsulation makes it possible to heat this house throughout most of the year with a small wood stove. The stair, serving as a plenum, and the fresh-air system move the heated air throughout the building. This convective space planning requires only a single, high-output, backup space heater.

Terra Firma

Perspective

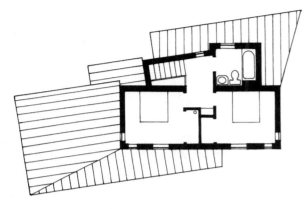

Second Floor

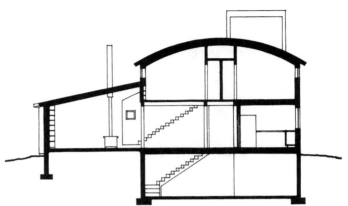

Section

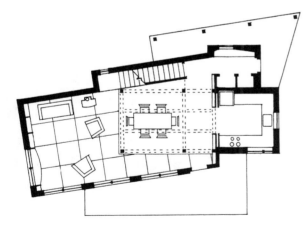

First Floor

Basement

Floor Plans and Section

Cozy Vermont Cabin

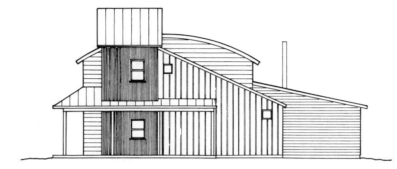

North

West

South

East

Elevations

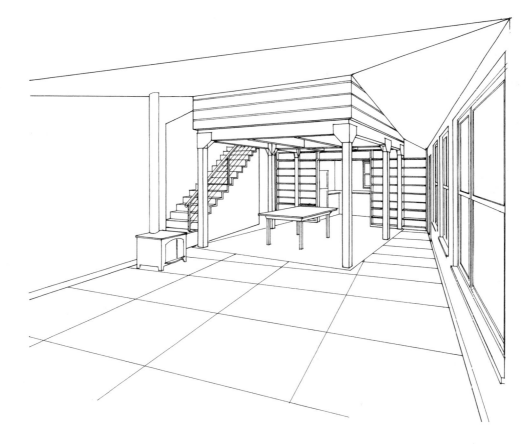

Axonometric

Elegant Urban Fortress

London, England
1,250 gross square feet

Completing a new street facade, the house answers the challenge of the aggressive road on which it sits by enfolding its occupants in a protective layer of books, buffering them from the inner-city noise outside. The south side is a stepped bookcase, or bookstep, forming a tiered living area that encourages appropriation (with sofa, work surface, etc.). On the north, the house grows toward the fresher air and quieter environment of Hoxton Square.

Climbing from the street up a flight of exposed and weathered Corten steel steps, one enters the body of the house. Concrete structural spines, which announce the route through the house as well as its eventual destination, act as plumb lines gauging the eccentricities of the site—a measuring device. The smaller interior rooms are lightly held by the larger stepped space of the bookcase room. The interior gently unfolds ahead: one inhabits, accumulates, mediates; rising at last to the perch, the widest shelf at the highest point of the bookcase room.

The house fractures away from its boundary to allow light to penetrate deep into the interior, and a rectangular light scoop lined with etched glass pierces the roof so that light runs down alongside the service core and top bedroom.

Megan Williams

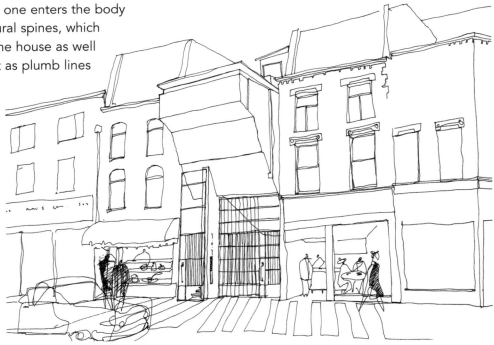

Perspective

120

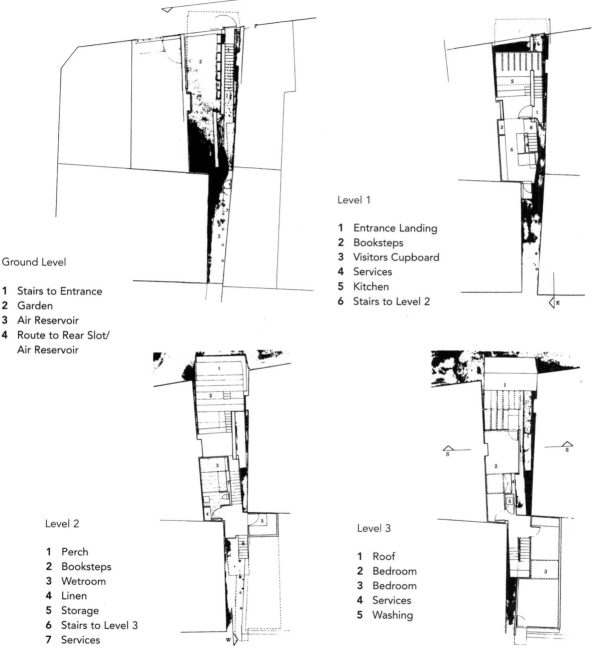

Ground Level

1 Stairs to Entrance
2 Garden
3 Air Reservoir
4 Route to Rear Slot/
   Air Reservoir

Level 1

1 Entrance Landing
2 Booksteps
3 Visitors Cupboard
4 Services
5 Kitchen
6 Stairs to Level 2

Level 2

1 Perch
2 Booksteps
3 Wetroom
4 Linen
5 Storage
6 Stairs to Level 3
7 Services

Level 3

1 Roof
2 Bedroom
3 Bedroom
4 Services
5 Washing

Floor Plans

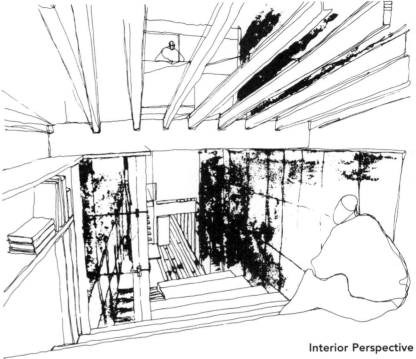

Interior Perspective

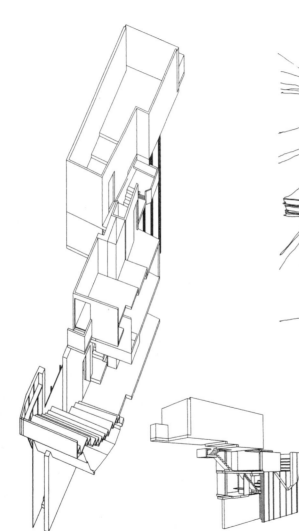

Axonometrics

Zen Temple

Japan

1,200 gross square feet

Every surface appears to be fading away in this design, leaving behind a world of silence and a feeling of utter solitude. A chilly grayness lies at the innermost heart of Japanese space. In the smoky light that pervades a Zen temple or tiny tea house, the human eye is engaged indirectly as if by stealth.

These whitened and emptied qualities of light must have been created by and for a human spirit ready to go beyond the outer aspects of things, and beyond a reality aimed to satisfy vision. Their tones express a taste for something deeper and more mysterious than traditional housing.

The structure is cable and steel. The roof is a galvanized steel sheet, and the flooring is of Japanese cedar and oak as well as exposed concrete. Landscaping includes gravel, a pond, bamboo, and maple trees.

Hideyuki Takita

Overhead Perspective

Zen Temple

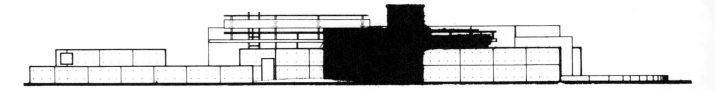

South

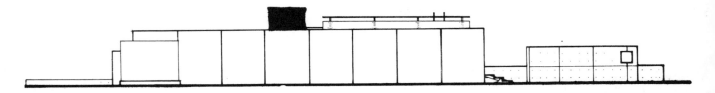

North

West

East

Elevations

124

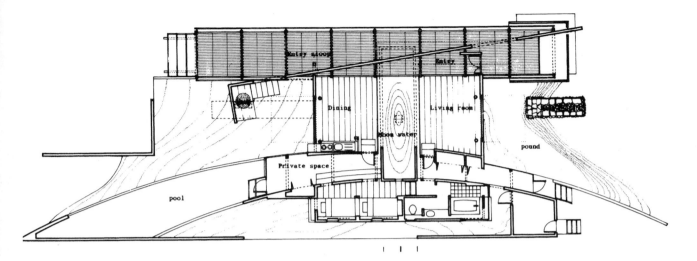

Floor Plan

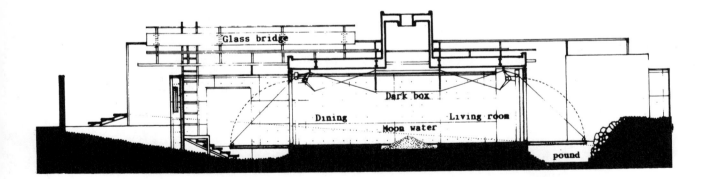

Section

Meditative Lakeside Retreat

Covert, New York
1,000 gross square feet

Here we chose to collage two typical forms: garden wall and sacred object building. Due to the tight, delicate site conditions, we kept the house modestly scaled, and placed the non-heated services against the wall. This provides a buffer to road noise and cold northern winds, and serves as a backdrop/foreground to the chapel, through containment of the outbuilding functions: potting shed, entry portal, wood storage loggia, and carport. It is deformed to accept changes in elevation and function.

The object building contains living accommodation, and heightens the contemplative introversion fostered by the wall, cliff edge, and woods. Each side of the pure volume is uniquely deformed due to internal considerations, and to focus on a particular aspect of its relation to landscape and wall: the wooden porch accepts entry courtyard; the wooden kitchen saddlebag addresses wall and evening sitting terrace; the glass dining area and bedroom dormer open southward to the garden; and the glass apse finds culmination in the distant view.

Lee B. Temple

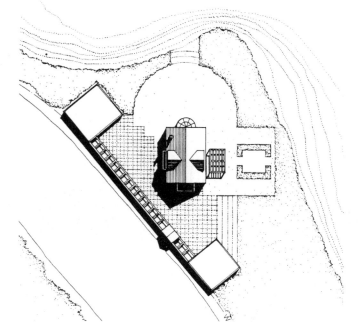

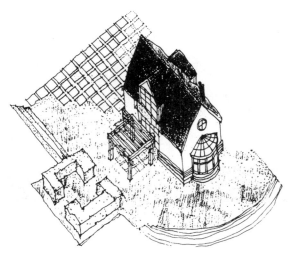

Site Plan

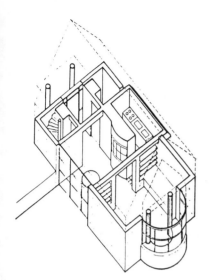
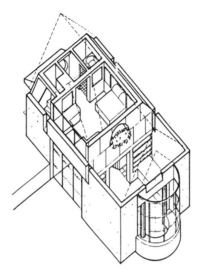
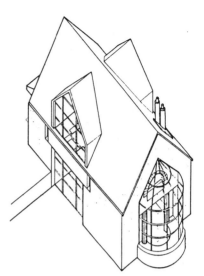

Perspectives

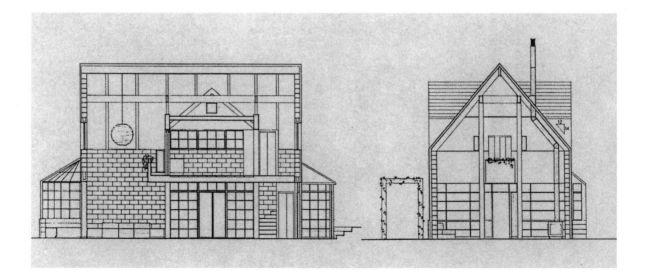

Elevations

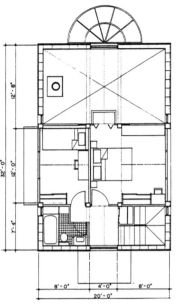

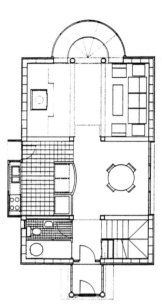

Floor Plan

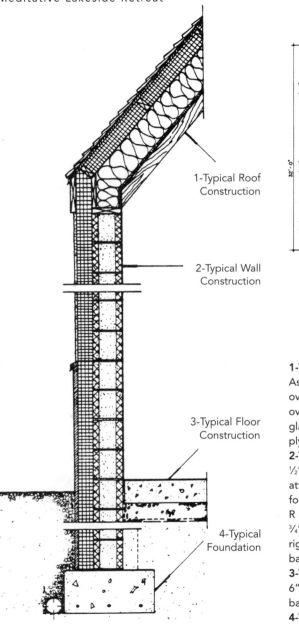

Wall Section

1-Typical Roof Construction
Asphalt shingles over ½" plywood over 4" foam and 2 x 4 sleepers over vapor barrier over 8" fiberglass and 4 x 10 rafters over ½" plywood R = 32

2-Typical Wall Construction
½" stucco over metal lathe attached to 8" CMU thru 4" rigid foam insulation and vapor barrier R = 24
¾" Pressure Treated board over 4" rigid foam insulation over vapor barrier over 8" CMU

3-Typical Floor Construction
6" conc. slab on grade over vapor barrier over 5" gravel

4-Typical Foundation
1' x 2' conc. footing poured in place/reinforcing bars, 4" drain tile

Neighborhood Privacy

Redwood City, California

1,000 gross square feet

Project Assumption
To provide an affordable compact house for middle-income buyers in a suburban housing development.

Approaches
Increased density to reduce cost of land per dwelling.

Use of mini-clusters to give more visual interest and mass to small units. Common open space created and number of curb cuts minimized.

Strongly defined streetscape created by assembling mini-clusters in manner to avoid monotonous rows of small detached units common to many subdivisions.

Architectural design based on most desired housing vernacular determined by market surveys.

Plan simplified by variation of space provided. Bedroom-bath areas separated for guests or shared use of home.

Maximum use of insulated exterior walls and roof for energy conservation.

Use of conventional wood construction.

Group-maintained, drought-free landscaping to reduce maintenance work for owners.

Owner-maintained patio provided at each unit.

Special Features and Advantages
Site is well drained non-agricultural land in area occupied by single-family dwellings.

Site has little initial visual interest. Landscaping, mounding, and street pattern are used to enhance views and create sheltered areas.

Higher sloping roof pitch over living areas and vent allow escape of warm air in summer. Heat recycled in winter by fan and duct from ceiling to floor at living area.

Parts of patio convert into multi-exposure solar greenhouses for passive solar design.

David Leash

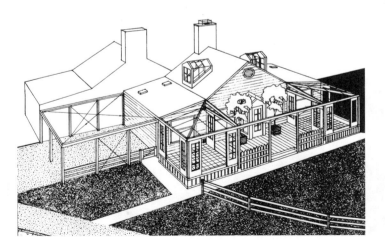

Perspective

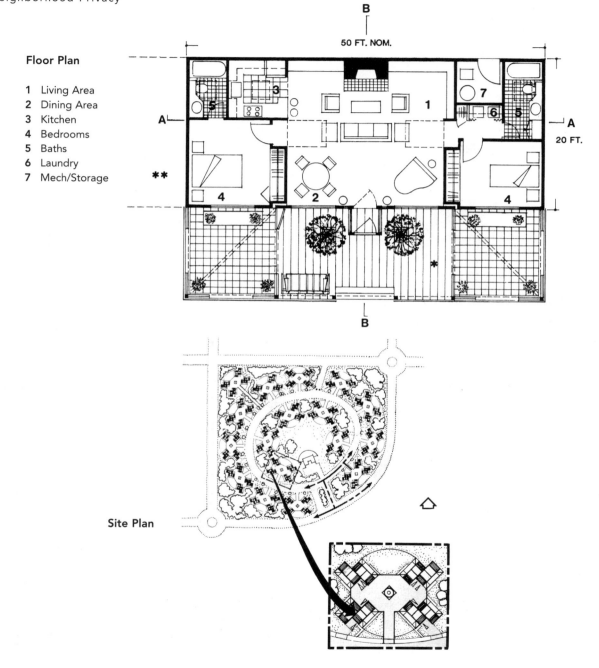

Floor Plan

1 Living Area
2 Dining Area
3 Kitchen
4 Bedrooms
5 Baths
6 Laundry
7 Mech/Storage

B

50 FT. NOM.

A

A

20 FT.

B

Site Plan

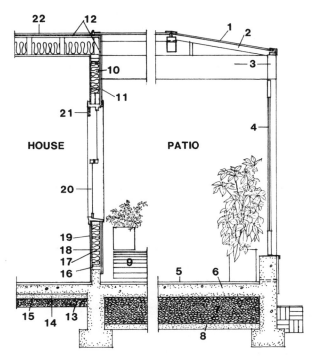

HOUSE   **PATIO**

Wall Section

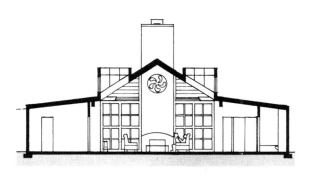

AA

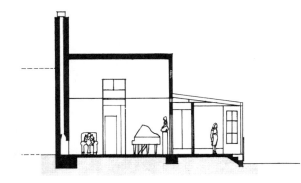

BB

1	Tempered Glass	14	Sand
2	Anodized Alum.	15	Vapor Barrier
3	Timber Framing	16	Wood Framing
4	Wood/Glass Doors	17	Insulation
5	Tile	18	Vapor Barrier
6	Conc. Slab	19	Gypsum Board Interior
7	Rock Thermal Storage	20	Operable Sash
8	Pumice	21	Adjustable Louver
9	Water Thermal Storage	22	Roofing
10	Vent Beyond		
11	Wood Siding		
12	Plywood Sheathing		
13	Gravel		

Sections

Dramatic Coastal Lookout

Marin County, California
990 gross square feet (including terraces and greenhouse)

T his site is located in the hills above the rugged California coast. The house is composed of terraces oriented due south to capture the spectacular view and maximize the mild climate. The architectural form of the house is generated by the northern California vernacular combined with passive solar access needs.

The minimum heating requirements of the house are served on the lower level by a greenhouse which collects heat and radiates through the thermal mass of the floor slab.

The upper level is also heated by the greenhouse in combination with the fireplace. In addition, there is a small auxiliary mechanical system if poor weather conditions persist.

Nancy Scheinholtz

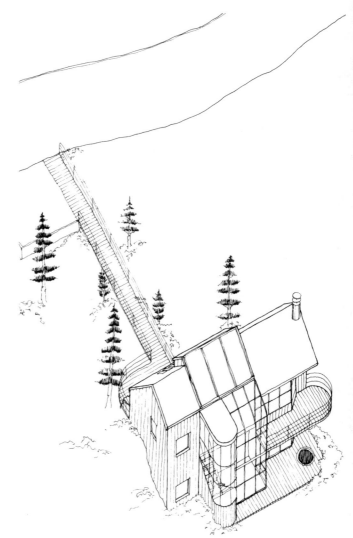

Axonometric

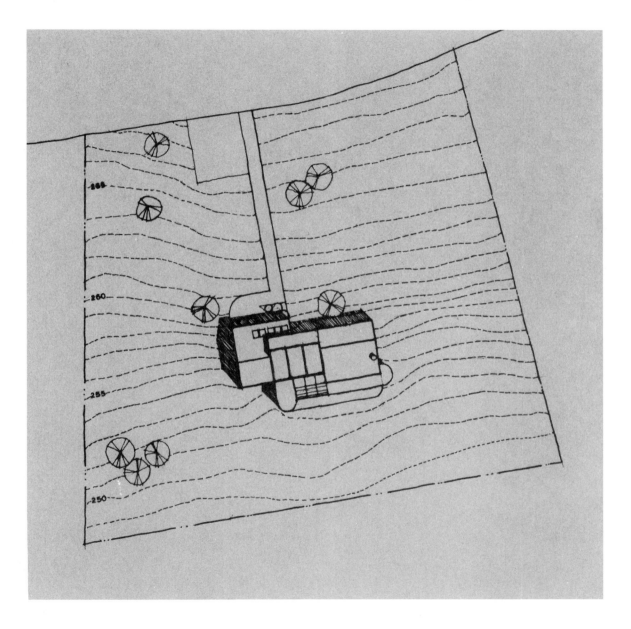

Site Plan

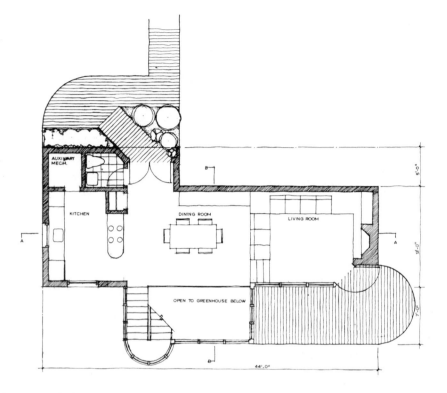

Upper Level Plan

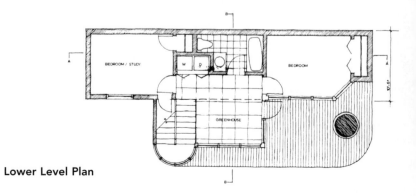

Lower Level Plan

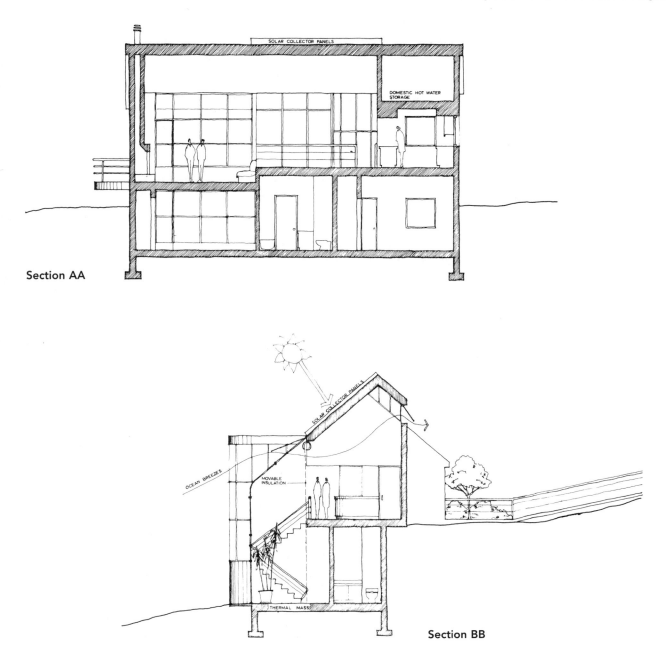

Section AA

Section BB

Dramatic Coastal Lookout

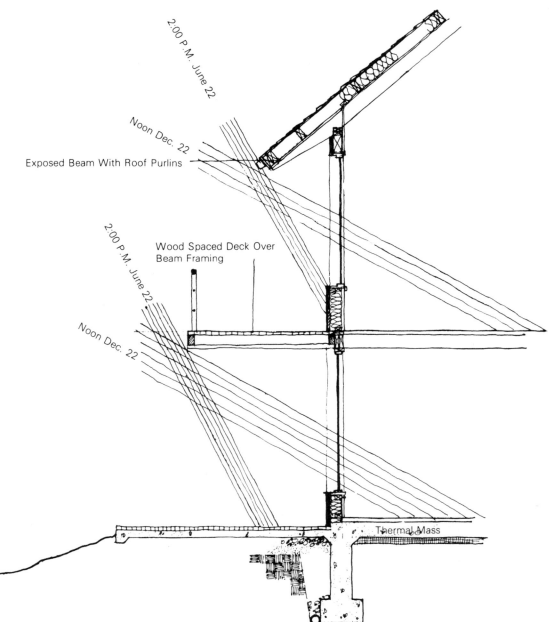

2:00 P.M. June 22

Noon Dec. 22

Exposed Beam With Roof Purlins

2:00 P.M. June 22

Noon Dec. 22

Wood Spaced Deck Over
Beam Framing

Thermal Mass

Wall Section

Classical Florida House

Gainsville, Florida
1,000 gross square feet

A proposal for a small house on a suburban subdivision on the outskirts of Gainesville, Florida.

It is designed in the belief that it is possible to build a small, formal house which combines many of the advantages of compact planning and energy-efficient design with the usual functional and psychological needs of a small, middle-class, suburban family.

It is based on the traditional southern house type, with a wide roof overhang for maximum shading. It is freestanding and set on a plinth above ground.

A series of vents at ground level bring air into the house and circulate it vertically through a thermal chimney.

The design attempts to solve the problem of size by using a big roof to give the impression of largeness, and overscaled elements, such as the entrance dormer and columns.

Gordon Ashworth

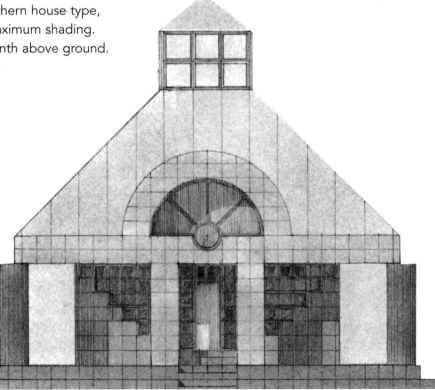

Elevation

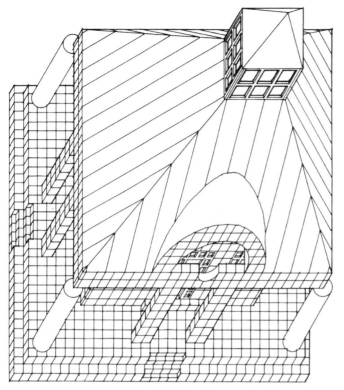

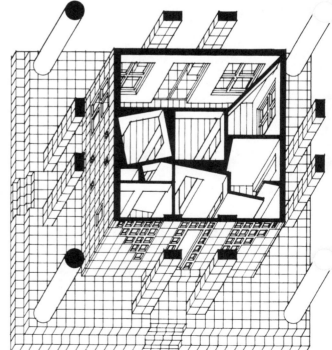

Axonometrics

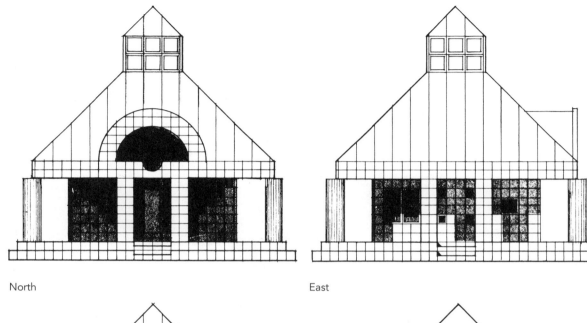

North

East

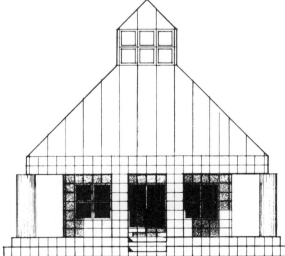

South

East-West Section

Elevations

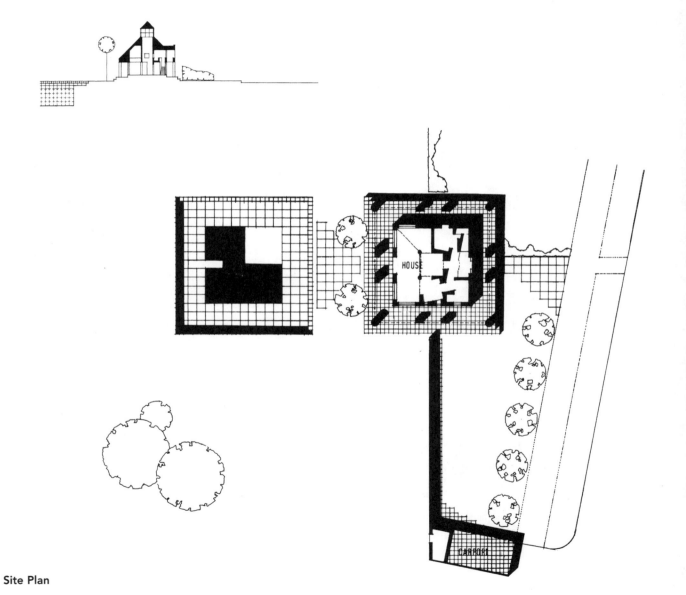

Site Plan

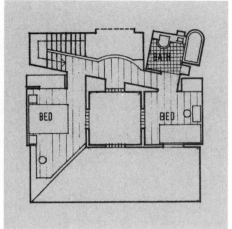

Upper Level

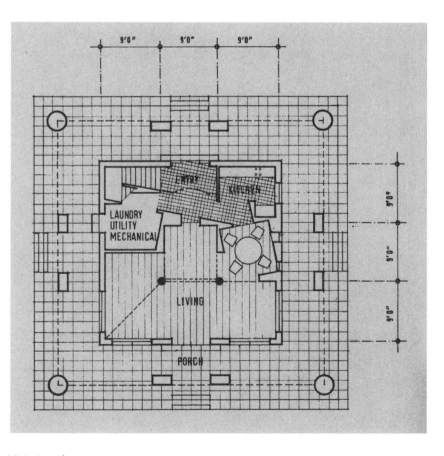

Main Level

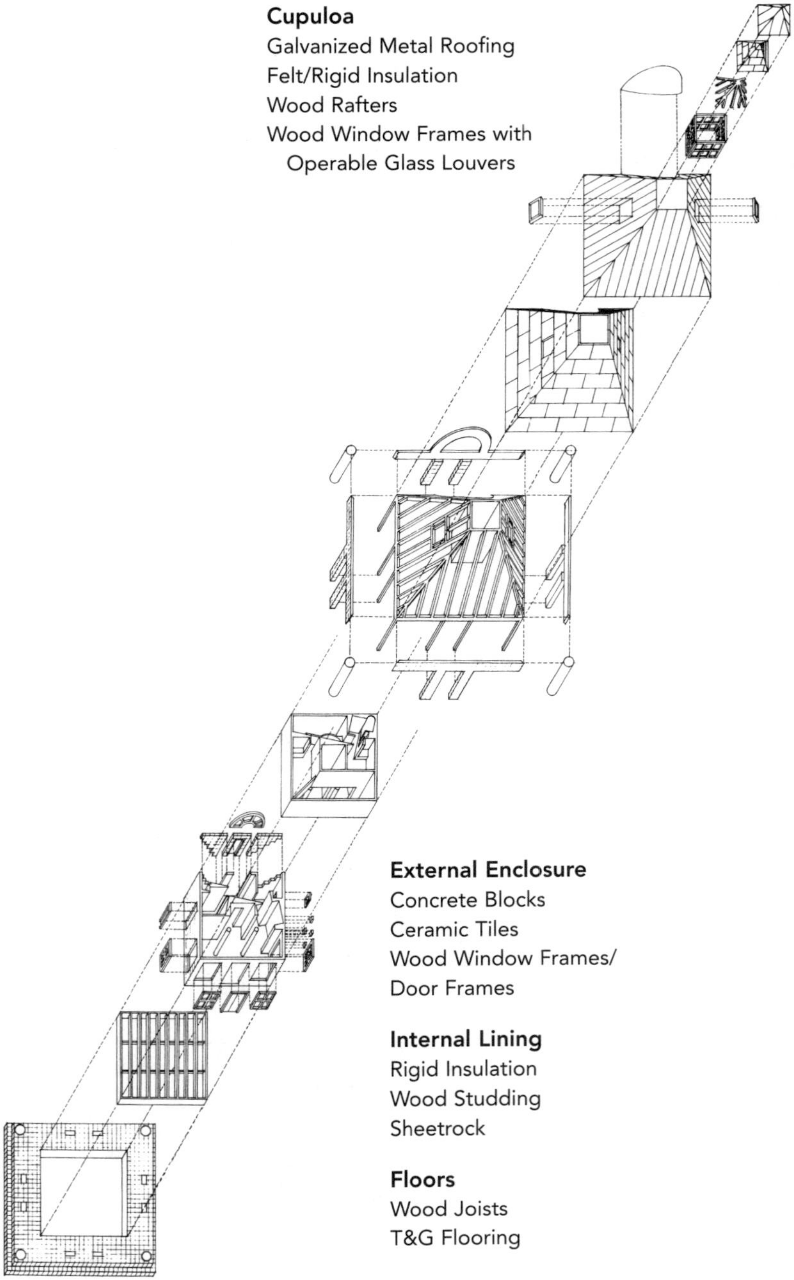

Classical Florida House

Cupuloa
Galvanized Metal Roofing
Felt/Rigid Insulation
Wood Rafters
Wood Window Frames with
  Operable Glass Louvers

Roof
Galvanized Metal
Roofing
Felt/Rigid Insulation
Wood
Rafters/Corner
Beams/Edge Beams
Metal Skylights

Structure
Tubular Steel
Columns
Steel Angle Beams
(All Faced with
Wood Studding,
Plywood and Tiles;
Except Corner
Columns Which Are
Faced with Circular
Glass Fiber Casings)

Internal Division
Wood studding
Sheetrock

External Enclosure
Concrete Blocks
Ceramic Tiles
Wood Window Frames/
Door Frames

Internal Lining
Rigid Insulation
Wood Studding
Sheetrock

Floors
Wood Joists
T&G Flooring

Foundation
Concrete Slab and
Edgebeams
Clay Tiles on External Areas

142

Cozy Woodland Home

North Bangor, New York
996 gross square feet

An Outline

- Earth-sheltered concept in harmony with south-sloping building site.

- Southern exposure has beautiful view of constantly running stream.

- Privacy. The six-acre site adjoins hundred of acres of pastures, meadows, and forest.

- A wind-sheltered forest cove.

- Natural landscaping. The open forest floor. The house area and play area are grassed.

- Sandy gravel loam soil. Good percolation.

- Russian fireplace with high ceiling hot air intakes down through fireplace mass.

- Mass storage. Tile and concrete floors, and masonry walls.

- Economical removable night insulation of fabric-covered urethane panels.

- Structural bay truss system, long span decking. Ease of construction.

Marc Camens

Perspective

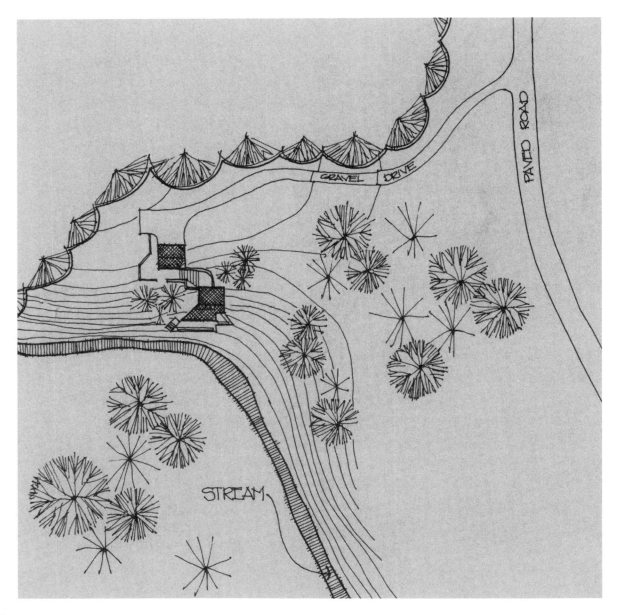

Site Plan

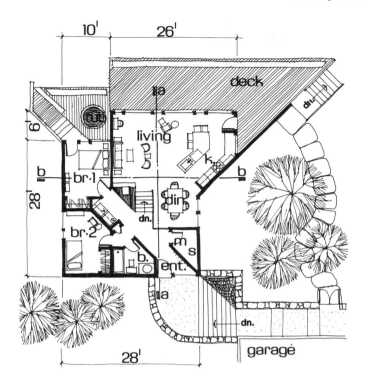

Floor Plan

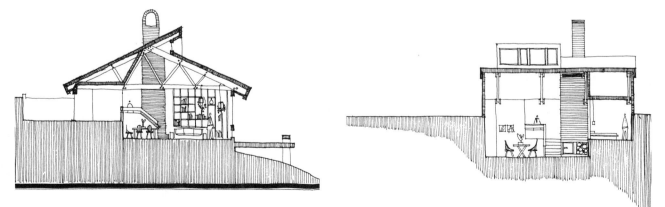

Section AA

Section BB

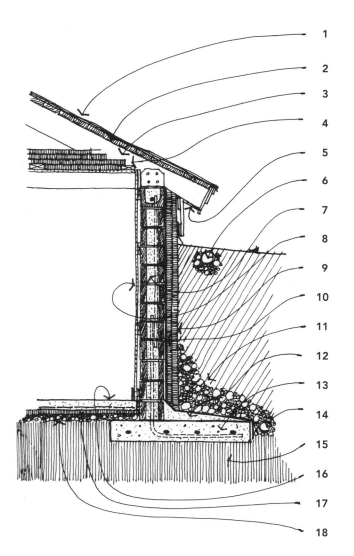

1 Asphalt Shingles Over 15# Felt
2 2 x 6 T&G Wood Deck
3 Heavy Timber Trusses
4 5" Urethane Foam-Foil Faced
5 Vent Strip Cont.
6 Upper 4" Perforated Drain
7 10" C.M.U. Reinf. & Conc. Filled
8 ½" Gyp. Bd. on Furring Strips
9 4" Polystyrene Insulation
10 Waterproof Membrane
11 Gravel Fill
12 Footer Drainage Cant.
13 Reinforced Cantilever Ftg.
14 4" Perforated Drain & Filter
15 Undisturbed Earth
16 4" Reinf. Conc. Slab
17 1" Polystyrene Insulation
18 Gravel Fill

Wall Section

"Prairie One"

Stilwater, Oklahoma
900 gross square feet

The concept of Prairie One is a passive thermo sink plenum/superinsulated solar syphon from which hot air rises to the top. It is vented by an operable sky-light in conjunction with awning windows in the passive solar wall to maintain positive ventilation. The awning windows are approximately three times larger in surface area than the skylight at the top solar syphon.

The air lock entries are on the east and west walls. They are made of 8-foot-square, precast concrete storm sewer pipes with sliding glass doors at either end.

Prairie One assumes a very active owner who is a "do-it-yourself" type person. The hermatic environment of Prairie One with its ivy-covered earth berm on three sides of the living space affords the use of earth and nature to enclose the house. The earth berm is constructed of loose rubble and compact fill so as to maintain its shape and insulation integrity. The passive solar wall is the open glazed side which faces the south with a view of an open field. Deciduous trees line the south side, shading the passive solar wall during the summer and allowing heat gain during the winter.

Richard Dunham

Perspective

"Prairie One"

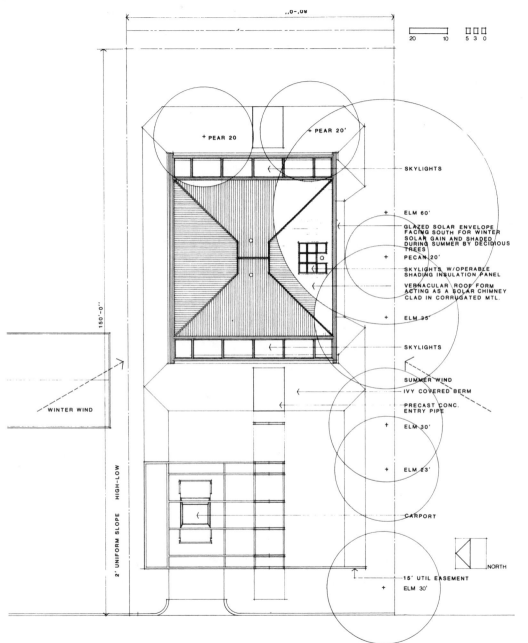

SKYLIGHTS

ELM 60'

GLAZED SOLAR ENVELOPE
FACING SOUTH FOR WINTER
SOLAR GAIN AND SHADED
DURING SUMMER BY DECIDIOUS
TREES

PECAN 20'

SKYLIGHTS W/OPERABLE
SHADING INSULATION PANEL

VERNACULAR ROOF FORM
ACTING AS A SOLAR CHIMNEY
CLAD IN CORRUGATED MTL.

ELM 35'

SKYLIGHTS

SUMMER WIND

IVY COVERED BERM

PRECAST CONC.
ENTRY PIPE

ELM 30'

ELM 23'

CARPORT

15' UTIL EASEMENT

ELM 30'

NORTH

+ PEAR 20

+ PEAR 20'

80'-0"

150'-0"

2' UNIFORM SLOPE HIGH-LOW

WINTER WIND

20   10   5 3 0

Site Plan

148

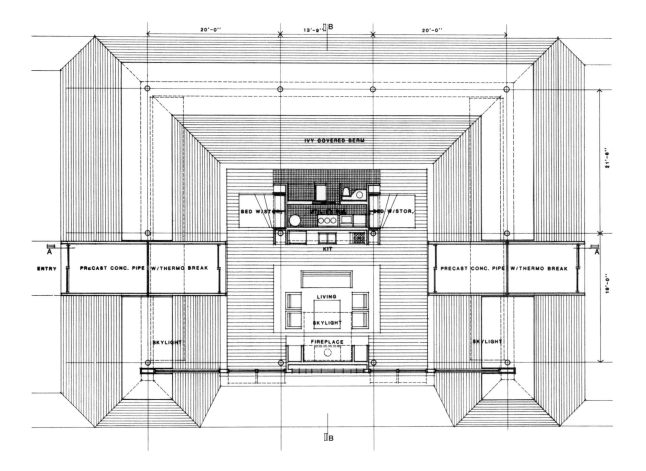

20'-0"   13'-9"   B   20'-0"

21'-8"

IVY COVERED BEAM

BED W/STOR.   BED W/STOR.

A   KIT   A

ENTRY   PRECAST CONC. PIPE W/THERMO BREAK   PRECAST CONC. PIPE W/THERMO BREAK   16'-0"

LIVING

SKYLIGHT

SKYLIGHT   FIREPLACE   SKYLIGHT

B

Floor Plan

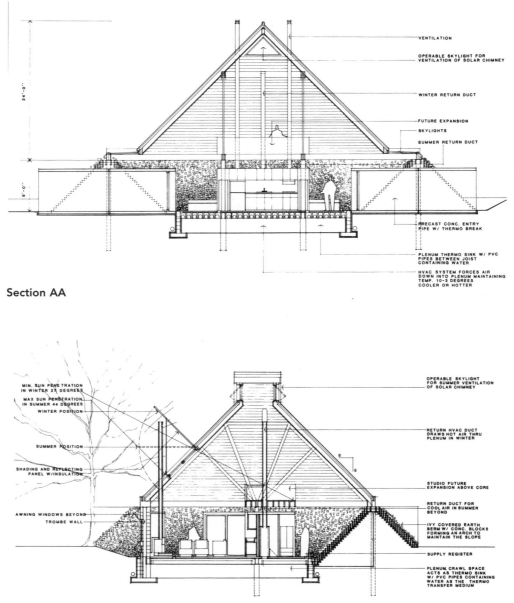

Section AA

VENTILATION

OPERABLE SKYLIGHT FOR
VENTILATION OF SOLAR CHIMNEY

WINTER RETURN DUCT

FUTURE EXPANSION

SKYLIGHTS

SUMMER RETURN DUCT

PRECAST CONC. ENTRY
PIPE W/ THERMO BREAK

PLENUM THERMO SINK W/ PVC
PIPES BETWEEN JOIST
CONTAINING WATER

HVAC SYSTEM FORCES AIR
DOWN INTO PLENUM MAINTAINING
TEMP. 10-3 DEGREES
COOLER OR HOTTER

MIN. SUN PENETRATION
IN WINTER 27 DEGREES

MAX SUN PENETRATION
IN SUMMER 44 DEGREES

WINTER POSITION

SUMMER POSITION

SHADING AND REFLECTING
PANEL W/INSULATION

AWNING WINDOWS BEYOND

TROMBE WALL

OPERABLE SKYLIGHT
FOR SUMMER VENTILATION
OF SOLAR CHIMNEY

RETURN HVAC DUCT
DRAWS HOT AIR THRU
PLENUM IN WINTER

STUDIO FUTURE
EXPANSION ABOVE CORE

RETURN DUCT FOR
COOL AIR IN SUMMER
BEYOND

IVY COVERED EARTH
BERM W/ CONC. BLOCKS
FORMING AN ARCH TO
MAINTAIN THE SLOPE

SUPPLY REGISTER

PLENUM CRAWL SPACE
ACTS AS THERMO SINK
W/ PVC PIPES CONTAINING
WATER AS THE THERMO
TRANSFER MEDIUM

Section BB

Enlarged Section

1   Built-Up Truss 2 x 4
2   Corrugated Mtl. Cladding
3   3" Rigid Insulation Roof
     Decking R6 w/Roofing Felt
4   6" Batten Insulation R19
5   2 x 8 Ceiling Rafters
     16" O.C.
6   Vapor Barrier
7   1 x 8 T&G Fin. Ceiling
8   Skylight
9   Mtl. Rake Closure
10 2-2 x 12 Built Up w/Rigid
     Insulation
11 45 Degree Slope Maintained
     By 8" Sq. Conc. Blocks
     Forming an Arch w/Keystone
12 Precast Conc. Storm Pipe
     w/Thermo Break
13 Compact Fill Earth Berm
14 Supply Register
15 Chain Link Fence
     w/Vapor Barrier and
     Rigid Insulation
16 Vapor Barrier
17 Conc. Footing w/Conc.
     Blk. Stem Wall Filled
     w/Vermiculite
18 Super Insulated
     Thermo Plenum
19 8" Concrete Pip. Pier
20 Drainage Pipe
21 8" Dia. PVC Pipe w/Water
     Capped on Ends, Wire Mesh
     Supports PVC Thermo Sink
22 Vapor Barrier
23 2 x 12 Floor Joist 12" O.C.
24 1 x 8 T&G Floor
     w/³⁄₄" Ply Wd. Subfloor
25 12" Conc. Pip. Pier

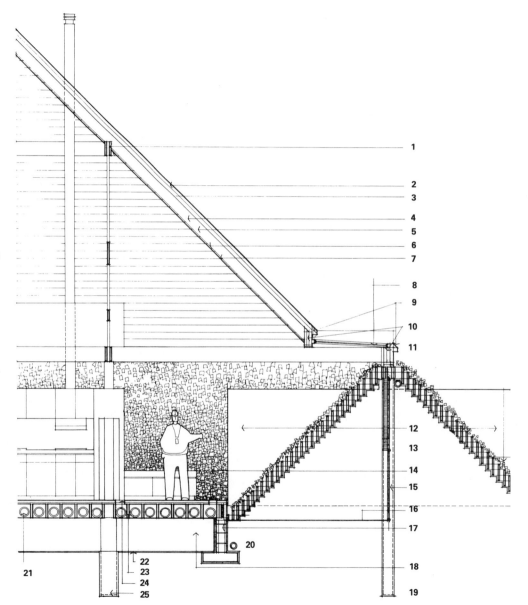

Flexible Family Living

Chapel Hill, North Carolina
1,000 gross square feet

The site is in a rural neighborhood on a 1½-acre lot which slopes gently away from the road to a creek on the south side and is heavily wooded with deciduous trees. Temperatures in the immediate area are generally 5°-10° cooler than the nearest reporting station, and the prevailing winds are from the northwest.

The house is of direct gain passive solar design with a covered or screened porch which can be converted into a solarium in the winter by attaching clear awning material or glass storm panels. An insulating shutter for the skylights over the living room pivots at the ridge to store against the opposite ceiling when open.

Brick floors are used in conjunction with clear water tubes in the cabinets behind the couches for thermal mass.

In the summer, awnings are placed over the skylights to prevent overheating, operable windows in the gable ends over the living room offer natural ventilation, and a whole-house attic fan is planned. Transoms are used over the bedroom doors to maintain privacy while providing ventilation. Supplemental heat comes from a centrally located wood stove. The projected heating costs are based on an electric air-to-air heat pump.

There's a great deal of flexibility in the living space: the kitchen table can be rotated to seat six, and two additional sleeping areas can be provided by rotating the two L-shaped couches face-to-face to create two full-sized beds.

This house was designed for an exciting and spacious-feeling living environment for people desiring the smaller house.

Bob Giddings

Perspective

152

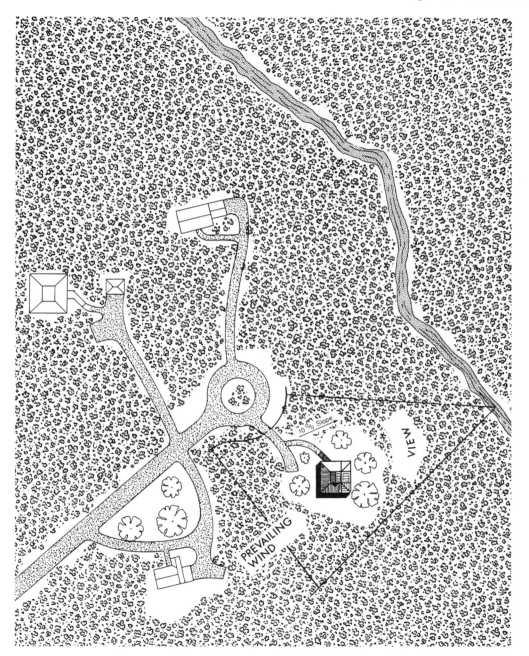

Site Plan

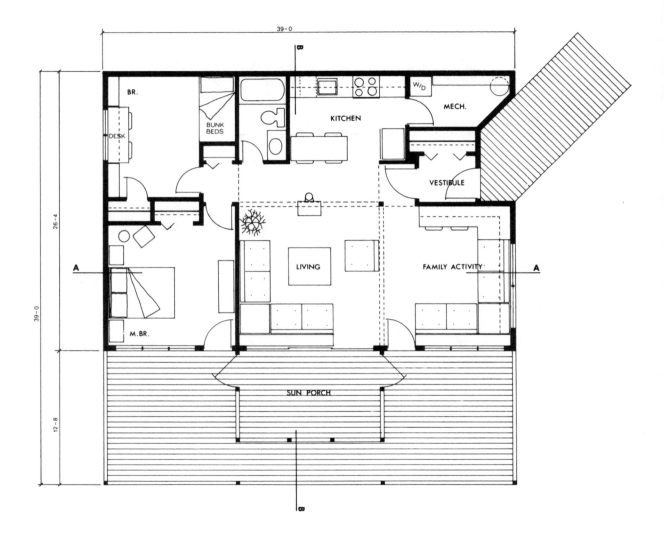

39-0

26-4

39-0

12-8

BR.

DESK

BUNK
BEDS

KITCHEN

W/D

MECH.

VESTIBULE

A

A

LIVING

FAMILY ACTIVITY

M.BR.

SUN PORCH

Floor Plan

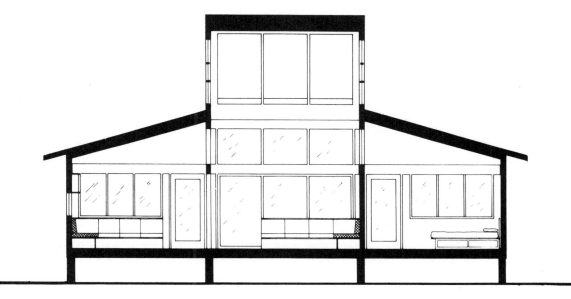

Section AA

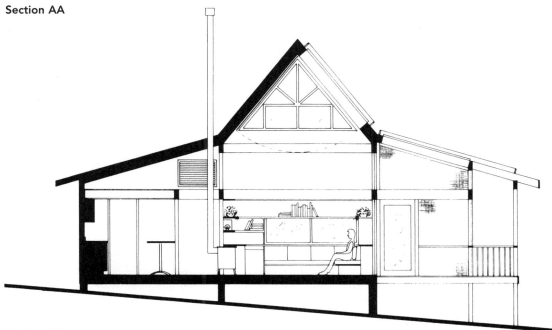

Section BB

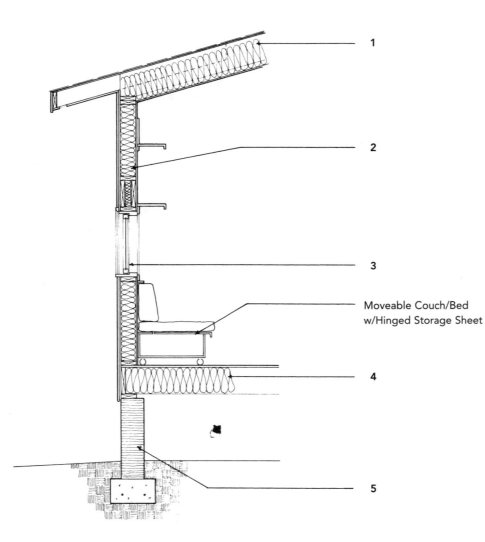

1 **Roof Construction**
240 # Asphalt Shingles on 15 # Bldg. Felt on ½" Plywood w/H-Clips on Roof Trusses or 2 x 12's @ 24" O.C. w/R-30 Batt. Insul. Over 4 Mil. Vapor Barrier

2 **Exterior Wall Construction**
Siding (Owner's Choice) on ½" Foil Faced Foam Sheathing on 2 x 6 Studs @ 24" O.C. w/Let in Diagonal Bracing & R-19 Batt. Insulation w/½" Drywall Over 4 Mil. Vapor Barrier

3 **Windows & Sliding Glass Doors**
Windows are Wood Casement, Awnings & Fixed w/Thermopane Glass Sliding Glass Doors are Bronze Finish Aluminum w/Thermal Break & Thermopane

4 **Floor Construction**
Finish Floor (Owner's Choice) on 1/4" T&G Plywood on 2 x 10's @ 16" O.C. w/R-30 Batt. Insul. w/4 Mil. Vapor Barrier on Ground

5 **Foundation Construction**
3" Scored Conc. Block on Continuous Concrete Footing w/Continuous Steel Reinforcing

Moveable Couch/Bed w/Hinged Storage Sheet

Wall Section

Modified Colonial Saltbox

Branford, Connecticut
962 gross square feet

The building site is part of a wooded acreage being subdivided for single-family homes. The 7,500-square-foot lot is situated in a clearing at the top of a knoll with Southeast views of Long Island Sound. Four large maples are to remain. The south-facing slope is ideal for passive solar techniques. Summer breezes blow off the water while winter storms buffet the shore from south and west. Underlying soil is a stable, gravelly clay with good bearing characteristics.

This compact design has been developed from the Connecticut saltbox of colonial times to place bedrooms below the main living space. The building volume is nearly square to reduce surface area. Interior spaces are continuous and an entry lock is provided.

A metal roof reflects uncontrolled radiation; windows and translucent panels admit and diffuse controlled sunlight. Night insulation (R-9) is provided by sliding and hinged panels.

The principle energy feature is a concrete masonry solar chimney which concentrates storage mass and admits daylight in the center of the house. Additional mass is provided in a thickened ground floor slab.

In summer the air is vented to promote natural cooling. Collectors for a solar water heater are mounted on the roof adjacent to the chimney.

Solar techniques provide 92 percent of the heating needs of this home. A wood stove located in the central chimney can easily supply the balance. A furnace provides back-up heat and ventilation.

Thomas M. Haskell

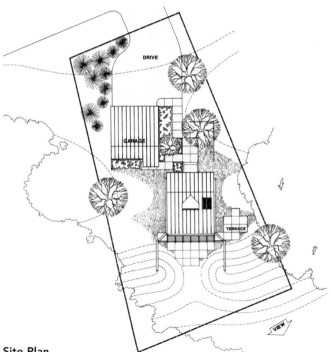

Site Plan

157

Modified Colonial Saltbox

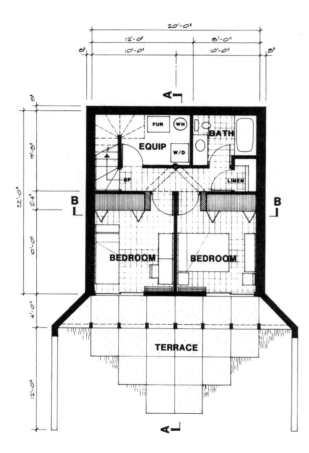

Ground Floor Plan

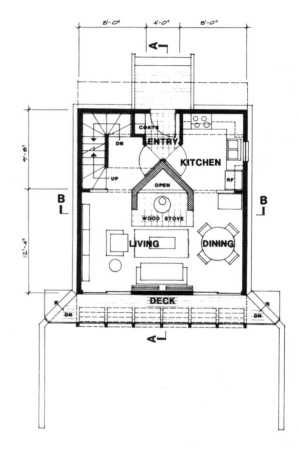

Main Floor Plan

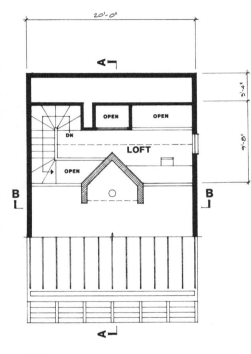

Loft

Perspective

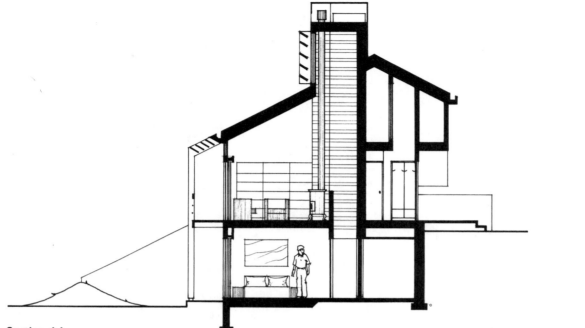

Section AA

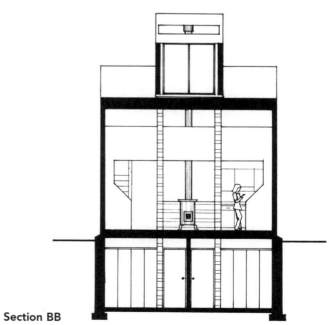

Section BB

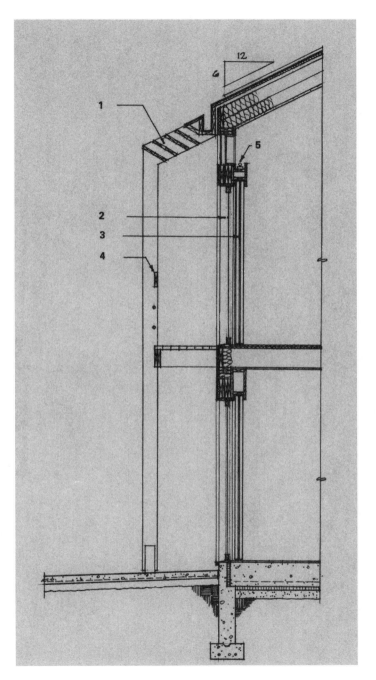

1 Wood Louvers
2 Wood Sliding Doors
3 Sliding Translucent Insulating Panels
4 Hand Rail
5 Light Cove

South Wall

1 **Roof**
Standing Seam Metal Roof
⅝" Plywood Underlayment
2 x 12 Rafter w/2 x 2 Nailer, 24" O.C.
12" Batt. Insulation
Vapor Barrier
⅝" Gypsum Bd.

2 **Loft**

3 **Wall**
⅝" Gypsum Bd.
Vapor Barrier
2 x 6 Studs, 16" O.C.
Batt. Insulation
⅝" Insul. Sheathing
Horizontal Cedar Siding

4 **Floor**
Hardwood Flr.
¾" Plywd. Subfloor
2 x 10 Joists, 16" O.C.
⅝" Gypsum Bd.

5 **Main Floor**

6 **Wall**
⅝" Gypsum Bd.
Vapor Barrier
3½" Studs, 16" O.C.
Batt. Insulation
60 Mil. Waterproofing
8" Conc. Foundation Wall

7 **Ground Floor**

8 **Floor**
Quarry Tile
4" Concrete Slab
Vapor Barrier
1½" Rigid Insulation
4" Sand Cushion

9 **Metal Gutter in Wood Frame**

10 **Contin. Vent**

11 **Plywood Soffit**

12 **Metal Cap Flashing**

13 **Footing Drain**

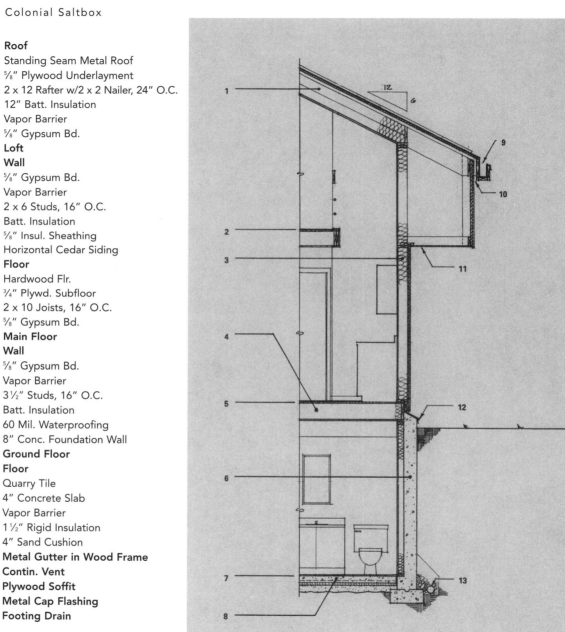

North Wall

Nature Lover's House

Lincoln, Massachusetts
960 gross square feet

A home for an amateur naturalist who requires a flexible program allowing for both social and solitary usage; here a high, quiet perch provides both and strikes a balance between protection and exposure.

A cost-efficient post foundation emphasizes both long water views and eye-level forest canopy. The house is summer shaded, protected from the northeast winter wind, and well above possible floods.

A large planned woodlot will thin over time to grazing land, retaining all trees along the water line and enough growth elsewhere for windbreaks, animal shade, and erosion control.

The parti points not just to a structure in harmony with the terrain, but also to ultimate treehouse of childhood, reinterpreted according to adult needs.

A long bridge from the driveway/parking area is playful in its suggestion of a moat, but quite serious in its practical linking with the pond below. The ample porch is balanced by a private deck off to the side, designed specifically as a retreat and as a site for a small, protected aviary.

The site is a mixture of meadow, marsh, and woodland on glacial till. The pond shore is either under conservation or in limited private hands dedicated to preservation. The pond supports much migratory and permanent wildlife, and is a routine nesting ground for geese, heron, duck, and osprey.

Neil Husher and Kathyanne Cowles

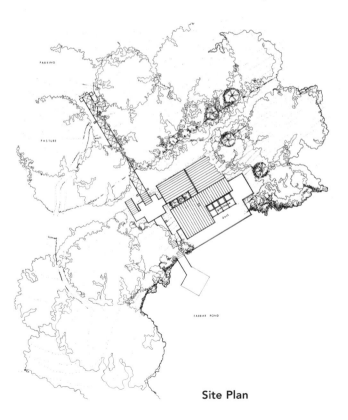

Site Plan

Section AA

Section BB

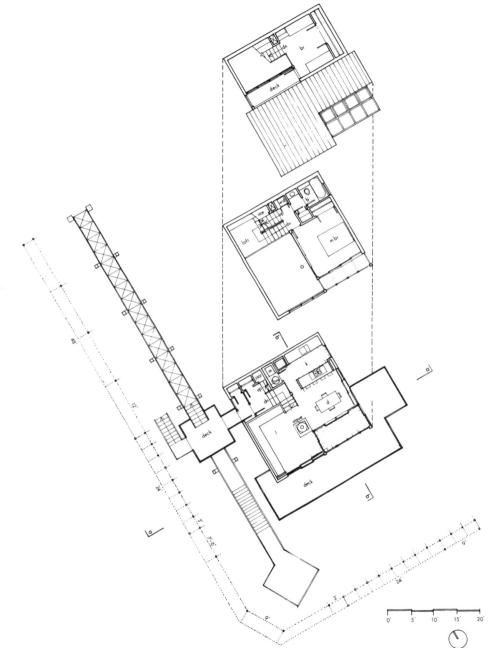

Floor Plan

Perspective

1. Standing Seam Metal Roof
2. 2 x 12 Rafters @ 24" O.C.
3. 10" Batt. Insulation
4. 1" Foam Insulation Taped for Vapor Barrier
5. Flash
6. Vent Holes
7. Tongue & Groove Siding
8. Wood Deck on Built-up Roof
9. 8" Batt. Insulation
10. 1" Foam Insulation Taped for Vapor Barrier
11. 2 x 8 Joists @ 24" O.C.
12. 5" Batt. Insulation
13. 1" Foam Insulation Taped for Vapor Barrier
14. 2 x 6 Studs @ 24" O.C.
15. ½" CDX Plywood
16. Tongue & Groove Siding
17. Vapor Barrier
18. 2 x 12 Joists @ 24" O.C.
19. 10" Batt. Insulation
20. Wire Mesh
21. 4, 2 x 12 Built-up Beams Bolted to Post
22. 18" Pressure-Treated Pole (creosote), Notched to Receive Wood Beams
23. Concrete Footing
24. Standing Seam Metal Roof
25. 10" Batt. Insulation
26. Insulated Shoji Screens
27. Wood Frame Window Fixed Glass, Double Glazed
28. Aluminum Frame Double-Glazed Sliding Glass Doors
29. Insulated Shoji Screens
30. Metal Grill Decking on Pad
31. ½" CC Plugged Ext. Plywood Painted
32. 18" Pole
33. Steel Cable Cross-Bracing

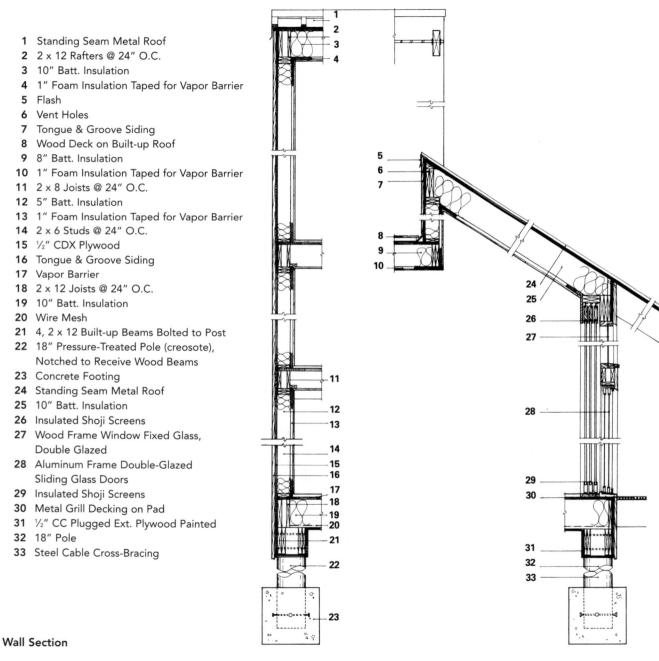

Wall Section

Underground Eden

Prescott, Arizona
1,000 gross square feet

The intent of this concept is to create an efficient, quality, garden environment that is adaptable to many different site conditions and family lifestyles, and is economical to build and operate.

A passive solar direct heat gain technique utilizes the sunken garden, floor-to-ceiling double-glazed glass, and the triple-glazed skylight. During the winter, when the tree has lost its leaves, the protected garden becomes a heat sink, which increases the outside temperature adjacent to the glass wall, thereby reducing interior heat loss.

Direct solar energy enters the house through the glass wall and skylight. It is stored in the exposed floor slab and rear wall mass. Cooler room temperatures cause the stored heat to radiate back into the interior.

The centrally located fireplace is actually a high efficiency wood-burning stove with glass screens, outside combustion air intakes, and an air chamber built into the hood. With the barometric evaporative cooler damper closed, the air inside the chamber is heated quickly by the fire and is drawn through the exposed sculptural duct system by natural convection.

In-line duct "assist" fans could be incorporated to accelerate air movement when necessary.

Wind power could supply electrical energy for auxiliary portable floor units when more heat is needed. The pole fan above the sleeping loft provides additional warm air circulation.

For cooling, the garden tree and canvas trellis shade flush south glazing without inhibiting the view, and the five-foot porch overhang protects living room glass. A removable wooden lattice screen is placed over the skylight to minimize direct solar exposure, and the earth-insulated wall stabilizes exterior wall temperatures.

Edward Madison Jones

Perspective

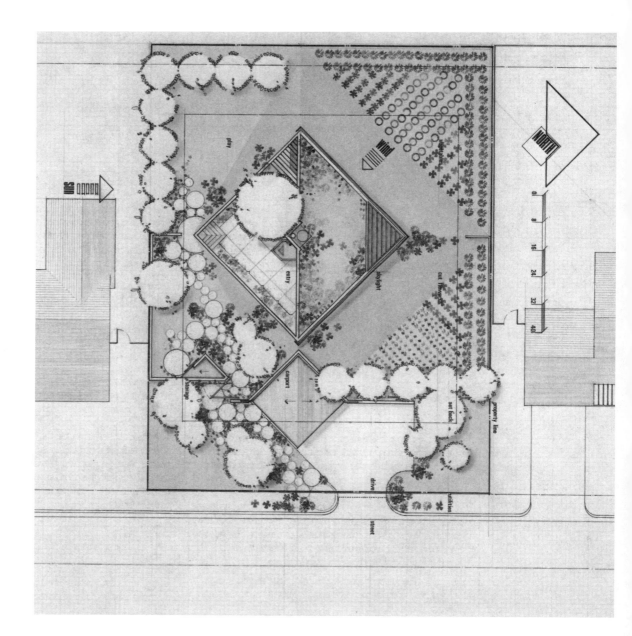

Site Plan

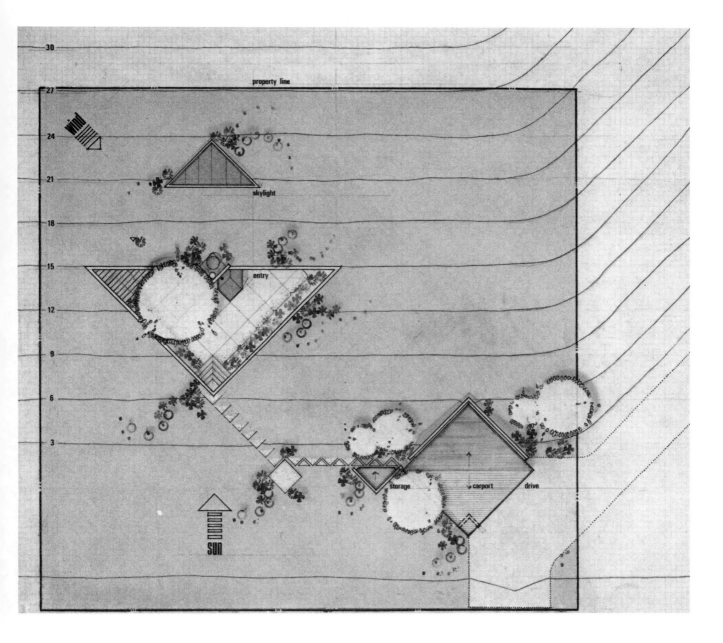

Section AA

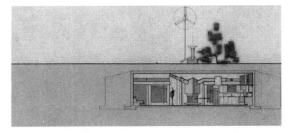

Section BB

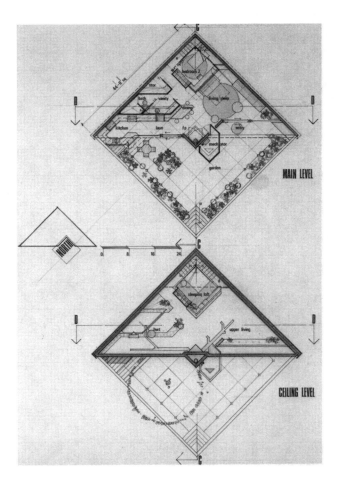

Floor Plan

Section CC

Section DD

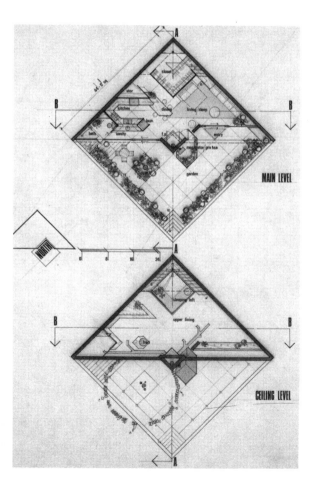

Floor Plan

Vermont Retreat

Central Vermont
993 gross square feet

The compact house should be an economic alternative to the mobile home. To compete, all systems must be based on standard building procedures, and easily constructed by a carpenter or owner-builder.

The heat storage system utilizes the first floor for a collector and storage for both passive and wood heat.

This house is in a central Vermont valley with western hills obstructing the afternoon sun. The soil is sandy, providing good septage, but a town system is nearby, and alternative pricing should be considered.

Considerable cost savings could be realized with alternate floor and sliding finishes, and altering the heat storage.

Tom Leytham

Perspective

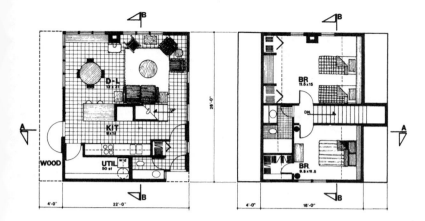

Floor Plans

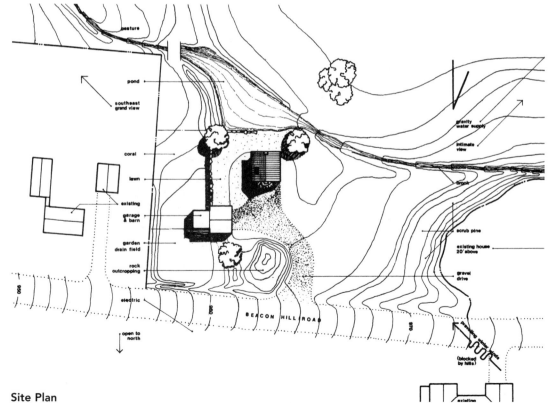

Site Plan

Wall Section

Sections

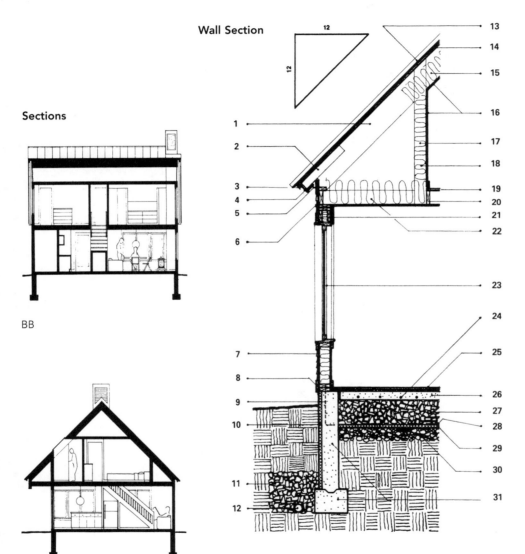

BB

AA

1   2 x 12s—16" O.C.
2   2 x 4 Scab
3   1 x 2 Trim
4   1 x 6 Trim
5   Eave Vent with Screen
6   Clapboard Siding
7   Insulating Sheathing (Brace)
8   Fiberglass Sill Seal
9   Anchor Bolt
10 2" Rigid Insulation
11 Crushed Stone
12 Footing Drain
13 Standing Seam Metal
    Roofing
14 ⅝" Plywood
15 9" Fiberglass in Sloped Roof
    and 12" in Flat
16 Gypsum Board
17 5½" Fiberglass Insulation
    with Vapor Barrier
18 2 x 6s—16" O.C.
    (Balloon Frame)
19 ¾" Tongue & Groove
    Plyw'd
20 2 x 10 Blocking
21 2-2 x 6s
22 2 x 10'—16" O.C.
23 Casement Window
24 Heat Piping
25 Masonry Floor Set
    in Cement Bed
26 Light Weight Concrete Slab
27 Crushed Stone
28 Vapor Barrier
29 2" Rigid Insulation
30 Gravel
31 Concrete Footing
    & Frost Wall

Storybook Cottage

New Haven, Vermont
978 gross square feet

This compact house design combines simple structural and energy-efficient planning with the detail and craftmanship of traditional New England building. A regional approach incorporates indigenous forms such as the breezeway, ellipse-shaped and engaged fan trim, and crafted details within a curved roof form. This house design is oriented towards people desiring design and craftmanship with quality and character. The orientation of the gable end to the south allows for the maximum visual impact by this small house.

The elongation of the plan maximizes the solar potential. Options include: earth berming with second-floor entry, garage, breezeway, greenhouse, alternate northwest entry, and attic expansion space.

The combination of superinsulation and solar contributions will reduce overall energy consumption to less than one or two cords of wood per year, depending on location and user characteristics.

William Maclay

Storybook Cottage

Perspective

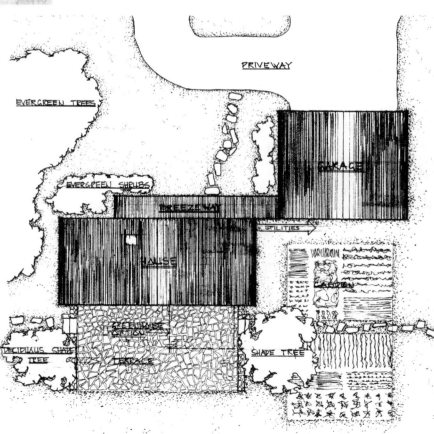

DRIVEWAY

EVERGREEN TREES

EVERGREEN SHRUBS

GARAGE

BREEZEWAY

UTILITIES

HOUSE

GARDEN

GREENHOUSE
ATRIUM

TERRACE

DECIDUOUS SHADE
TREE

SHADE TREE

Bermed Site With Garage

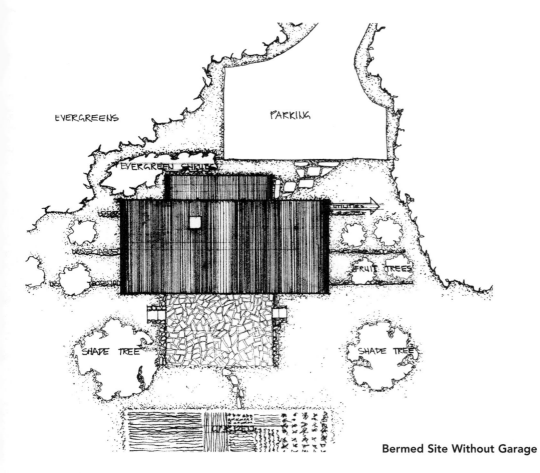

EVERGREENS

PARKING

EVERGREEN SHRUBS

UTILITIES

FRUIT TREES

SHADE TREE

SHADE TREE

Bermed Site Without Garage

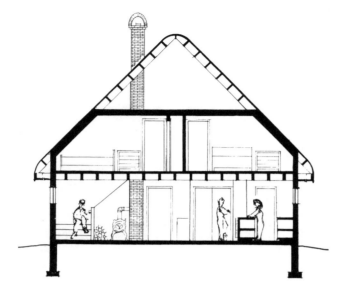

Section AA

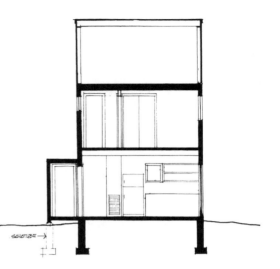

Section BB

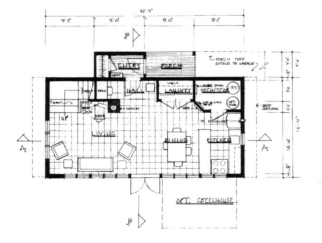

First Floor Plan

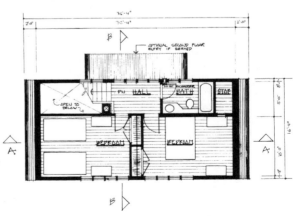

Second Floor Plan

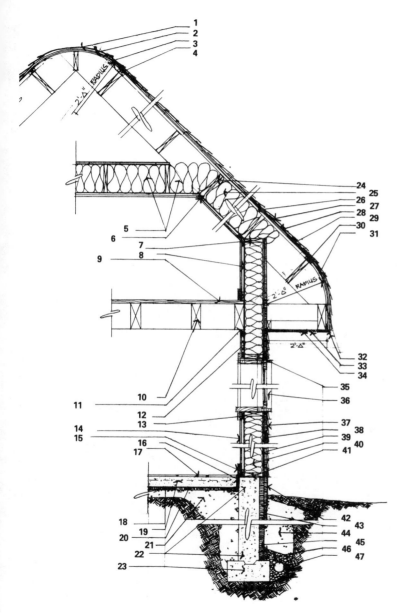

1 Roll Roofing @ Cap
2 15# Felt
3 2 Layers ¼" AC Ply @ Curve-Curved Blocking @ Joints
4 Furring
5 12" Fiberglass Insulation
6 ¾" Furring-16" O.C.
7 2 x 8 Balloon Framed Wall @ East & West w/Cont. V.P.
8 Air Space for Elect. Chase
9 2 x 6 T&G Flrg.
10 Exposed 4 x 10 Joists 24" O.C.
11 J or L Bead
12 6 Mil. Vapor Barrier x/No Penetrations-Lap All Joints
13 ¾" Furring for Elect. Chase
14 ½" Gyp. Bd.
15 Baseboard
16 ½" Premolded Expansion Joint
17 Tile or Slate-Mastic Set
18 1" EPS Rigid Insulation
19 4" Slab w/6 x 6 8/8 WW Fabric
20 6 Mil Poly-Lap @ Wall
21 Compacted Gravel Fill-4" MIU
22 8" Wall w/2-#4 Bars-Top & Bot.
23 PTG w/Key or #14 Stl. Dowels-24" O.C. Typ.
24 2 x 12 Rafter-24" O.C.
25 12" Fiberglass Insulation

26 Air Space for Vent
27 Asphalt Shingles
28 15# Felt
29 ½" CDX Sheathing
30 Furring
31 2 Layers ¼" AC Ply-curved Blocking @ Joints
32 Drip Edge
33 Soffit Vent
34 1" T&G Soffit or ½" AC Ply
35 No Header @ Window-Non Structural Wall
36 Permashield Windows or Eq. Seal w/Polycel Sealant and Vapor Barrier
37 Clapboards-3" Exposed
38 1" Blueboard Insulation
39 ½" CDX Ply Sheathing
40 9" Fiberglass Insulation
41 Sill Insulation
42 Aluminum Flashing to 1'-0" B.G.
43 3" Blueboard to 2'-0" B.G.
44 Gravel Fill
45 2" Blueboard Insulation
46 Crushed Stone
47 Perimeter Drain

Wall Section

A Taste of the Far East

Sandstone, West Virginia

875 gross square feet

The site is a ridge top in Summers County, West Virginia, with excellent views of the New River and the village of Sandstone to the northeast, and tree-covered Chestnut Mountain to the south.

This area has cool winters; pleasant springs and falls; and warm, hazy summers. Annual rainfall is about 35 to 45 inches. The wettest month is July; the driest, October.

Planned for owner-builders, the house is conceived as a modest but comfortable shelter, retreating into itself in cold weather and opening up to the site in warm weather. The overhanging roof not only provides protection for upper-level sleeping porches, summer kitchen, entry, and north porch, but collects rainwater to be filtered and stored as the primary domestic supply.

Inside the house, storage areas are located on the north, living areas on the south.

The k'ang, or Korean-style heated masonry floor, forms the center of the house. Furniture is kept to a minimum; seating is built in or a function of floor level change.

Folding beds create more usable space upstairs and allow flexibility of sleeping location. Folding chairs and an expandable table provide extra space for dinner guests.

Bruce Osen

Perspective

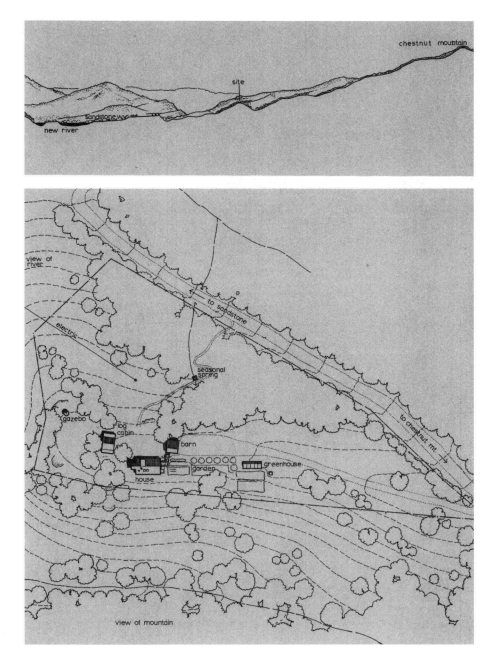

Site Plan

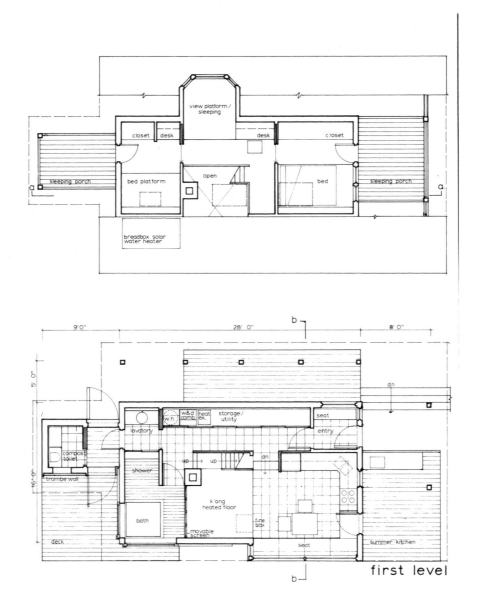

Floor Plans

184

Perspective

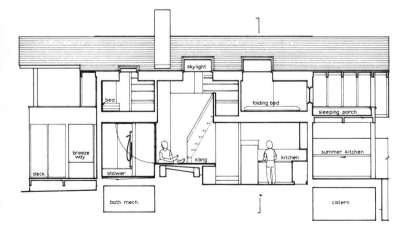

Section AA

Section BB

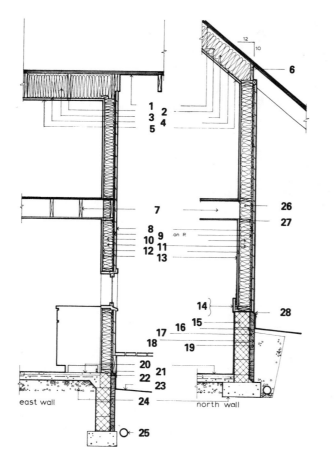

1   ⅝" CDX Plywood
2   2 x 12" Rafters
3   12" Fiberglass Insulation R-38
4   6 Mil. Poly Vapor Barrier
5   ½" Drywall
6   Vents
7   2 x 10 Floor Joists
8   1" Drop Siding
9   1" Rigid Insulation R-6.5
10 6" Fiberglass Insulation R-19
11 2 x 6 Studs
12 6 Mil. Vapor Barrier
13 ½" Drywall
14 Elec. Wiring Where Required on Exterior Wall
    is Placed in Raceways on the Interior Side of
    Vapor Barrier
15 Stack Bonded 8" Conc.
16 Bentonite Waterproofing
17 2" Rigid Insulation
18 6 Mil. Poly
19 Cement Asbestos Board
20 4" Conc. Slab
21 Pressure Treated Board
22 Sill Sealer
23 Grade
24 6 Mil. V B
25 4" Drain
26 North Wall Balloon Framed
27 Firestops
28 Drip Strip/Termite Shield

Wall Section

"Bridge House"

Malvern, Pennsylvania
997 gross square feet

Approaching the house, the garage and porch suggested in the developed plan stretch across the entry elevation, allowing the house to command an impressive aspect of the landscape. Seen this way, this compact house appears large.

The house is organized with service spaces on the north, sheltering the house and allowing the public rooms facing south to overlook a terrace that leads to an allée of fruit trees and a picturesque view of farmland.

The garage blocks winter winds and directs summer breezes to the house.

House

The double-height living and dining spaces make this compact house feel spacious and open, while the second-floor bridge articulates the space into more intimate functional areas.

The kitchen, although tucked in a corner and somewhat out of sight, is still open to the main activity areas.

The bedrooms also share the double-height space by having casement windows which can be closed for acoustical privacy.

A window seat on the stair landing doubles as a bed for an extra overnight guest.

J. Douglas Peix and William R. Crawford

Perspective

"Bridge House"

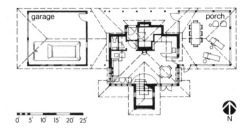

Developed Plan

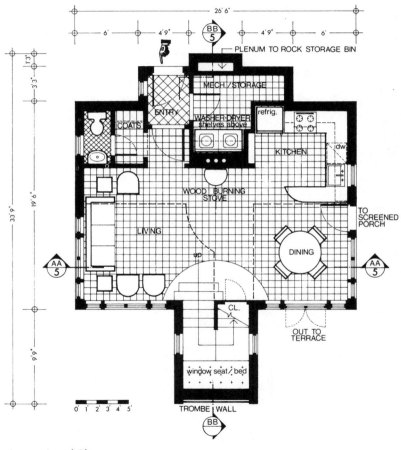

Lower Level Plan

188

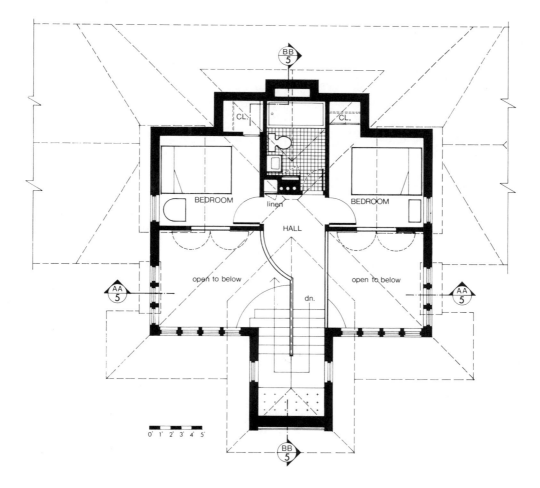

0' 1' 2' 3' 4' 5'

Upper Level Plan

"Bridge House"

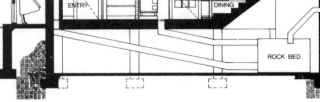

ATTIC VENT

R60 INSULATION

TROMBE WALL PLENUM

CL.

BEDROOM

TROMBE WALL

seat

ENTRY

DINING

ROCK BED

East   BB

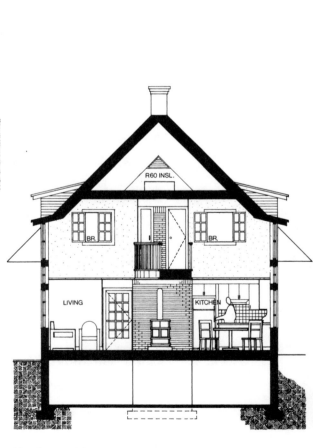

R60 INSL.

BR.

BR.

LIVING

KITCHEN

North   AA

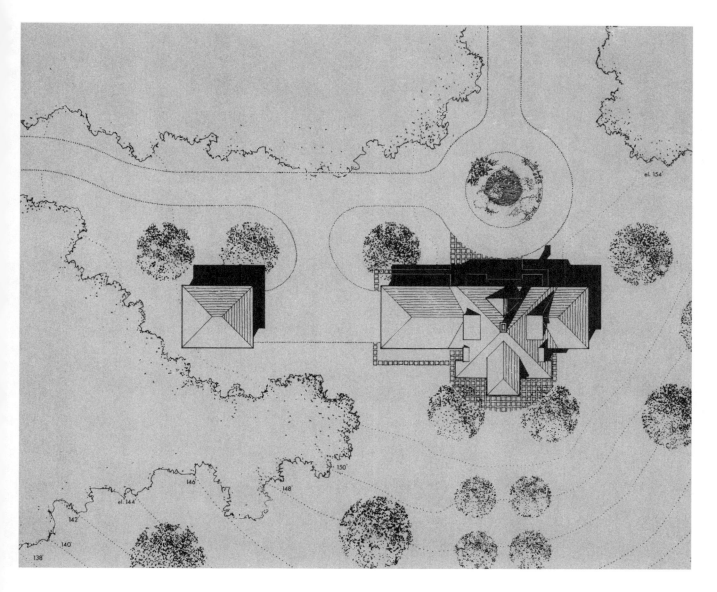

el. 154'

150'

146'

148'

el. 144'

142'

140'

138'

Site Plan

1 Inflatable Insulating Curtain in Insulated Housing
2 Upper Outside Vent Continuous Hinge
3 Cedar Face
4 ¾" Exterior Plywood
5 1½" Rigid Insulation
6 Insect Screening Weather Strip
7 Latch
8 4" Air Space
9 ⅝" Tempered Insulating Glass
10 Cedar Mullion with Removable Stop
11 1 Part Portland Cement, 1 Part Sand Slurry with Black Masonry Pigment & Black Concrete Stain
12 Heavy Weight Concrete Masonry Unit Grouted Solid
13 2 #4 Rebars @ 24" O.C.
14 #4 Rebars @ 16" O.C.
15 Lower Outside Vent Similar to Upper Vent
16 Flashing & Counterflashing
17 ⅜" Diameter Weeps 2'0" O.C. with Insect Screening

18 R-60 Roof Insulation
19 Thermosiphon Plenum with Automatic Damper to Rock Bed Heat Storage
20 2 x 10 Joists
21 R-19 Batt. Insulation
22 Chicken Wire Support for Insulation
23 6 Mil. Polyethylene Vapor Barrier
24 Painted GWB Laminated Directly to Concrete Block
25 Typical Wood Floor
26 Back Draft Damper
27 Thermosiphon Loop Return
28 R-19 Insulated Crawl Space
29 Rock Bed
30 Automatic Damper
31 Sand
32 6 Mil. Poly Film
33 R-15 Rigid Insulation
34 ¾" Plywood Enclosure
35 Dry, Clean, Non-Radon Producing Rocks
36 Metal Lath
37 Concrete Block Plenum
38 ¼" Masonite

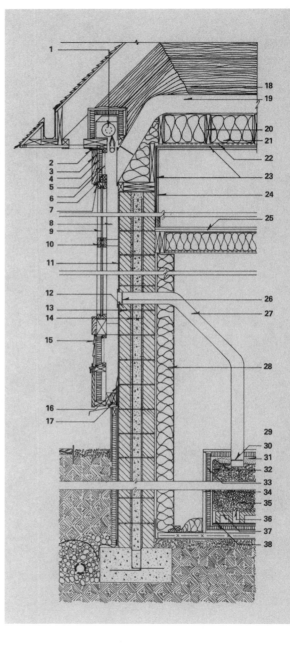

Trombe Wall

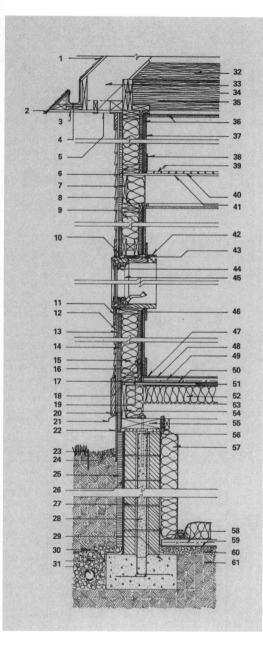

Wall Section

1 Asphalt & Fiberglass Overlay, Fed. Spec. SS-S-001534, Class A, Type I; UL Class A, Over No. 15 Asphalt Saturated Felt; Fasten with Hot Galvanized Steel Roofing Nails
2 Copper Flashing
3 ¾" Exterior Grade Plywood Roof Deck
4 Inset Copper Gutter with Flashing & Counterflashing
5 Continuous Eave Roof Vent with Insect Screening
6 2 x 6 Sole Plates
7 2 x 10 Header & Floor Joists
8 2 x 6 Cap Plates
9 2 x 6 Studs, 24" O.C.
10 Flashing
11 Cedar Trim 6" x ¾"
12 Cedar Rabbeted Bevel 5" x ⁹⁄₁₆" Siding
13 ½" Exterior Grade Plywood Sheathing
14 1" Tongue & Groove Rigid Polystyrene Sheathing
15 R-19 Batt. Insulation
16 1" Rigid Polystyrene Insulation
17 6 Mil. Polyethylene Vapor Barrier
18 ⅝" Gypsum Wall Board
19 2 x 6 Sole Plates
20 2 x 12 Cedar Trim
21 Copper Shield
22 ¼" Mineral Fiber Board
23 Metal Border Strip
24 Crushed Stone Drainage
25 2" Waterproof Rigid Insulation
26 Bituminous Waterproofing
27 12" Reinforced Concrete Masonry Foundation Wall with #4 Rebars
28 Vermiculite Cavit Insulation
29 Poured, Reinforced, Continuous Concrete Footing; Set 2" Below the Frost Line
30 6 Mil. Polyethylene Silt Shield
31 Graded Gravel Drainage Perforated PVC Drainage Pipe

32 R-38 & R-19 Batt. Insulation; Total Roof R-60
33 2 x 12 Rafters, 12" O.C.
34 Blocking
35 Nailer for Ceiling
36 6 Mil. Polyethylene Vapor Barrier
37 ⅝" Gypsum Wall Board Taped & Compounded with 3 Coats. To Be Painted
38 6" x ½" Painted Poplar Base
39 Select Oak Strip Flooring 25/32" x 2½". Sand, Stain & Finish with 3 Coats of Moisture Curing Polyurethane
40 5 Lb. Building Paper
41 ¾" Plywood Subfloor
42 3 Layer Insulated Retractable Film Shades
43 Shim
44 Triple Glazed Insulating, Vinyl Clad Casement Windows, R = 3.12
45 Insect Screen
46 Painted Hardwood Sill & Trim
47 8" x 8" x ½" Black Slate Flooring
48 Cement Mortar
49 1½" Thick Reinforced Concrete Bed
50 6 Mil. Polyethylene Cleavage Membrane
51 ¾" Exterior Grade Plywood Subfloor
52 R-19 Batt. Insulation
53 Chicken Wire Support
54 2 x 12 Header & Floor Joists
55 2 x 8 Sill
56 ½" Diameter Anchor Bolt Fixed in Mortar
57 Foil Faced Insulation
58 2" Reinforced Cement Bed
59 6 Mil. Polyethylene Vapor Barrier
60 Crushed Stones
61 Earth

Michigan Lake House

St. Joseph, Michigan
1,000 gross square feet

The building is located on a fairly level site which gently slopes down to Lake Michigan. Dunegrass and a few small evergreen and cottonwood trees are the only vegetation that exists in the sandy soil.

Lake Michigan has a tempering effect on the climate. Air conditioning is not really a necessity; a fan should be used to circulate the humid air.

The winters are not as cold as they are inland; however, lake effect precipitation results in a heavy snowfall and frequent cloud cover, making the site unattractive for solar heating.

The design is intended for people interested in a starter house or a small second home. It is appealing because the whole design scheme can be implemented in phases, thereby reducing the initial capital expenditure. A different composition of house, garage, and walks will make the house adaptable to most of the lakefront sites in the area.

Through the use of a low house profile and natural materials (wood shingles), the house is integrated into the beach environment. Cutouts in the basic rectangular form are used to address the entry and the lake.

Other features include optional basement floor plan (without compromising the design scheme) and an unfinished attic space that can be finished later to accommodate future spatial needs.

Arunas Rumsa

Perspective

Floor Plan

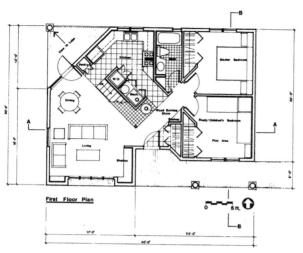

First Floor Plan

0   5 ft.

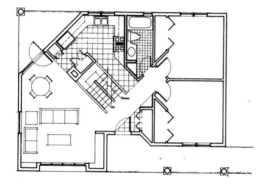

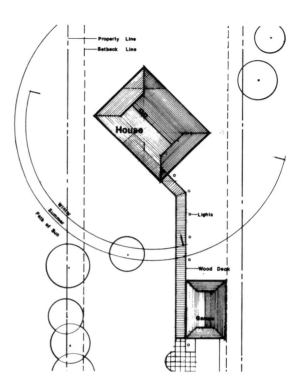

Site Plan

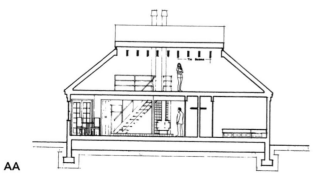

AA

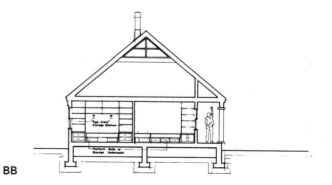

BB

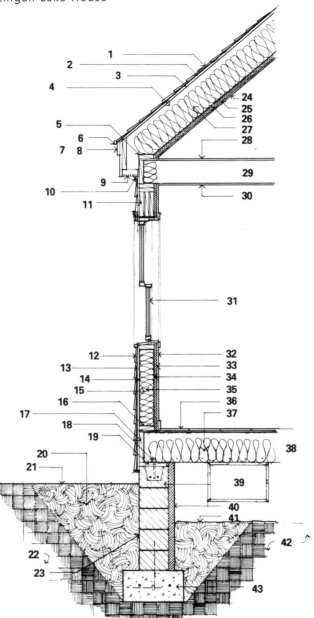

Wall Section

1   Cedar Shingles (Dipped)
2   Building Paper
3   ½" Plywood Roof Sheathing
4   Air Space
5   2" x 6" Wd. Plate
6   Galy. Stl. Drip-Edge
7   1" x 4" Wd. Trim Over
8   1" x 12" Wd. Trim
9   Contin. Vent w/Insect Screen
10 Wd. Trim Pc.
11 (3) 2" x 12" w/ ½" Spacers
12 Cedar Shingles (Dipped)
13 Building Paper
14 ½" Plywd. Sheathing
15 2" x 6" Wd. Framing
16 2" x 6" Wd. Plate
17 2" x 12"
18 Stl. Anchor Bolt
19 2" x 12" Treated Wd. Plate Over Sill Sealer
20 Backfill
21 Grade
22 Sand
23 Waterproofing
24 ½" Gypsum Board (Screwed to Rafters)
25 6 Mil. Vapor Barrier

26 1" Rigid Insulation
27 10" Batt. Insulation
28 ¾" Plywood Subfloor
29 2" x 10" Wd. Joists
30 ½" Gypsum Board
31 Double-Hung Window (Triple Glazed Shown) Caulk Around Windows
32 ½" Gypsum Board (Screwed to Studs)
33 6 Mil. Vapor Barrier
34 1" Rigid Insulation
35 5½" Batt. Insulation
36 Tile or Carpet over ¾" Plywood Subfloor
37 5½" Batt. Insulation
38 2" x 12" Wd. Joists
39 Duct-Space 12" G.M.U. Fd'n Wall w/Horizontal Reinf. Bond Beam w/(2) #4 Rebars at Top Course
40 2" Rigid Insulation (Optional)
41 6 Mil. Vapor Barrier
42 Sand
43 2'-0" 3 1'-0" Conc. Ftg. in (2) #5 Stl. Rebars. #4 Dowel

Ocean Views

Rhode Island
980 gross square feet

The house site is 300 feet from the edge of 150-foot bluffs overlooking the Atlantic. The view from the ground floor is screened by a dense, 8-foot high thicket of wild bayberry. As a result, all of the common spaces have been placed on the second floor, with large east- and south-facing windows.

The site is quite hilly, covered in the summer with lush vegetation, and surrounded by few other houses. The soil contains some clay.

In order to save energy, the house has been kept small, well-insulated, caulked, and weather-stripped. Harsh winter temperatures are moderated somewhat by the Gulf Stream, but severe gales are frequent, requiring the letting in of wind bracing in addition to the plywood sheathing. Sufficient and carefully installed flashing is essential to keep out wind-driven rain; gutters and downspouts are useless.

There are few windows on the west and north sides.

Building materials have been selected for their thermal efficiency, weathering capabilities, and construction tightness.

The house is solar oriented, and a coal stove will be supplemented by a 20,000 Btu/h kerosene mobile home heater.

Homer Russell and Carol Nugent

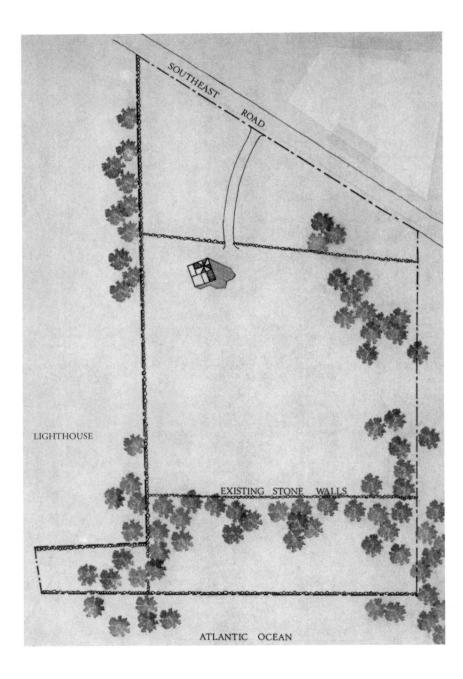

SOUTHEAST ROAD

LIGHTHOUSE

EXISTING STONE WALLS

ATLANTIC OCEAN

Site Plan

1 6" Foil-Faced Batt. Insul. (R-19 Min.)
2 ½" GWB
   Note: All Foil on Insul. to Face
   Living Space
3 Double Glazing
4 6" Batt. Insul. (R-19 Min.)
5 2 x 6 Studs 16" O.C.
6 ⅝" Oak Fin. Floor
7 ⅝" Ply. Subfloor
8 6" Batt. Insul. (R-19 Min.)
9 2" Rigid Insul.
10 Vapor Barrier
11 Frost Line 3'-6" Below Grade
12 290# Asphalt Roofing
13 15# Bldg. Paper
14 ½" Ply Sheathing
15 2 Layers Cedar Shingles Under First
   2 Rows of Roofing
16 Eave Vent
17 8" Lead Flash & Caulk
18 10" Alum. Pan Flash & Caulk
19 White Cedar Shingles, 5" Exp.
20 ½" Ply Sheathing
21 2 x 6 P.T. Sill
22 Sill Sealer
23 C.M.U.

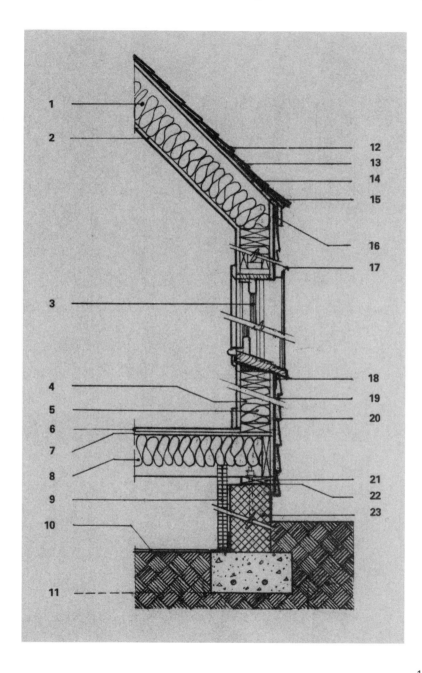

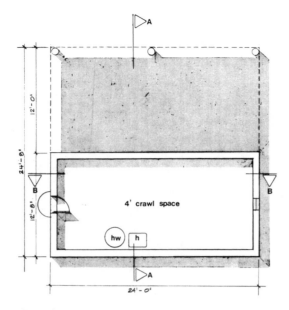

Foundation

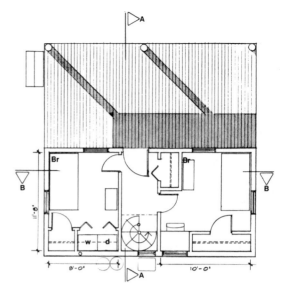

First Floor Plan

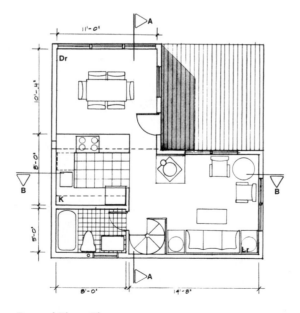

Second Floor Plan

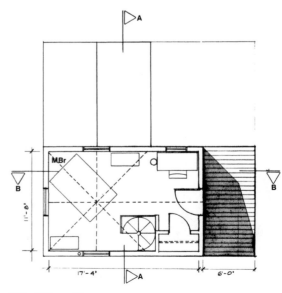

Third Floor Plan

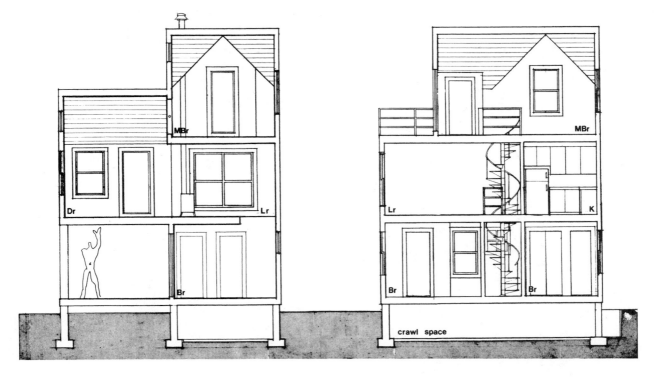

AA

BB

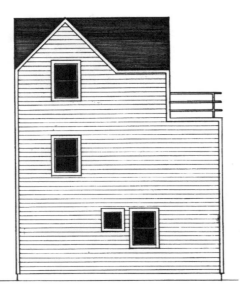

North

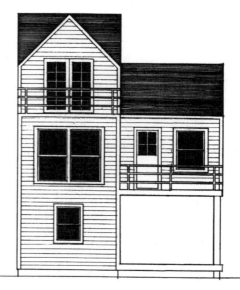

West

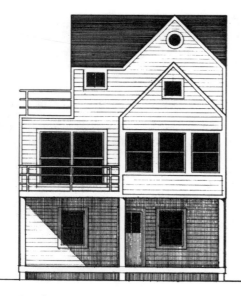

South

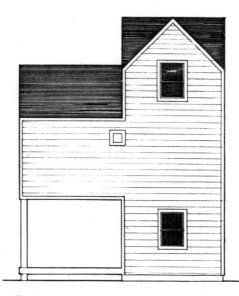

East

Formal Ocean-side Home

Charleston, South Carolina

996 gross square feet

The house is designed as a prototype dwelling for the hot, humid climate of the southeastern United States. The specific site chosen is a beach lot near Charleston, South Carolina, with a climate of warm, humid summers and moderate winters.

The house, especially the public area, is oriented to provide the best views of the ocean and take advantage of prevailing breezes. A garden greenhouse on the south and deck/hot tub on the north enhance the north/south axis of the floor plan. The berm and new evergreens help protect the house from winter winds. Existing live oaks and overhangs shade the house from afternoon sun. The house is raised to protect it from coastal flooding and to improve natural ventilation.

The seating area, under the octagonal belvedere, becomes a symbolic focus and increases natural ventilation.

A storage zone divides the public and private areas. The bathroom serves as a buffer during the afternoon to cool the public space.

Zoning also allows the private area to be cooled or heated separately.

The bedrooms are characterized by ceiling spaces with hot air exhausts for cooling.

The optional greenhouse augments winter heating and allows vegetables and fruits to be grown year-round. A solar hot water system is used for hot water needs, and a heat pump facilitates heating and cooling demands.

Roberto L. Sotolongo

View from Southwest

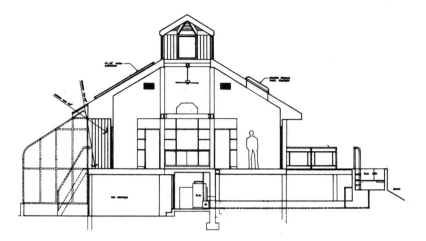

Section AA

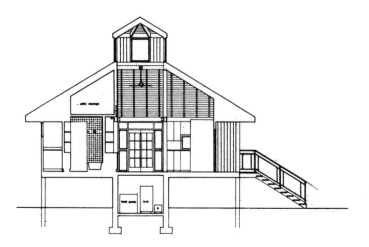

Section BB

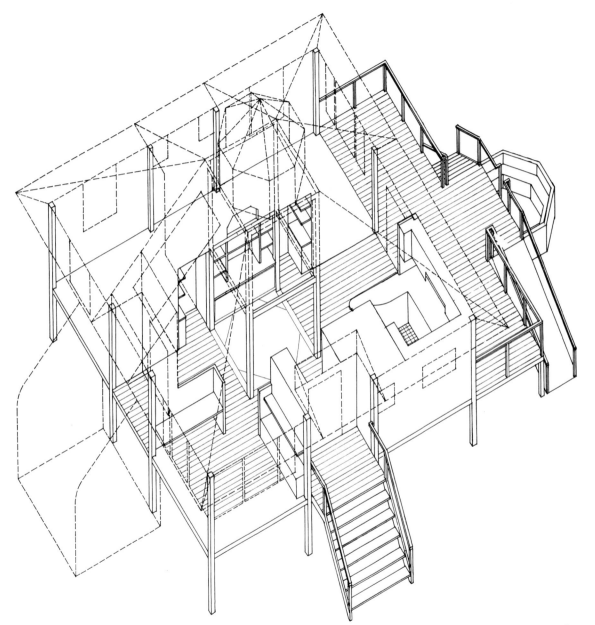

Axonometric

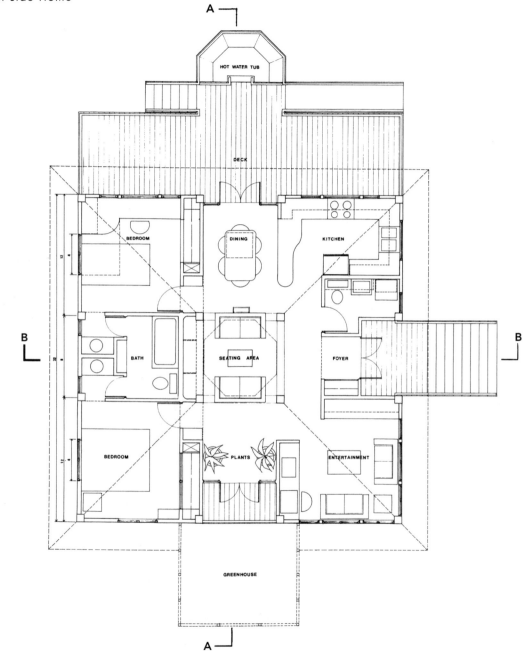

HOT WATER TUB

A

A

DECK

BEDROOM

DINING

KITCHEN

B

B

BATH

SEATING   AREA

FOYER

BEDROOM

PLANTS

ENTERTAINMENT

GREENHOUSE

A

Floor Plan

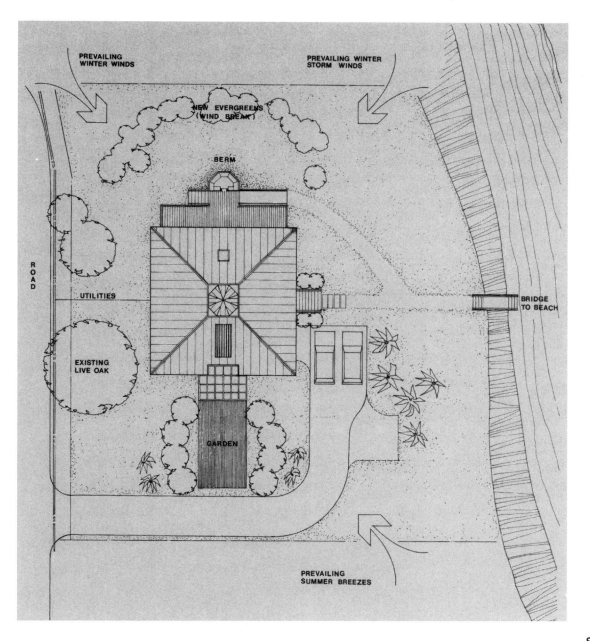

Midwest Modular

Upper Midwest
998 gross square feet

This house has been designed for a new community of affordable homes in the upper Midwest. The land, a former farm, is flat, without special views, and without any significant micro-climate.

The house has been designed to be componentized, and delivered to the site on one flatbed truck.

The design consists of four small boxes that can be built with minimum effort, are easy to frame, and economical to build. All framing is on 24-inch centers and has minimum waste.

The living room, kitchen, and family/dining room have sloping ceilings and are open to one another, creating an additional feeling of space.

The main outdoor living area also serves as an entrance court. Added privacy can be achieved by erecting a fence on the east side of the deck. A second outdoor living area opens off the living room.

The house can be faced and sited on small lots in many different ways, and the garage can be placed in several different locations to form the private entrance court.

George Hugh Tsuruoka

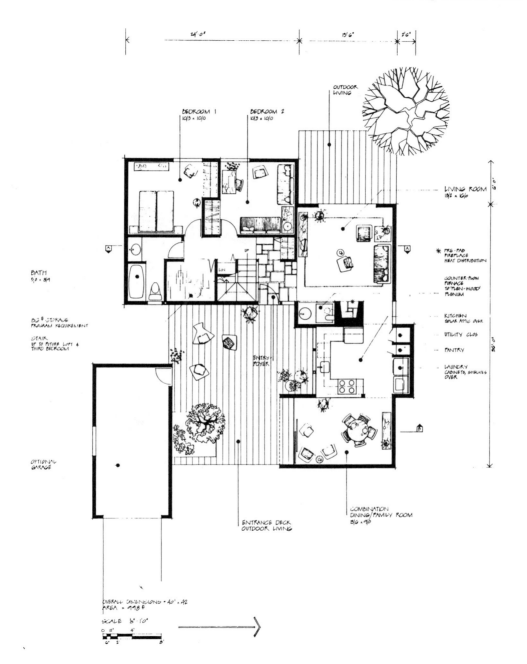

24'0"   15'6"   2'6"

OUTDOOR
LIVING

BEDROOM 1
10/3 x 10/0

BEDROOM 2
10/3 x 10/0

LIVING ROOM
13/2 x 16/0

FIRE-PAD
FIREPLACE
HEAT DISTRIBUTION

COUNTER-FLOW
FURNACE
TO MAIN-WOOD
PLENUM

BATH
5/0 x 8/9

KITCHEN
SOLAR ATTIC OVER

BIG # STORAGE
PROGRAM REQUIREMENT

UTILITY CLOS

STAIR
UP TO FUTURE LOFT &
THIRD BEDROOM

PANTRY

LAUNDRY
CABINETS, SHELVES
OVER

ENTRY
FOYER

OPTIONAL
GARAGE

ENTRANCE DECK
OUTDOOR LIVING

COMBINATION
DINING/FAMILY ROOM
8/6 x 9/6

OVERALL DIMENSIONS = 40' x 42'
AREA = 998 #

SCALE 8' = 1'0"
0 1' 4'
6' 2' 8'

Floor Plan

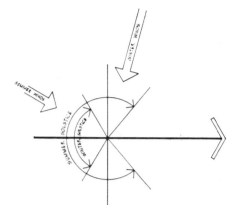

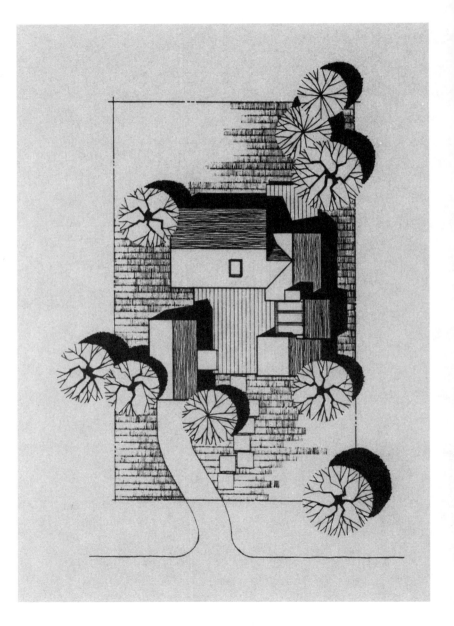

Site Plan

Section AA

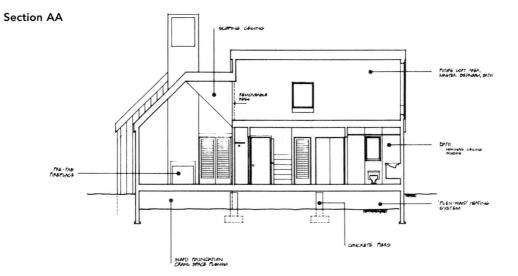

SLOPING CEILING

FUTURE LOFT AREA, MASTER BEDROOM, BATH

REMOVABLE WALL

BATH
REMOVED CEILING
WINDOW

PRE-FAB FIREPLACE

'PLEN-WOOD' HEATING SYSTEM

CONCRETE PIERS

WOOD FOUNDATION CRAWL SPACE PLENUM

Section BB

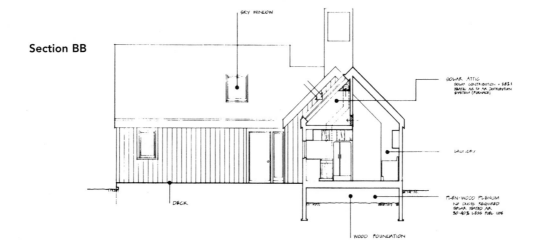

SKY WINDOW

SOLAR ATTIC
SOLAR CONTRIBUTION · 28%
HEATED AIR TO AIR DISTRIBUTION
SYSTEM (FURNACE)

LAUNDRY

DECK

PLEN-WOOD PLENUM
NO DUCTS REQUIRED
SOLAR HEATED AIR
30-40% LESS FUEL USE

WOOD FOUNDATION

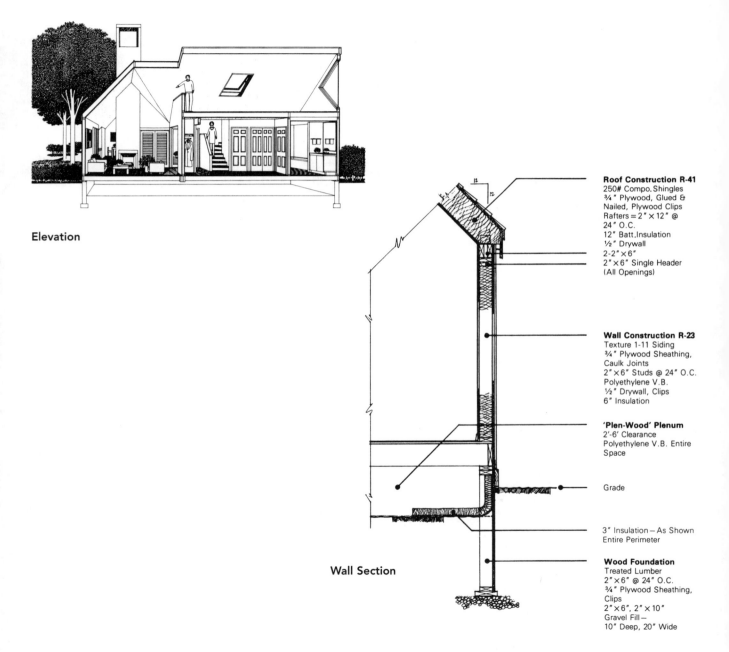

Elevation

Wall Section

Roof Construction R-41
250# Compo. Shingles
¾" Plywood, Glued &
Nailed, Plywood Clips
Rafters = 2" × 12" @
24" O.C.
12" Batt. Insulation
½" Drywall
2-2" × 6"

2" × 6" Single Header
(All Openings)

Wall Construction R-23
Texture 1-11 Siding
¾" Plywood Sheathing,
Caulk Joints
2" × 6" Studs @ 24" O.C.
Polyethylene V.B.
½" Drywall, Clips
6" Insulation

'Plen-Wood' Plenum
2'-6' Clearance
Polyethylene V.B. Entire
Space

Grade

3" Insulation — As Shown
Entire Perimeter

Wood Foundation
Treated Lumber
2" × 6" @ 24" O.C.
¾" Plywood Sheathing,
Clips
2" × 6", 2" × 10"
Gravel Fill —
10" Deep, 20" Wide

The Modified Dog-Trot

Houston, Texas
982 gross square feet (not including breezeway of 522 sq. ft.)

In a small second house for a remote site in a rural area near Houston, the traditional Texas dog-trot configuration is adapted to eliminate the need for air conditioning. Large sliding doors at both ends of a central breezeway and swing-up shutters over the windows can be manipulated to secure the house when vacant, open the house to sunlight but not to wind on cool days, and maximize breezes through the house on hot, humid days.

Michael Underhill

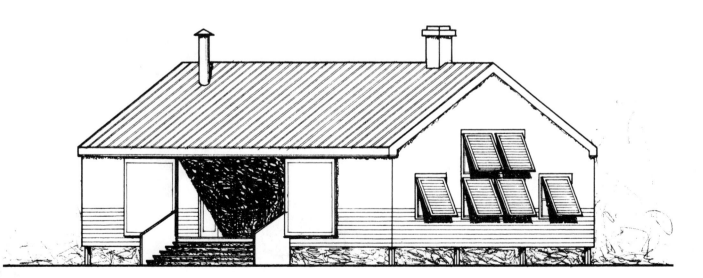

Perspective

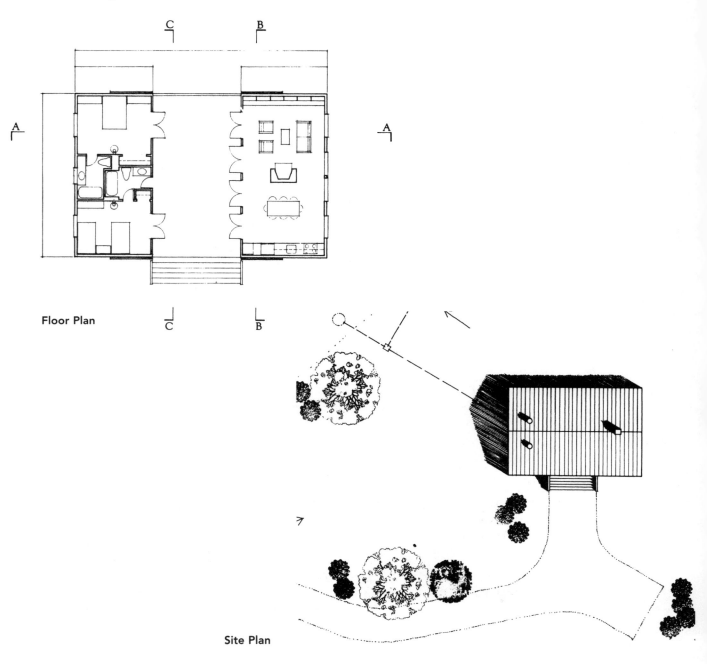

Floor Plan

Site Plan

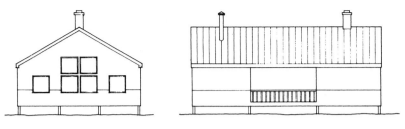

East

North

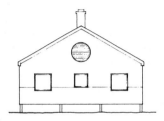

West

South

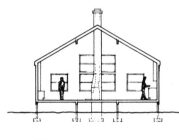

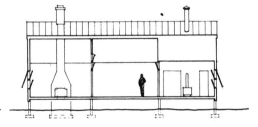

BB

AA

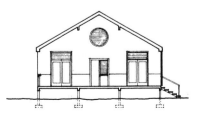

CC

Sections

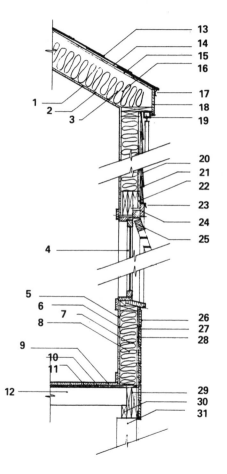

1 ½" Gypsum Board
2 Vapor Barrier
3 8" Batts Insulation Between 2 x 10 Rafters 16" on Center
4 Standard Wood Hopper Window Units
5 ½" Gypsum Board
6 Vapor Barrier
7 5" Batts Insulation
8 2 x 6 Studs 16" on Center
9 Wood Flooring
10 Building Paper
11 ¾" Plywood Deck
12 2 x 6 Joists 16" on Center
13 Asphalt Shingles or Standing Seam Metal
14 Roofing Felts
15 ½" Plywood Deck

16 2 x 10 Rafters 16" on Center
17 Metal Drip Edge
18 1 x 8 Wood Fascia
19 Sliding Door Tract
20 Wood Shingles
21 Foil Faced Building Paper
22 ½" Plywood Sheathing
23 Metal Drip Cap
24 1¼ x 4" Wood Casing
25 Swinging Wood Shutter
26 Shiplap Wood Siding
27 Foil Faced Building Paper
28 ½" Plywood Sheathing
29 Double 2 x 10 Header
30 2 x 4 Ribbon
31 6 x 6 Treated Piles
32 Concrete Foundation Pads (not shown)

Wall Section

Elegant Hacienda

Terrazas Del Sol, New Mexico
960 gross square feet (per unit)

The concept of Terrazas Del Sol was to offer the freedom of condominium living and the benefits of single-family residence country life, all in a compact, reasonably priced, energy-efficient package.

The project was designed to accentuate the "wide open spaces" of the Southwest while maintaining moderate high-density for land efficiency. The condominium concept retains control over any possible future unsightliness through the rule of the homeowners' association, and assures future maintenance, thus guaranteeing values.

The cluster takes on a "hacienda" or estate appearance, a style indigenous to the Southwest.

Partial berming of the houses aids the heating and changes the scale as each house marries with the site, giving each a lower profile on the horizon. Landscaped berms were constructed to modulate an otherwise flat terrain, to control drainage, to define space, and give a sense of privacy and "place."

The concept of Terrazas Del Sol is to provide for its owners the amenities of a planned unit development in a rural setting where open space, beautiful views, clean air, and efficient solar construction make for a desirable lifestyle.

James M. Wehler

Perspective

217

Floor Plan

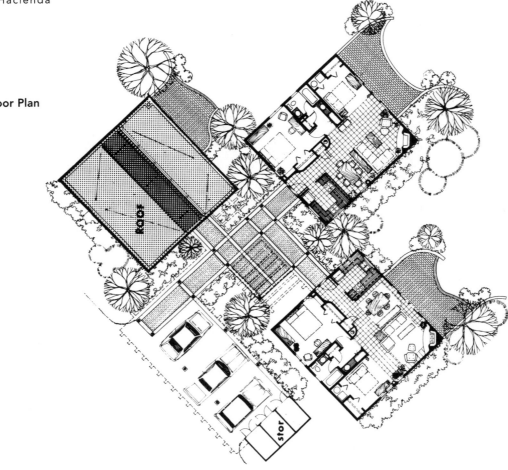

pool

stor

Site Plan

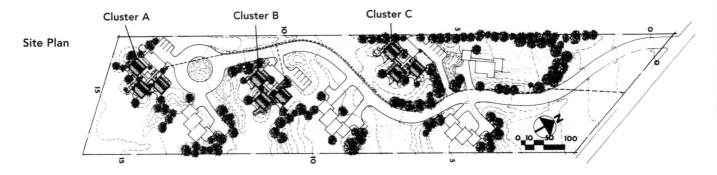

Cluster A

Cluster B

Cluster C

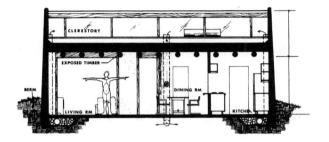

Section AA

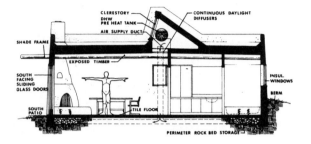

Section BB

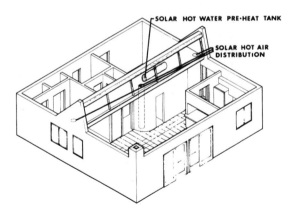

Isometric

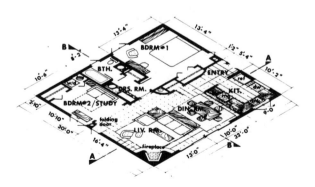

Floor Plan

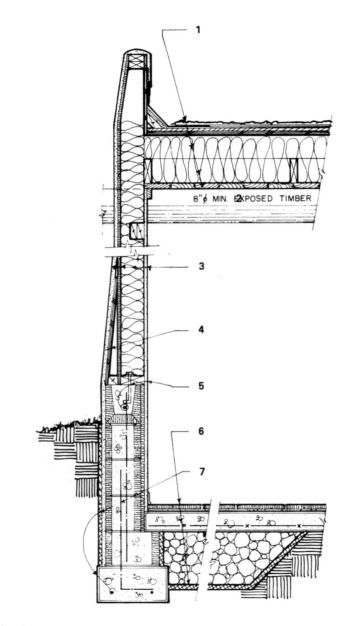

8"ø MIN. EXPOSED TIMBER

1   Built-up Roof & Gravel, 4-ply on ½
    Fibre Bd. Base on ½" CDX Plywood
    Deck on 2 x 6 Rafters @ 2'-0" O.C.
    on 2 x 6 Blocking @ 6'0" O.C. w/R-40
    Cellulose Fibre Insulation & 1 x 6 T&G
    Aspen Ceiling Deck
2   8" Ø Min. Exposed Timber
3   ½" Gyp. Board on 2 x 6 @ 16" O.C.
    Wd. Frame w/R-19 Cellulose Fibre
    Insul. & ½" Fibre Bd. Sheathing w/¾"
    Cement Stucco over Galv. Stucco Wire,
    Sand Float Finish
4   ½" CDX Plywd. Batter-Bd. w/2 x Blk.
5   8" CMU Bd. Bm. w/1-#4 Cont., Faced
    with/½" Fibre Bd. & ½" Gyp. Bd. w/½"
    Ø A.B. @ 4'-0" O.C.
6   12" x 12" Conc. Tiles in Thinset on 4"
    Conc. Slab w/6" x 6" 10/10 WWF on
    Rock Bd. Perimeter w/1" Rigid Insul.
    Lining
7   8" CMU Filled Stem w/1-#4 @4'-0"
    Vert. on One Course 12" CMU on
    8" x 16" Conc. Ftng. w/2-#4 Contin.
    & 1" Rigid Insul.

Wall Section

Solar Staircase House

Vermont
988 gross square feet

The Solar Staircase House addresses several issues often ignored in the rush for efficient plans and low heating bills. Siting is very flexible, and the solar staircase/hearth is a unique way of providing environmental comfort and several useful small spaces which make the compact house enjoyable to live in.

Siting

The corner porch entry along with a careful sequence of landscaping allows the house to be sited with any combination of site access/solar orientation while offering a warm and inviting entry and maintaining privacy for outdoor living/working areas.

Environmental

The staircase is slightly inflated to serve as a solar collector/storage unit filtering light into the living areas and offering a window seat in the sun.

This solves the compact house dilemma of not having enough square feet for a usable sunplace, but not wanting a direct gain situation where the living areas are hot, stuffy, and full of glare.

Social

The house is very open, but care was taken in the planning to respect the needs for privacy, and to provide a place for children. Bedrooms are cozy, private, and large enough for a study. Under the solar staircase we find a secluded window seat (doubles as a sleeping nook for a guest) and below that a "children's cave" with its own window. Above the bath is an area for a future crow's nest playroom.

Michael Wisniewski

Perspective

221

Solar Staircase House

1 Loft (Unfinished)
2 Window Nook
3 Child Cave
4 Phase Change Storage
5 Thermal Curtain
6 Air Duct
7 Canvas Awning-Optional

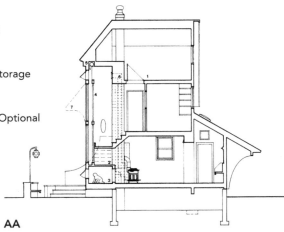

AA

BB

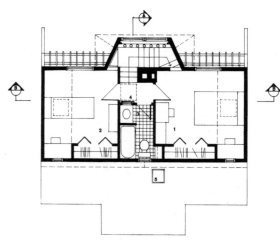

1 MBR
2 BR
3 Bath w/Obscure Glass
4 Loft (Unfinished) Ladder
5 Porch Skylight

1 Corner Porch
2 Wood Storage
3 Entry w/Bench
4 Living
5 Hearth
6 Country Kitchen
7 Utility (Tankless
   H2O Heater)
8 Window Seat/Child Cave
9 Solar Staircase
10 Air Duct
11 Trellis
12 Deck
13 Garden

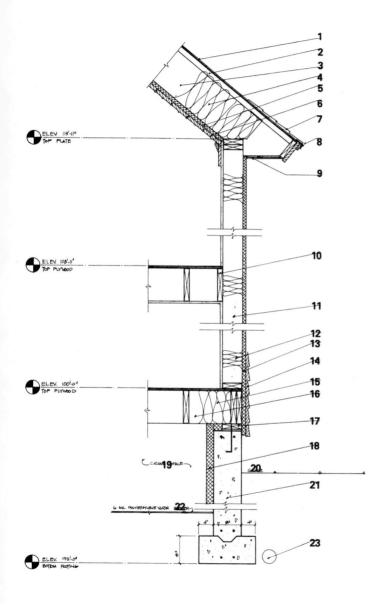

1 ½" Sheathing
2 2 x 3 Strapping Nailed into Roof Rafters for Vent Space
3 2 x 12 Rafters—2'0" O.C.
4 12" Fiberglass Batt
5 1.2" R-7 Insulating Sheathing
6 Painted Exterior "Porch" Grade Beaded T&G Spruce
7 Shingles
8 Gal. Metal Drip Edge
9 Soffit Vent w. Insect Screen
10 2 x 10 Joists 16" O.C. Spanning North South-Bridging at Midspan
11 2 x 6 Stud Wall 2'-0" O.C. Balloon Frame East and West Walls, Platform Frame North-South Walls
12 6" Fiberglass Batt.
13 1.2" R-7 Insulating Sheathing
14 Wood Clapboard 4" to Weather
15 9" Fiberglass Batt.
16 2 x 10 Joists 16" O.C. Spanning North/South. Provide Bridging at Midspan. Double Rim Joist, ¾" T&G Plywood
17 Pressure Treated 2 x 6 w/Sill Seal
18 2" Rigid Polystyrene perimeter Insulation 2'-0" Below Exterior Grade
19 Crawl Space
20 Grade
21 Concrete or Concrete Block Frost Wall-2 Coats of Asphalt Bituminous Waterproofing on Below Grade Exterior
22 6 Mil. Polyethylene Vapor Barrier
23 4" PVC Drain Tile

Wall Section

Elegant Postmodern

North-central Texas
1,250 gross square feet

The basic concepts utilized in the design of this house are: clarity of organization and circulation, zoning according to public and private spaces, and the notion of images which depict dwelling.

The front plane of the house enfronts the street with a single layer that reveals subsequent layers beyond. The image suggests two house forms, the primary two-story block for people and the smaller house for vehicles and ancillary functions. Symmetrical devices are used to provide a formal entry and receiving space for visitors. The living area is two stories high, with a balcony above that serves as a small library leading to the master bedroom on the second floor.

The master suite is well away from the children. The library loft allows a pleasant place to read, write, talk on the telephone, or watch the children below. The plan provides for a darkroom adjacent to the library. We have included an alternate plan for this area illustrating how this space might be utilized for additional closet space in the master bath area.

Circulation is at the edge of rooms rather than corridors. In is the variation of spatial definition and different views from the spaces which allow for a variety of experiences.

Richard B. Ferrier

Perspective

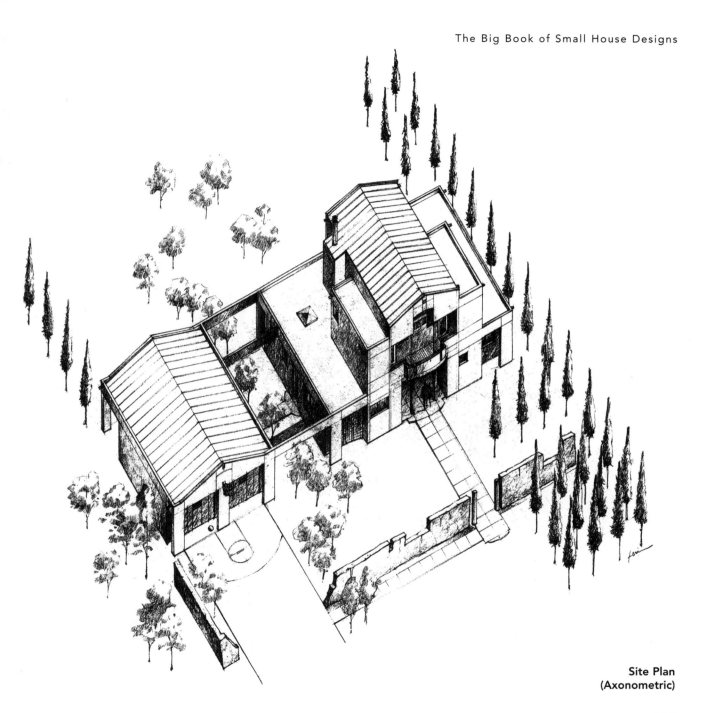

Site Plan
(Axonometric)

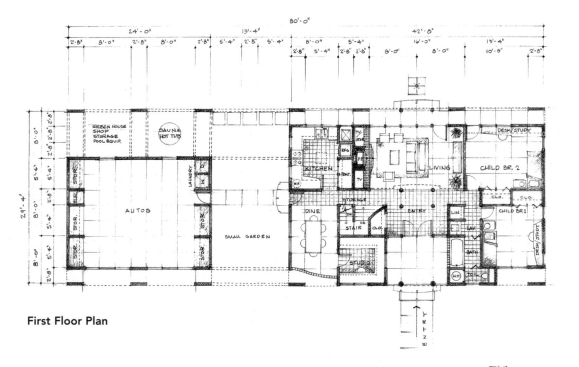

First Floor Plan

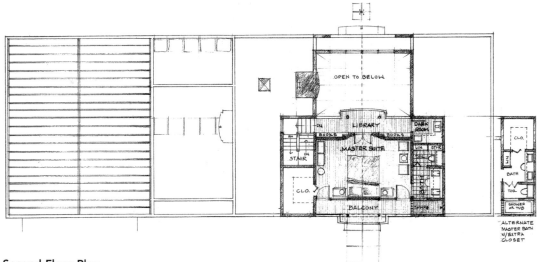

Second Floor Plan

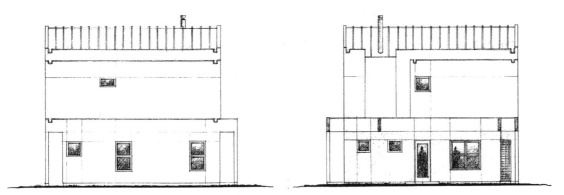

Elevation: Side

Elevation: Side (Kitchen/Dining)

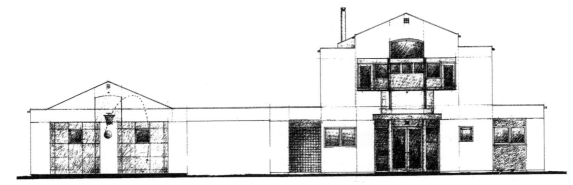

Elevation: Entry/Front

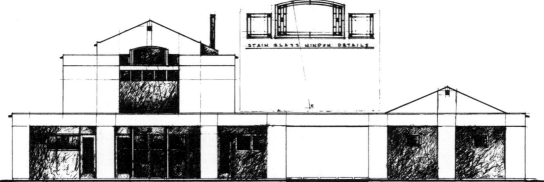

Elevation: Garden/Rear

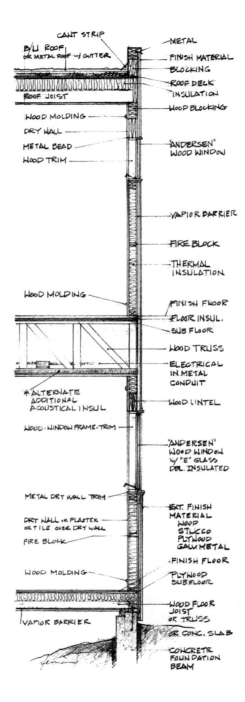

CANT STRIP
METAL
B/U ROOF OR METAL ROOF W/ GUTTER
FINISH MATERIAL
BLOCKING
ROOF DECK
INSULATION
ROOF JOIST
WOOD BLOCKING
WOOD MOLDING
DRY WALL
METAL BEAD
"ANDERSEN" WOOD WINDOW
WOOD TRIM
VAPIOR BARRIER
FIRE BLOCK
THERMAL INSULATION
WOOD MOLDING
FINISH FLOOR
FLOOR INSUL.
SUB FLOOR
WOOD TRUSS
ELECTRICAL IN METAL CONDUIT
* ALTERNATE ADDITIONAL ACOUSTICAL INSUL
WOOD LINTEL
WOOD WINDOW FRAME TRIM
"ANDERSEN" WOOD WINDOW W/ "E" GLASS DBL. INSULATED
METAL DRY WALL TRIM
EXT. FINISH MATERIAL WOOD STUCCO PLYWOOD GALV METAL
DRY WALL or PLASTER or TILE over DRY WALL
FIRE BLOCK
FINISH FLOOR
WOOD MOLDING
PLYWOOD SUBFLOOR
WOOD FLOOR JOIST or TRUSS
VAPIOR BARRIER
OR CONC. SLAB
CONCRETE FOUNDATION BEAM

Wall Section

Earth and Wood Essential

Napa Valley, California
1,241 gross square feet

The construction elements here are earth and wood.

Our essential house, simple yet inspiring, is located in the Napa Valley region of northern California on a narrow, south-facing city lot. The residence derives its strength and functionality in this urban setting from sound-absorbing, monolithic earth walls. These 2-foot-thick walls, in conjunction with active and passive solar systems, retain the warmth of sunny winter days as well as the coolness of the foggy summer nights.

Imagine quiet, cozy seats in most windows, niches and bookcases carved from the thick walls, private kid's spaces under the sloping roof, and a kitchen designed to make recycling a natural.

A practical design for comfortable living, massive earth masonry for energy efficiency, and sustainable materials for environmental responsibilities.

Rammed Earth Works

Perspective

Site Plan

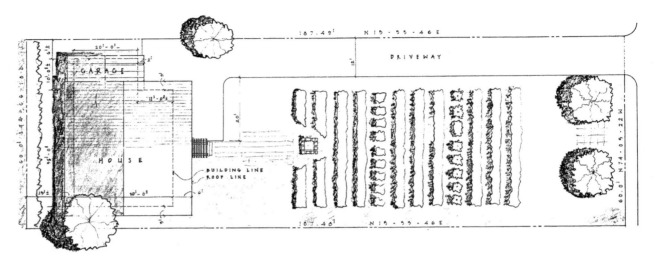

Installing Radiant Slab and Earth Tile Floor

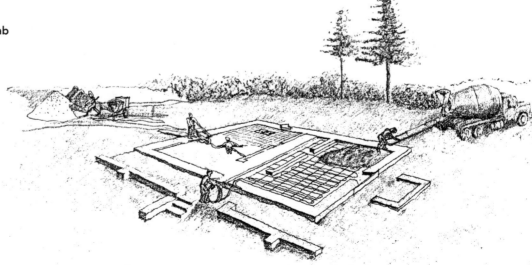

First Floor Plan

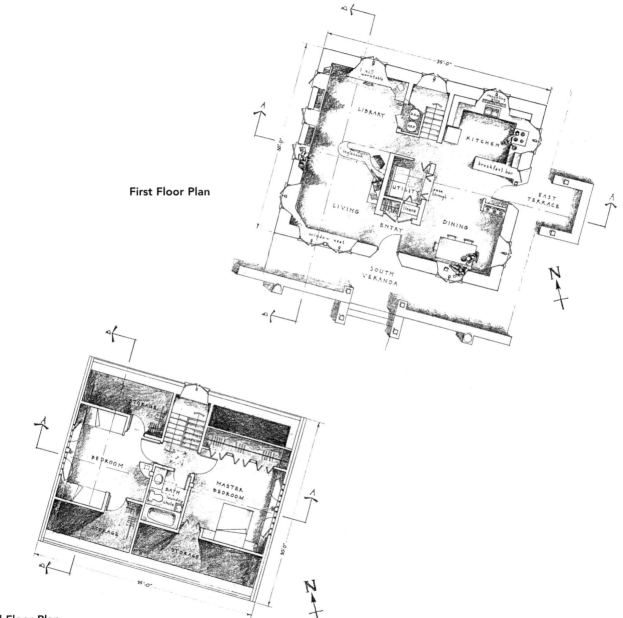

Second Floor Plan

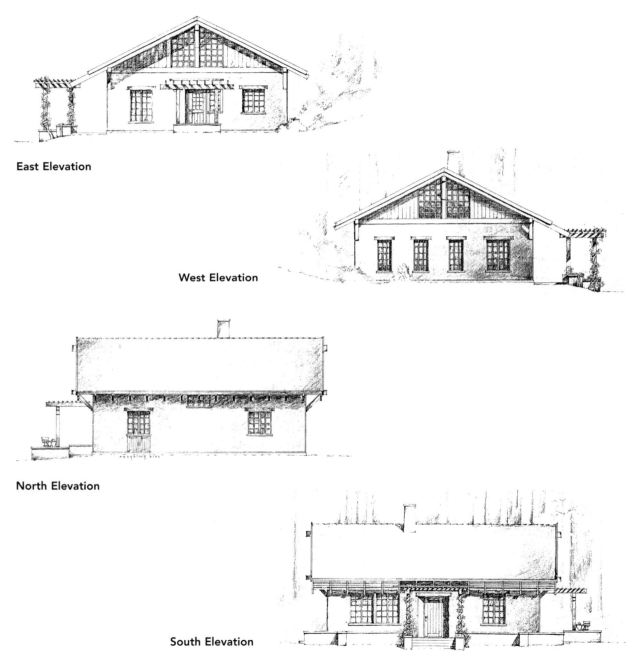

East Elevation

West Elevation

North Elevation

South Elevation

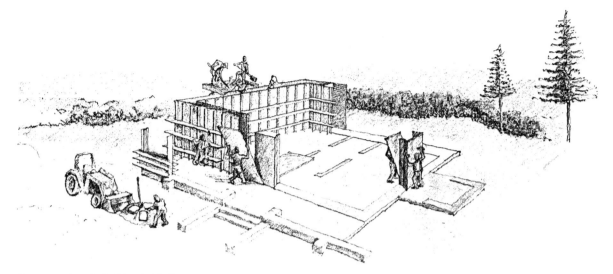

Constructing Solid Earth Walls

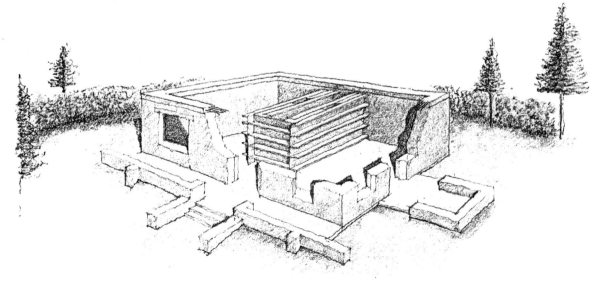

Casting Interior Walls

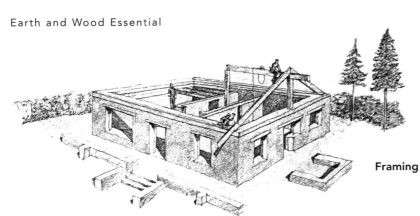

Framing Upper Floor and Roof

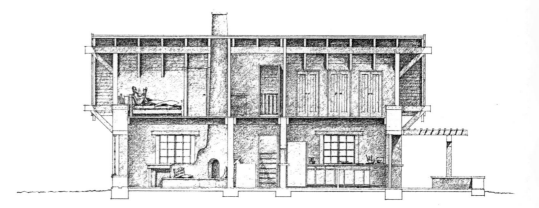

Section A-A

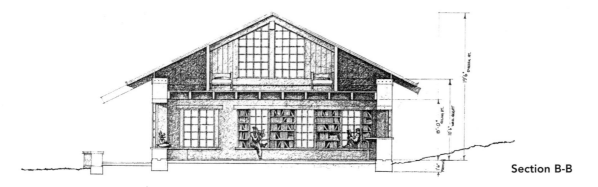

Section B-B

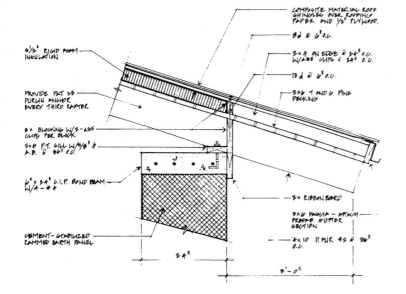

COMPOSITE MATERIAL ROOF SHINGLES OVER ROOFING PAPER AND 1/2" PLYWOOD.

8d @ 6" O.C.

2 x 4 ON EDGE @ 24" O.C. W/ A35 CLIPS @ 24" O.C.

16d @ 6" O.C.

2 x 6 T AND G PINE DECKING

6 1/2" RIGID FOAM INSULATION

PROVIDE PST 28 PURLIN ANCHOR EVERY THIRD RAFTER

2 x BLOCKING W/ 2 - A35 CLIPS PER BLOCK

2 x 8 P.T. SILL W/ 5/8" Ø A.B. @ 46" O.C.

6" x 24" C.I.P. BOND BEAM W/ 4 - # 4

CEMENT-STABILIZED RAMMED EARTH PANEL

2 x RIBBON BOARD

2 x 6 FASCIA — ATTACH PRE-FAB. GUTTER SECTION

4 x 10 D.F.R. # 2 @ 24" O.C.

24"

8' - 0"

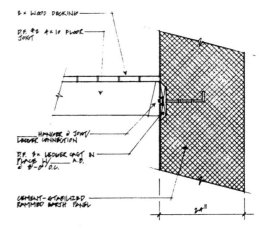

2 x WOOD DECKING

D.F. # 2 4 x 10 FLOOR JOIST

HANGER @ JOIST/ LEDGER CONNECTION

D.F. 2 x LEDGER CAST IN PLACE W/ A.B. @ 8' - 0" O.C.

CEMENT-STABILIZED RAMMED EARTH PANEL

24"

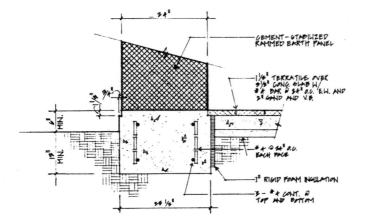

24"

CEMENT-STABILIZED RAMMED EARTH PANEL

1 1/2" TERRATILE OVER 3 1/2" CONC. SLAB W/ # 4 BAR @ 24" O.C. E.W. AND 2" SAND AND V.B.

3/4"

MIN.

18" MIN.

4 @ 24" O.C. EACH FACE

1" RIGID FOAM INSULATION

3 - # 4 CONT. @ TOP AND BOTTOM

25 1/2"

Wall Details

Ever-Efficient Home

South Florida
1,240 gross square feet

This design is a study in providing an energy-, cost-, and space-efficient house that is responsive to the functional and aesthetic needs of the people that use it. Its spaces intimate and dynamic are intended to romance and excite the users as they experience the routine of daily living.

The centrally located courtyard is the transition of exterior and interior spaces. The courtyard links the living spaces on the ground floor and allows them to expand functionally and visually. Upstairs, the use of a shared tub/shower allows the typical bathroom to double and provide private access from either bedroom. The organization of the house as a single room depth helps minimize circulation and increase cross-ventilation.

South Florida's extensive heat and humidity require a series of design parameters that can at times detract from the overall appearance of the house. An example of this is the limited use of windows. In this design, the energy components are used to embellish the overall appearance:

- elevated floors, large overhangs, and clerestory windows help articulate and balance the overall building form;

- trellises derived from Spanish influence allow for exterior shaded use of courtyards and porches;

- radiant barriers, insulation, and ceiling fans when combined with volume ceilings help create dynamic, energy-efficient spaces.

The goal in the overall character of the house was to reach back into history and provide an appearance that is vernacular to the South Florida area.

Primitivo Emilio Conde

Perspective

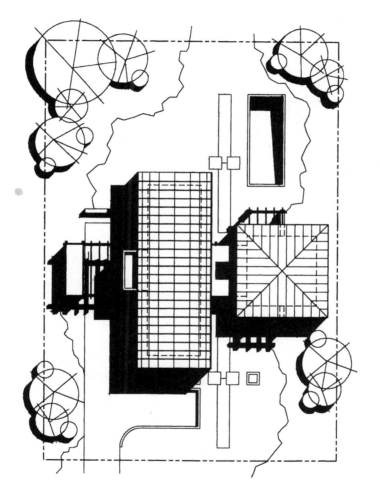

Site Plan

237

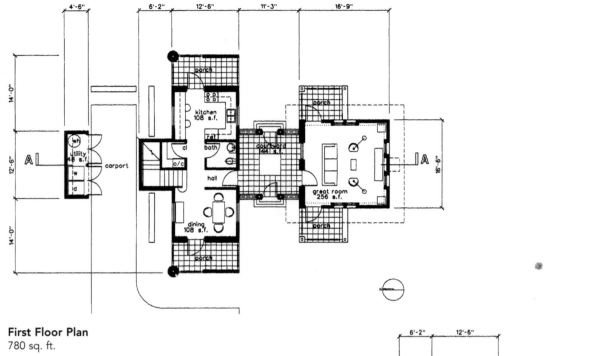

First Floor Plan
780 sq. ft.

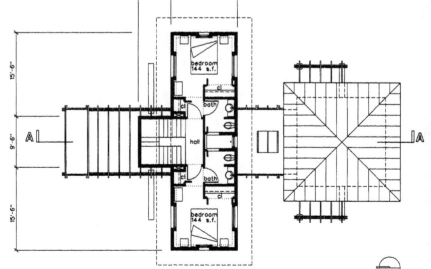

Second Floor Plan
460 sq. ft.

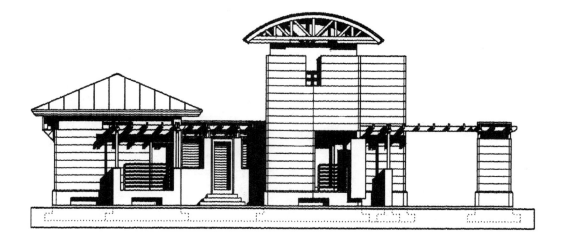

East Elevation

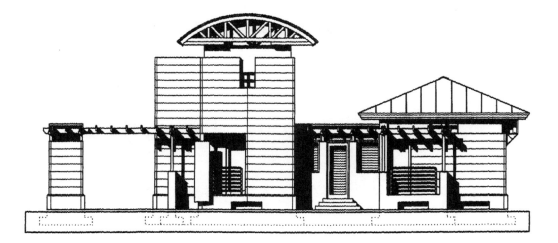

West Elevation

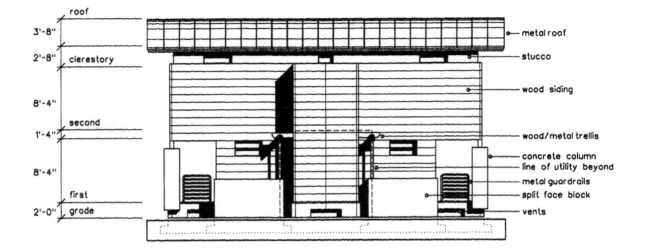

roof

3'-8"

2'-8"   clerestory

8'-4"

second

1'-4"

8'-4"

first

2'-0"   grade

metal roof
stucco
wood siding
wood/metal trellis
concrete column
line of utility beyond
metal guardrails
split face block
vents

North Elevation

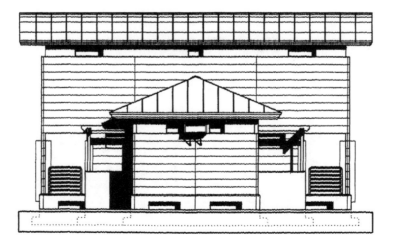

South Elevation

Section

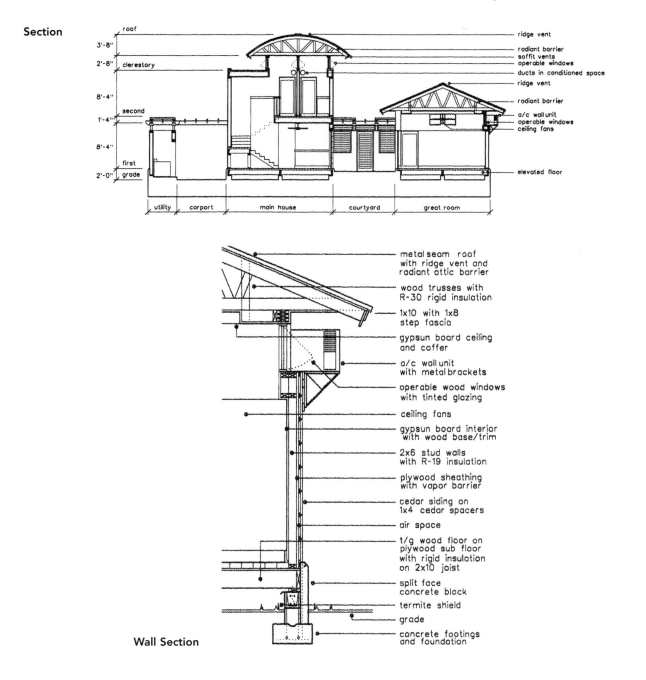

roof

3'-8"

2'-8" clerestory

ridge vent
radiant barrier
soffit vents
operable windows
ducts in conditioned space
ridge vent
radiant barrier
a/c wall unit
operable windows
ceiling fans

8'-4"

second

1'-4"

8'-4"

first

2'-0" grade

elevated floor

utility   carport   main house   courtyard   great room

metal seam roof
with ridge vent and
radiant attic barrier

wood trusses with
R-30 rigid insulation

1x10 with 1x8
step fascia

gypsun board ceiling
and coffer

a/c wall unit
with metal brackets

operable wood windows
with tinted glazing

ceiling fans

gypsun board interior
with wood base/trim

2x6 stud walls
with R-19 insulation

plywood sheathing
with vapor barrier

cedar siding on
1x4 cedar spacers

air space

t/g wood floor on
plywood sub floor
with rigid insulation
on 2x10 joist

split face
concrete block

termite shield

grade

concrete footings
and foundation

Wall Section

"Charleston House"

Southeastern U.S.
1,250 gross square feet

This house is intended as an infill unit for the low-density urban environments so common in the cities of the Southeast. It is loosely based on the Charleston townhouse model with its private garden to the side, as opposed to the rear, of the house. This garden can be defined as shown with a one-car garage, or simply with a high fence. The large areas of glass facing south onto this garden and the flagstone floor are calculated to give this house passive solar characteristics without looking like a "solar house." The second-story balcony of the master bedroom and deciduous trees shade these openings in summer.

The plan is a simple two room over two room with the stair in between. Mechanical systems are located in a pit below the stairs and share the zero-clearance fireplace flue with the chimney as shown by the minimal masonry chimney.

Of wood frame construction, this house is sided with 6-inch beaded flush siding treated with two coats of deep base stain. The roof is preformed standing seam metal. The windows are true divided-light single panes with insulating interior shutters.

The design of this house is generated from the geometry of the double square. Thus all elements, from the smallest detail to the entire plan and elevations, are unified. This house will evoke in all who experience it a sense of harmony, even though it is of a limited size and scale.

Nancy Nugent

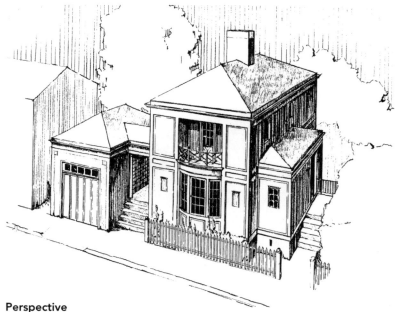

Perspective

242

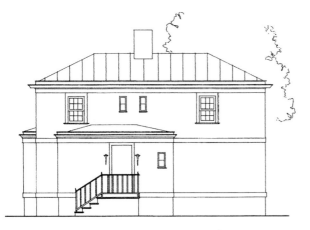

North Elevation

South Elevation

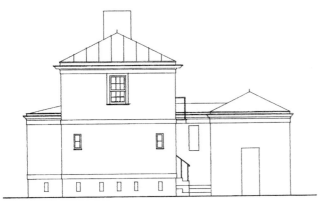

West Elevation

East Elevation

"Charleston House"

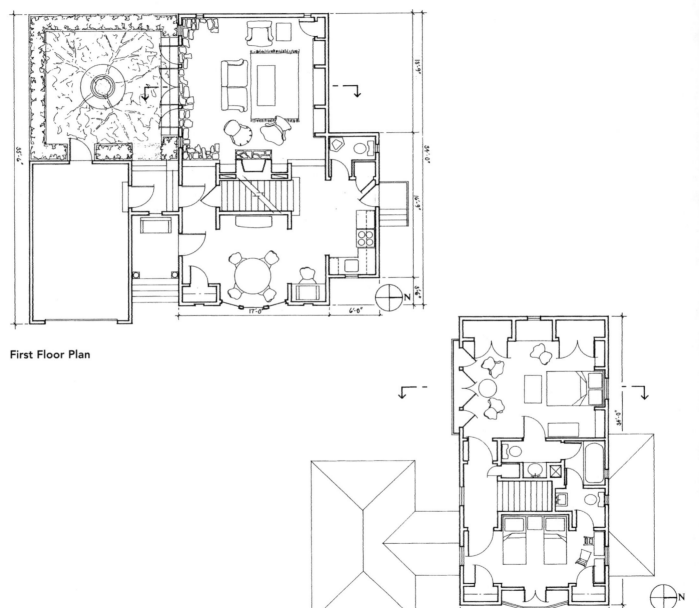

First Floor Plan

Second Floor Plan

Wall Section

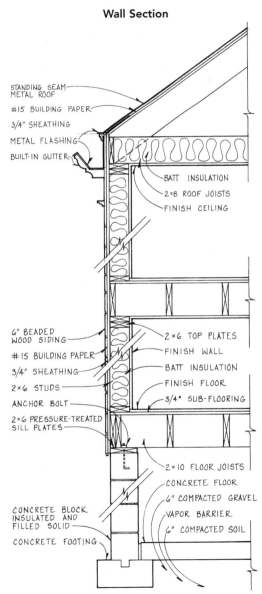

STANDING SEAM METAL ROOF

#15 BUILDING PAPER

3/4" SHEATHING

METAL FLASHING

BUILT-IN GUTTER

BATT INSULATION

2×8 ROOF JOISTS

FINISH CEILING

6" BEADED WOOD SIDING

#15 BUILDING PAPER

3/4" SHEATHING

2×6 STUDS

ANCHOR BOLT

2×6 PRESSURE-TREATED SILL PLATES

2×6 TOP PLATES

FINISH WALL

BATT INSULATION

FINISH FLOOR

3/4" SUB-FLOORING

2×10 FLOOR JOISTS

CONCRETE FLOOR

6" COMPACTED GRAVEL

VAPOR BARRIER

6" COMPACTED SOIL

CONCRETE BLOCK INSULATED AND FILLED SOLID

CONCRETE FOOTING

Section

Wisconsin Farm House

Washington Island, Wisconsin
1,200 gross square feet

This house is inspired in part by typical farm complexes of northern coastal Wisconsin. Three structures house living spaces, bedrooms, and bathrooms, respectively.

The separation of this tiny program (1,200 square feet) into three distinct structures establishes a reassuring community of buildings on this remote 13-acre site on Lake Michigan. Accordingly, this design is as much about the spaces between buildings as it is about the buildings themselves.

Frederick Phillips

**Perspective
(Axonometric)**

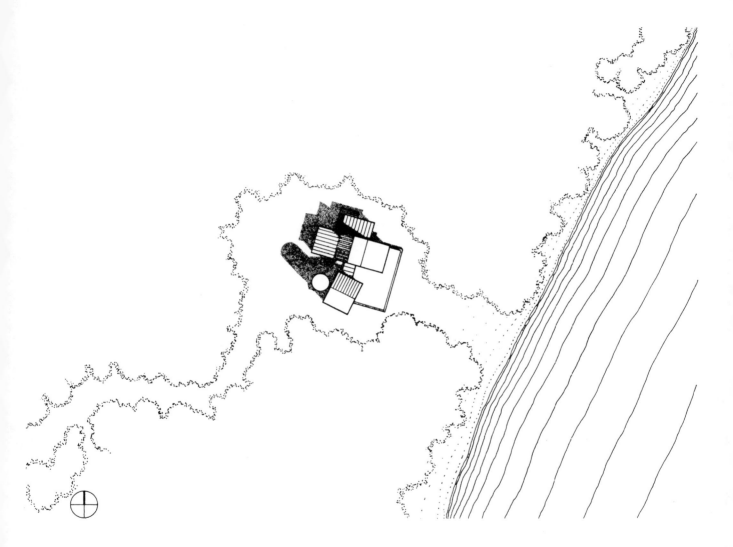

Site Plan

Wisconsin Farm House

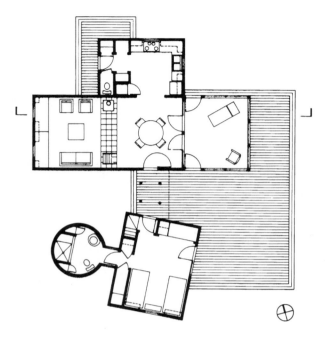

First Floor Plan

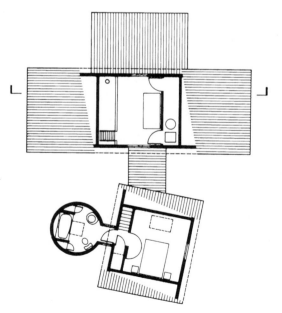

Second Floor Plan

East Elevation 1

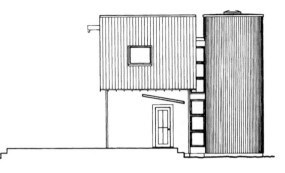

North Elevation 1

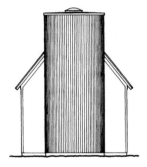

West Elevation 1

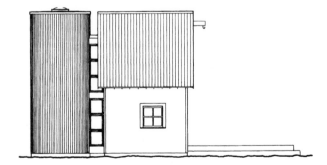

South Elevation 1

East Elevation 2

North Elevation 2

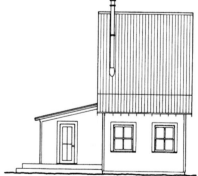

West Elevation 2

South Elevation 2

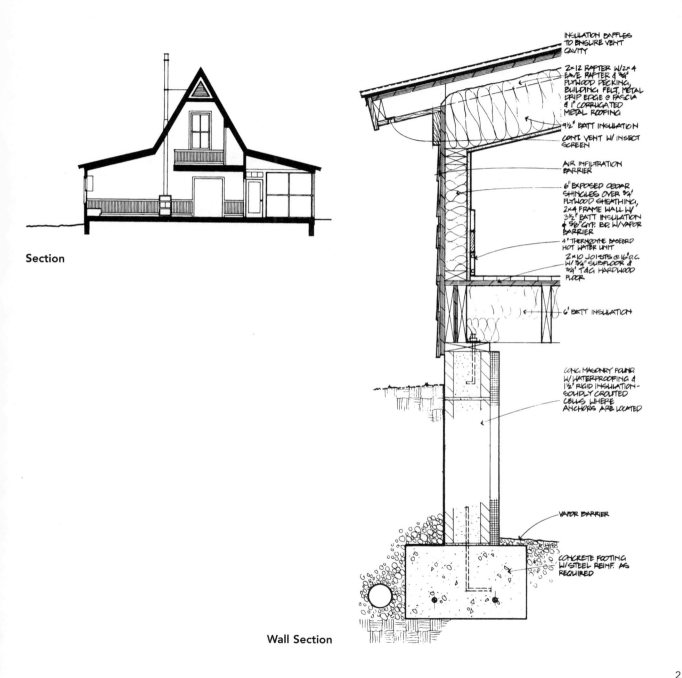

Section

Wall Section

INSULATION BAFFLES TO ENSURE VENT CAVITY

2×12 RAFTER W/ 2×4 EAVE RAFTER & 3/4" PLYWOOD DECKING, BUILDING FELT, METAL DRIP EDGE @ FASCIA & 1" CORRUGATED METAL ROOFING

9½" BATT INSULATION

CONT VENT W/ INSECT SCREEN

AIR INFILTRATION BARRIER

6" EXPOSED CEDAR SHINGLES OVER 3/4" PLYWOOD SHEATHING, 2×4 FRAME WALL W/ 3½" BATT INSULATION & 5/8" GYP. BD. W/ VAPOR BARRIER

4" THERMODYNE BASEBRD HOT WATER UNIT

2×10 JOISTS @ 16" O.C. W/ 3/4" SUBFLOOR & 3/4" T&G HARDWOOD FLOOR

6" BATT INSULATION

CONC. MASONRY FOUND. W/ WATERPROOFING & 1½" RIGID INSULATION— SOLIDLY GROUTED CELLS WHERE ANCHORS ARE LOCATED

VAPOR BARRIER

CONCRETE FOOTING W/ STEEL REINF. AS REQUIRED

Adobe

Santa Fe, New Mexico
1,220 gross square feet

This 1,220 square foot house was designed for the outskirts of a small town near Santa Fe, New Mexico. It is situated at the corner of two dirt roads that come together at an obtuse angle. The southwest walls of the house follow the line of the roads. Following the lead of John Gaw Meem, the great Santa Fe architect of the beginning of this century, the design freely adapts the local vernacular, in plan and detail.

The house is built of adobe, with the principal rooms opening to the courtyard. One enters through a tower, which can be reached by a steep stair in the vestibule. Inexpensive adobe fireplaces give focus to both the dining and living rooms, and the southfacing window-wall of the latter gives the house some passive solar possibilities. Awnings provide shade and outdoor living in the summer. Primary heating and mechanical systems are situated in a pit below the tower. Air conditioning is not necessary. The perimeter walls have small openings, which focus attention into the courtyard.

Richard Sammons

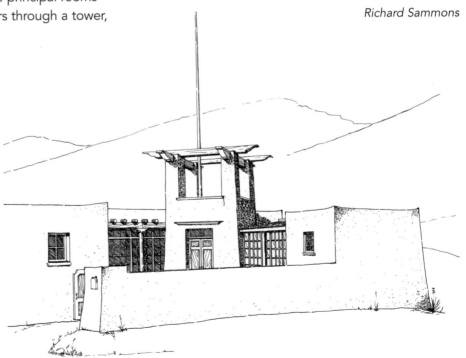

Perspective

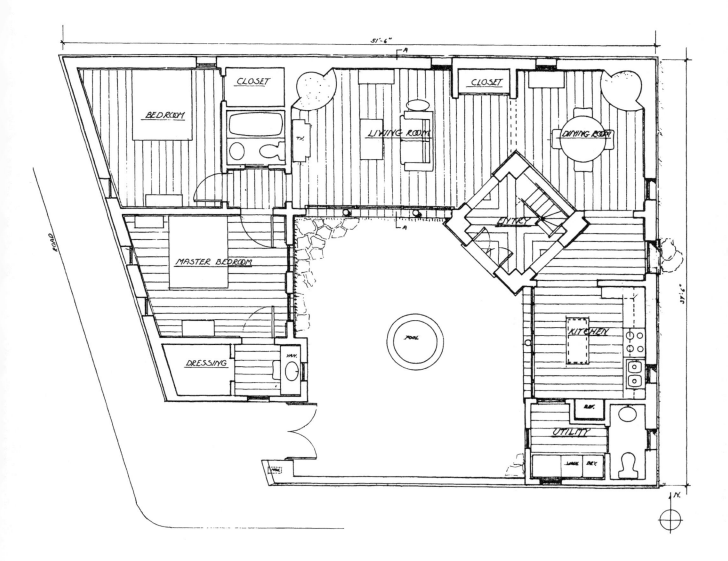

Floor Plan

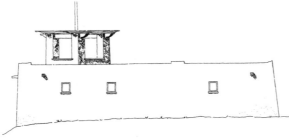

North Elevation

South Elevation

East Elevation

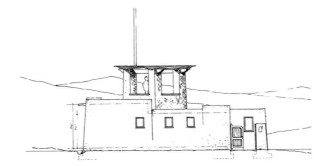

West Elevation

Section

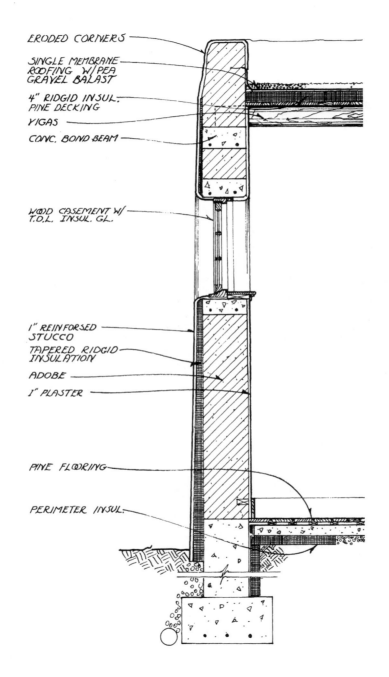

ERODED CORNERS

SINGLE MEMBRANE
ROOFING W/PEA
GRAVEL BALAST

4" RIDGID INSUL.
PINE DECKING

YIGAS

CONC. BOND BEAM

WOOD CASEMENT W/
T.O.L. INSUL. GL.

1" REINFORSED
STUCCO

TAPERED RIDGID
INSULATION

ADOBE

1" PLASTER

PINE FLOORING

PERIMETER INSUL.

Wall Section

Sophisticated Steel Frame

Clear Lake, California
1,205 gross square feet

The conventional house form with its numerous partitions cuts up space and works against a feeling of expansiveness. The plan here is long and rectilinear. Within this volume, a great space is kept, and distance itself serves to isolate areas of the house. The functions of kitchen and bath form a core placed so as to act itself as a divider of space. The expansive sense is enhanced by the "floating" of the upper level. Double-high space moves continuously around the perimeter of the house's interior. Space flows horizontally and vertically.

Another key element is the use of large glazed exterior walls. Sandwiched between the lakefront and a grove of trees, the sun-shaded glazed walls allow the interplay of interior and exterior space. The house is not so much a defined, limited enclosure but rather a place within and expanding into its natural setting.

Gerard Bolsega

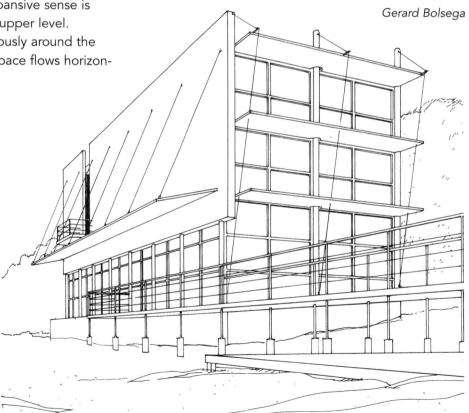

Perspective

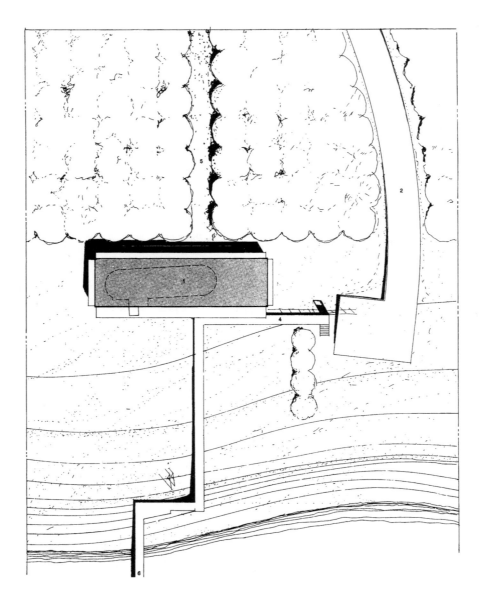

Site Plan

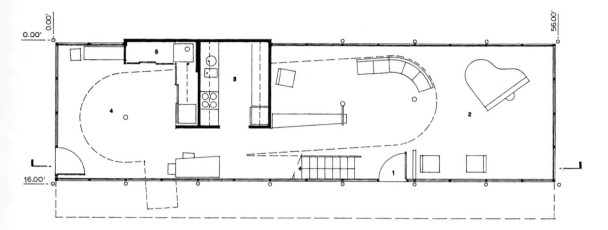

Ground Floor Plan

1 Entry
2 Living Area
3 Kitchen
4 Multi-Use
5 Storage/Utility
6 Bath
7 Sleeping Area
8 Open to Below
9 Terrace

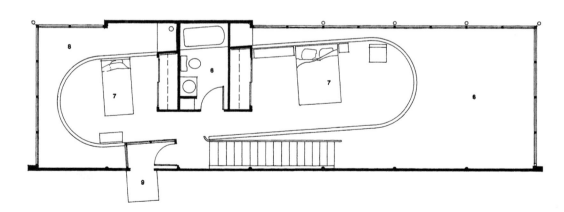

Upper Floor Plan

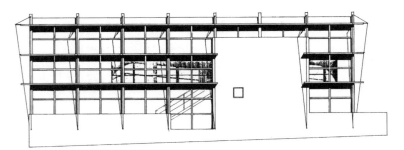

North Elevation

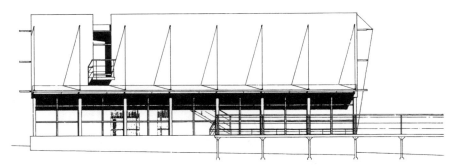

South Elevation

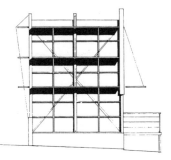

Side Elevation

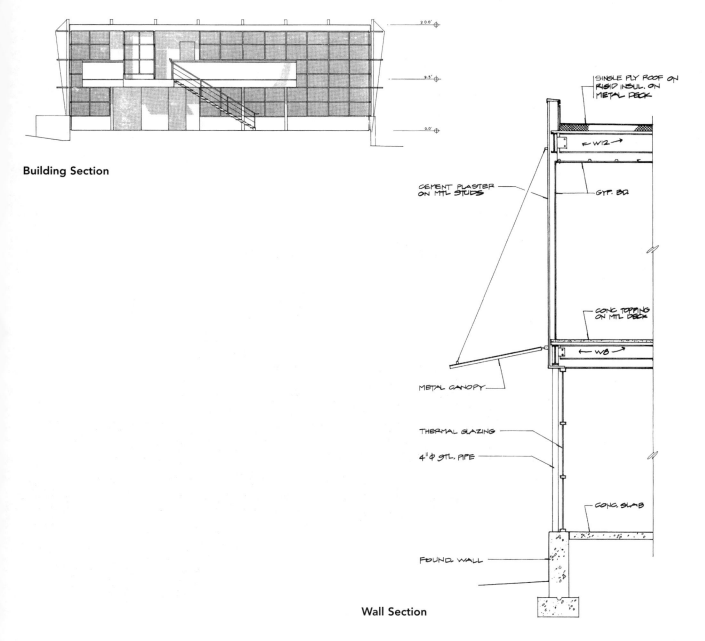

Building Section

20.0'

9.5'

0.0'

SINGLE PLY ROOF ON
RIGID INSUL. ON
METAL DECK

← W12 →

CEMENT PLASTER
ON MTL STUDS

GYP. BD

CONC TOPPING
ON MTL DECK

← W8 →

METAL CANOPY

THERMAL GLAZING

4" ∅ STL. PIPE

CONC. SLAB

FOUND. WALL

Wall Section

Woodsy Home/Studio

Orlando, Florida
1,175 gross square feet

The residence for a professional couple is situated on a densely wooded 5-acre site in central Florida.

The 1,175 square foot, two bedroom, two bath home-studio radiates from a spiral, central living area. Conventional trusses of uniform pitch and varying height and length span the living room by way of a steel "moment transference ring," allowing a central shaft of light to complement the perimeter clerestory.

A recessed floor allows seating around the low table.

The master bedroom opens onto a patio built around an existing palm tree. The master bath's sunken tub features floor-to-ceiling glass facing a private garden.

The powder room becomes a "ship's bath," with a floor drain and tiled walls with a shower head.

Windows encompass the studio area on three sides. A fireplace provides warmth during brisk winter mornings.

A V-grooved stucco exterior wall finish, rough-sawn red cedar fascia and metal roofing, and native coquina floor tile combine with the formal and spatial experience to produce an organic statement in a subtropic forest.

Jeffrey Burton

Perspective

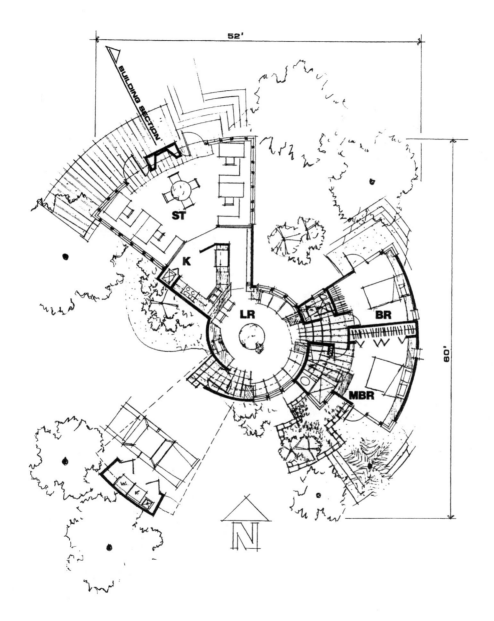

52'

BUILDING SECTION

ST

K

LR

BR

MBR

80'

N

Floor Plan

East Elevation

West Elevation

North Elevation

South Elevation

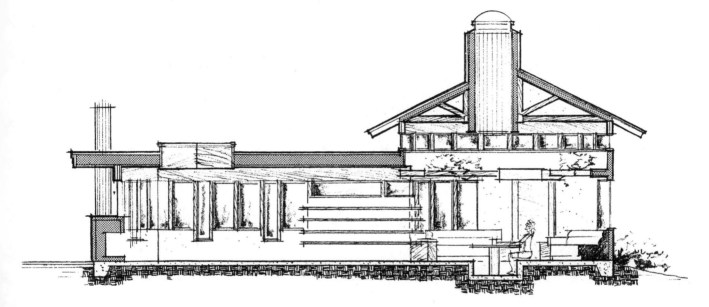

Section

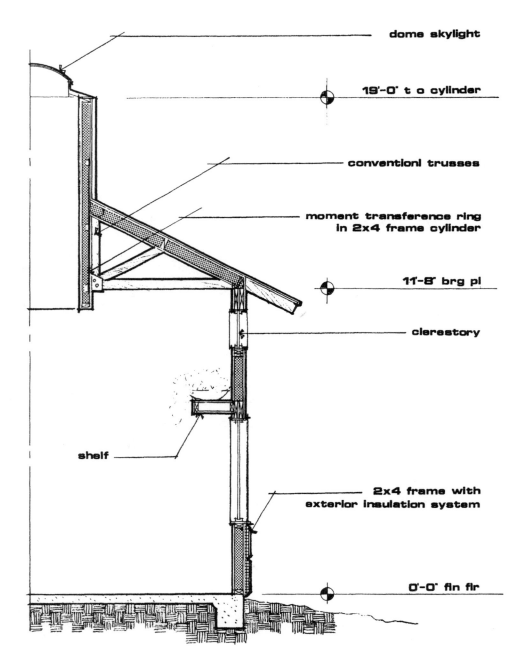

dome skylight

19'-0" t o cylinder

conventionl trusses

moment transference ring
in 2x4 frame cylinder

11'-8" brg pl

clerestory

shelf

2x4 frame with
exterior insulation system

0'-0" fin flr

Wall Section

Energy Efficient (on a South-Sloping Site)

Nonspecific Location
1,250 gross square feet (house)
1,200 gross square feet (garage)

This project was conceived in response to the call for submissions to the Second Compact House Competition. The house is not built; there is no specific location, site, or client.

I submitted this design in order to communicate some strongly held beliefs. Among these is that efficiency is valuable in and of itself. When one builds, whether to provide low-cost housing or a piece of expensive architecture, one has a moral obligation not to be wasteful. This is a basic tenet of my personal philosophy of architecture.

Another strongly held belief embodied in this design is that one should choose quality rather than quantity. My fictitious clients would like to build three bedrooms and two baths all at once and not have to deal with limited space, but to do so they would have to sacrifice quality. My design represents an acceptable alternative to this problem. The compact, efficient core design allows for incremental expansion. Delayed gratification versus instant gratification has, in the end, its own rewards.

Finally, in terms of environmental cost, the issue of energy efficiency is of great concern to all of us. This home relies on a number of passive design strategies in order to be energy-efficient. Primary among these is the placement of the house into a south-facing slope. Important, too, is the use of trees and overhangs to regulate seasonal solar gain.

Michael Clark Connor

Perspective

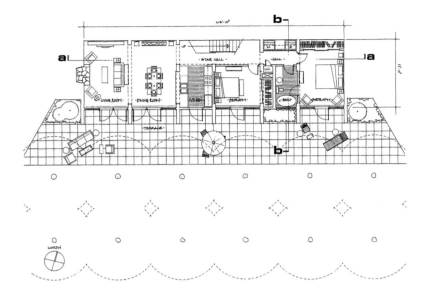

Lower Level Plan

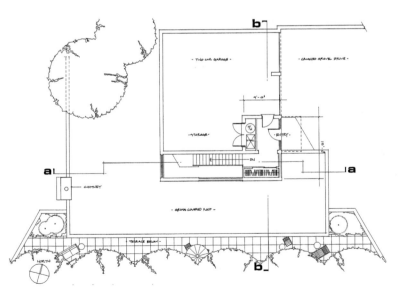

Upper Level Plan

South Elevation

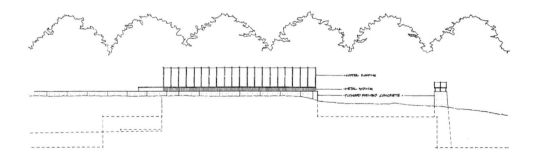

North Elevation

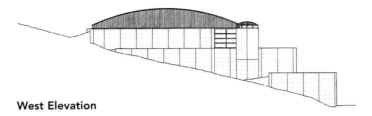

West Elevation

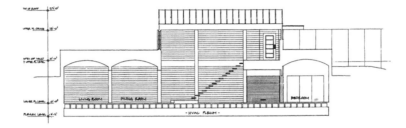

Section A-A

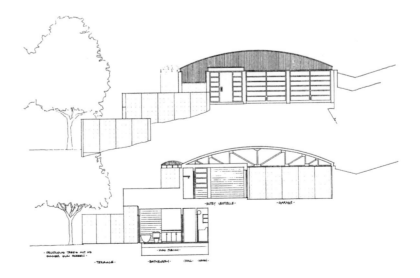

East Elevation (top)
Section B-B (bottom)

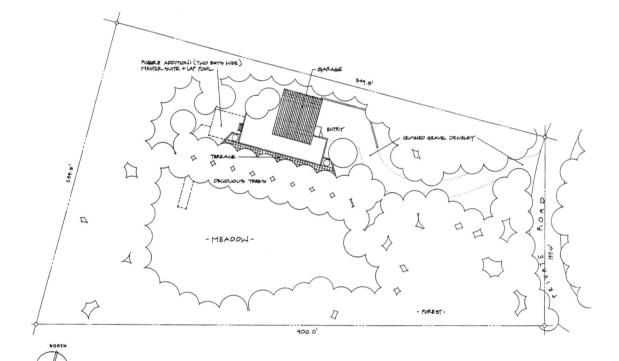

FUTURE ADDITION: (TWO BAYS WIDE)
MASTER SUITE + LAP POOL

GARAGE

349.5'

ENTRY

CRUSHED GRAVEL DRIVEWAY

TERRACE

DECIDUOUS TREES

254.5'

- MEADOW -

PRIVATE ROAD

147.0'

- FOREST -

400.0'

NORTH

Site Plan

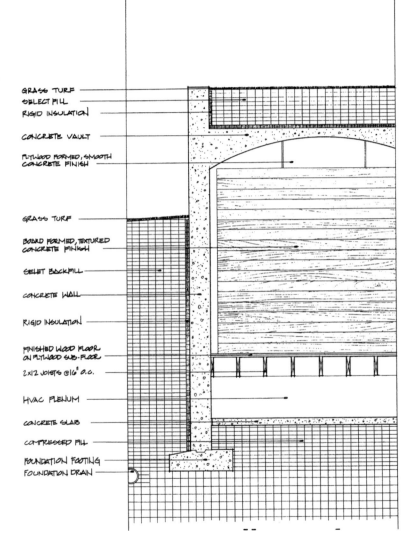

GRASS TURF

SELECT FILL

RIGID INSULATION

CONCRETE VAULT

PLYWOOD FORMED, SMOOTH
CONCRETE FINISH

GRASS TURF

BOARD FORMED, TEXTURED
CONCRETE FINISH

SELET BACKFILL

CONCRETE WALL

RIGID INSULATION

FINISHED WOOD FLOOR
ON PLYWOOD SUB-FLOOR

2X12 JOISTS @16" O.C.

HVAC PLENUM

CONCRETE SLAB

COMPRESSED FILL

FOUNDATION FOOTING

FOUNDATION DRAIN

Wall Section

Big Little House

Southern or Western U.S.

1,222 gross square feet

This residence is designed to meet the needs of the first-time buyer and the retired couple buying their last home.

The materials used in the design give the homeowner many of the luxuries found in a more expensive home. The home achieves a much larger appearance through the use of varying roof heights, the slope of the roof, and the horizontal lines produced by the siding.

Economic considerations being important, a water source heat pump is used to provide for the heating and cooling as well as the hot water requirements. The fireplace in the living area should also be integrated into the heating system. Awning windows are positioned to provide for cross-ventilation of the home during the spring and fall months. These windows, in conjunction with the open floor plan, do not confine one's eyes to a small area but allow them to visit all parts of the living area.

The residence is divided into the sleeping area upstairs and the living area on the first level. The living area with its open plan allows for freedom of movement. The use of a patio door in the living room brings the out-of-doors inside and makes the room appear more spacious and comfortable.

The use of wood flooring throughout the majority of the house adds a feeling of warmth and continuity to the home. The wood floors also allow for the use of area rugs to accent different sections within the home.

James M. Corkill

Perspective

273

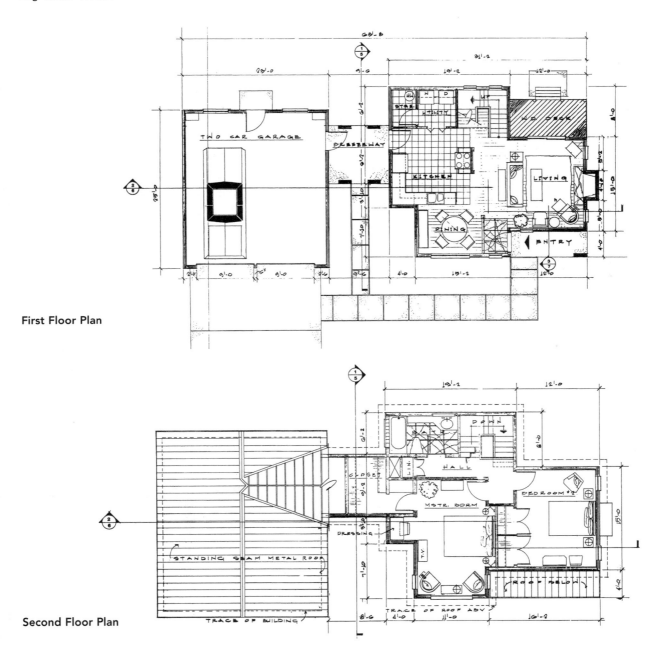

First Floor Plan

Second Floor Plan

North Elevation

South Elevation

East Elevation

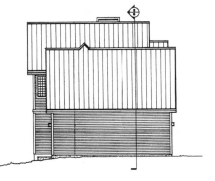

West Elevation

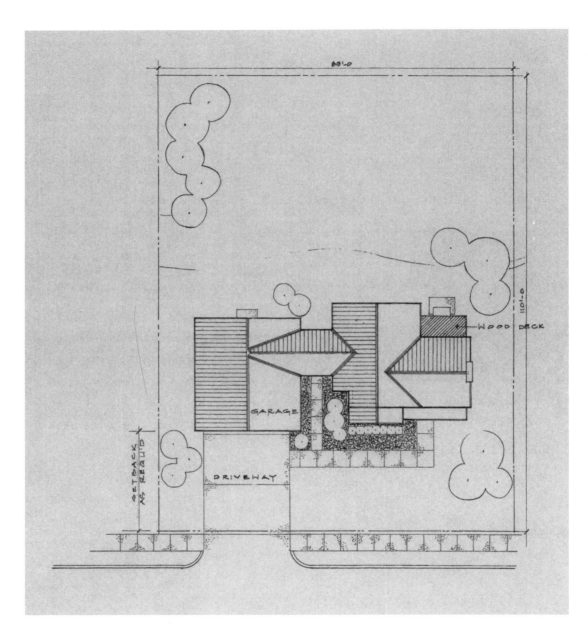

Site Plan

Section A-A

Section B-B

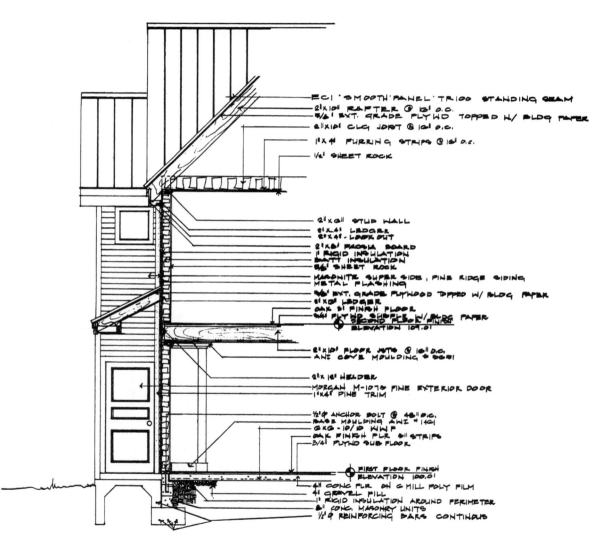

ECI 'SMOOTH' PANEL TR100 STANDING SEAM
2"x10" RAFTER @ 16" O.C.
5/8" EXT. GRADE PLYWD TOPPED W/ BLDG PAPER
2"x10" CLG JOIST @ 16" O.C.

1"x4" FURRING STRIPS @ 16" O.C.

1/2" SHEET ROCK

2"x8" STUD WALL
2"x4" LEDGER
2"x4" LOOK OUT
2"x8" FASCIA BOARD
1" RIGID INSULATION
BATT INSULATION
5/8" SHEET ROCK
HARDNITE SUPER SIDE, PINE RIDGE SIDING
METAL FLASHING
5/8" EXT. GRADE PLYWOOD TOPPED W/ BLDG PAPER
2"x8" LEDGER
OAK 3" FINISH FLOOR
3/4" PLYWD SHEATHING W/ BLDG PAPER
SECOND FLOOR FINISH
ELEVATION 109.0"

2"x10" FLOOR JOIST @ 16" O.C.
ANT COVE MOULDING # 5681

2"x10" HEADER
MORGAN M-1075 PINE EXTERIOR DOOR
1"x4" PINE TRIM

1/2" Ø ANCHOR BOLT @ 48" O.C.
BASE MOULDING AWI "1461
6x6 - 10/10 WWF
OAK FINISH FLR 3" STRIPS
3/4" PLYWD SUB FLOOR

FIRST FLOOR FINISH
ELEVATION 100.0"
4" CONC FLR ON 6 MILL POLY FILM
4" GRAVEL FILL
1" RIGID INSULATION AROUND PERIMETER
8" CONC. MASONRY UNITS
1/2" Ø REINFORCING BARS CONTINUOUS

Wall Section

Desert Module

Phoenix, Arizona
1,248 gross square feet

Designed for the Sonoran Desert, this home responds to the rigorously hot climate and a leftover, oddly shaped building site. The combination of sun and site helped suggest the stepped three-module plan and large-angled, sun-shading roof. Stepping and nesting the 24-foot-square modules to follow the southeast lot line afforded the opportunity to continuously open the cooler northeast side to the outdoors. The sun shade roof floats protectively over the living modules for maximum ventilation and covering for the HVAC and DWH equipment. Its angled shape yields huge effective overhangs to protect wall areas and also helps direct the eye along a longer,

more dynamic line. In addition to the sun shade, desert-tolerant trees are planted around the west, southwest, south, and east sides of the house to protectively shade walls and cool the adjacent ground.

A single floor material, colored and patterned concrete, flows from inside to out, enhancing the feeling of spaciousness. Nine-foot-high ceilings and continuous clerestory windows allow natural light without sun to further connect the occupant with the outside.

David B. DiCicco

Perspective

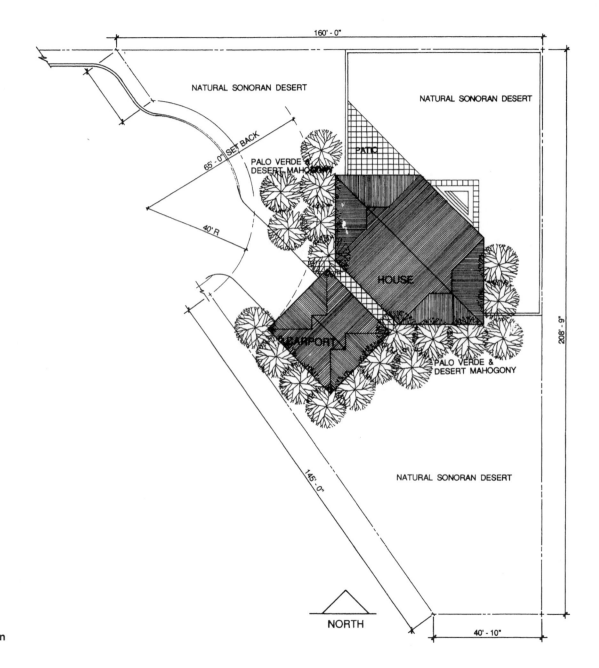

160' - 0"

NATURAL SONORAN DESERT

NATURAL SONORAN DESERT

65' - 0" SET BACK

PALO VERDE &
DESERT MAHOGONY

PATIO

40' R

HOUSE

208' - 9"

CARPORT

PALO VERDE &
DESERT MAHOGONY

NATURAL SONORAN DESERT

145' - 0"

NORTH

40' - 10"

Site Plan

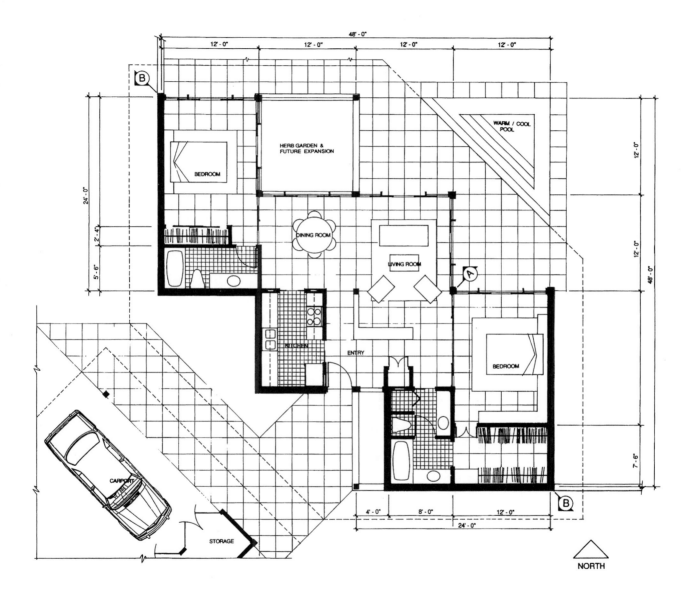

Floor Plan (and Partial Carport)

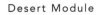

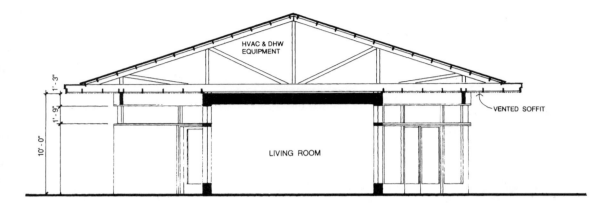

Cross Section

HVAC & DHW EQUIPMENT

VENTED SOFFIT

1'-3"

1'-9"

10'-0"

LIVING ROOM

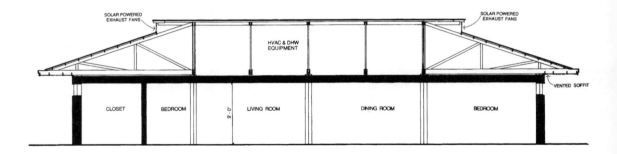

SOLAR POWERED EXHAUST FANS

SOLAR POWERED EXHAUST FANS

HVAC & DHW EQUIPMENT

VENTED SOFFIT

CLOSET   BEDROOM   LIVING ROOM   DINING ROOM   BEDROOM

Longitudinal Section

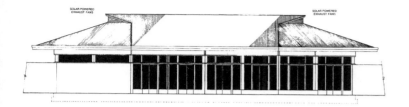

Northeast Elevation

Northwest Elevation

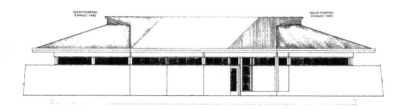

Southwest Elevation

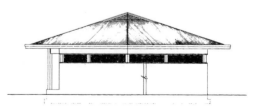

Southeast Elevation

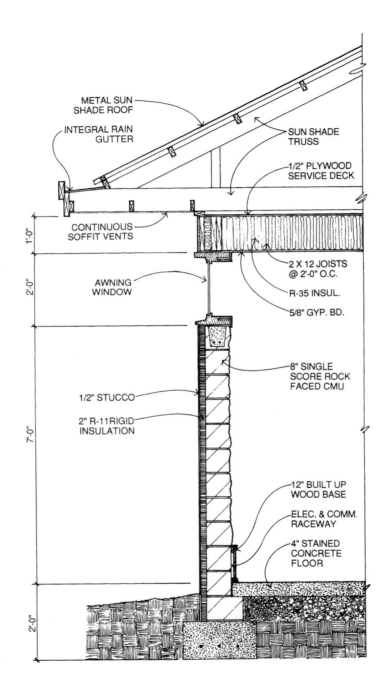

METAL SUN SHADE ROOF

INTEGRAL RAIN GUTTER

SUN SHADE TRUSS

1/2" PLYWOOD SERVICE DECK

CONTINUOUS SOFFIT VENTS

2 X 12 JOISTS @ 2'-0" O.C.

AWNING WINDOW

R-35 INSUL.

5/8" GYP. BD.

8" SINGLE SCORE ROCK FACED CMU

1/2" STUCCO

2" R-11 RIGID INSULATION

12" BUILT UP WOOD BASE

ELEC. & COMM. RACEWAY

4" STAINED CONCRETE FLOOR

1'-0"

2'-0"

7'-0"

2'-0"

Wall Section

Basic Ranch

Manitoba, Canada
1,200 gross square feet

This home is designed for a retiring couple with a love for the outdoors in both winter and summer. The home's formal front, verandah, and entry court address the vernacular architecture in the surrounding community. Extensive natural landscaping provides privacy from the street to the sun deck and patio. The house then acts as a gateway, opening up to spectacular views to the south. The verandah's design allows for it to be enclosed, extending its use into both the spring and autumn seasons.

In the interior, the wood stove acts as the central focus for the living area and country kitchen.

Through the arrangement of furnishings, the open plan creates a casual atmosphere with the possibility for both large or smaller, more intimate gatherings taking place. As a space-saving measure, the bathroom serves as both a guest powder room and an ensuite for the master bedroom. The extensive use of glazing on the south facade allows for winter sun to penetrate the home and summer breezes off the lake to filter through the house, cooling it. The home is planned on a single level, allowing for the mobility of residents in later years.

Michael J. Fritschij

Perspective

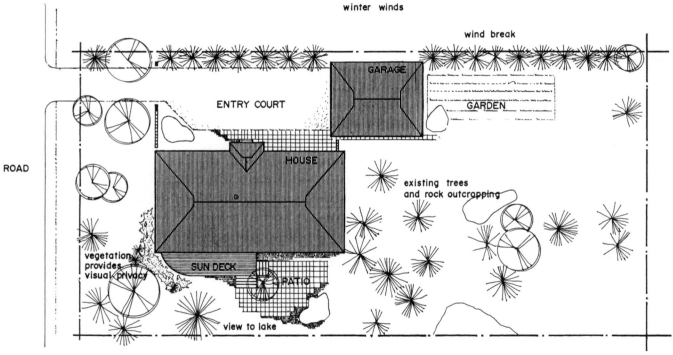

winter winds

wind break

GARAGE

ENTRY COURT

GARDEN

ROAD

HOUSE

existing trees
and rock outcropping

vegetation
provides
visual privacy

SUN DECK

PATIO

view to lake

summer breeze off lake

Site Plan

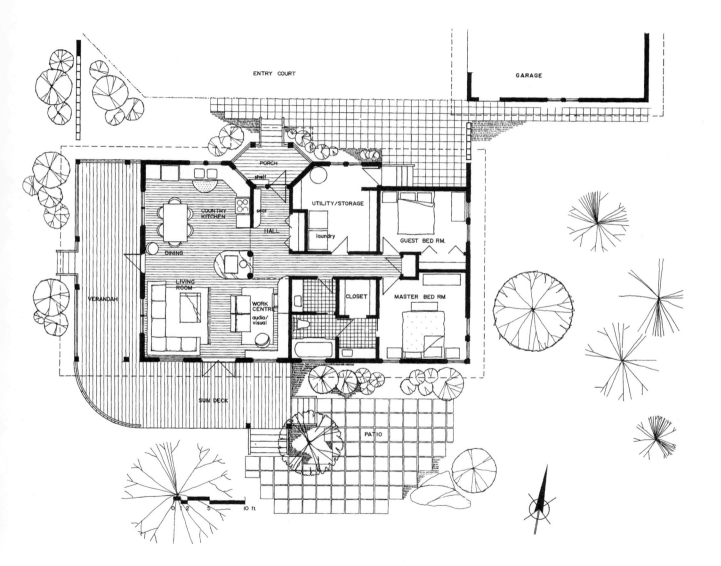

ENTRY COURT

GARAGE

PORCH

shelf

seat

COUNTRY KITCHEN

UTILITY/STORAGE

HALL

laundry

GUEST BED RM.

DINING

LIVING ROOM

WORK CENTRE

audio/visual

CLOSET

MASTER BED RM.

VERANDAH

SUN DECK

PATIO

0 2   5   10 ft.

Floor Plan

Basic Ranch

East Elevation

West Elevation

North Elevation

South Elevation

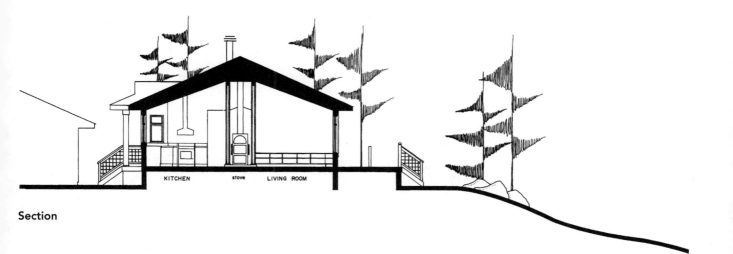

KITCHEN   stove   LIVING ROOM

Section

Live-in Sculpture

A Coastal, Moderate Climate

1,250 gross square feet

The site is a coastal point which has a fair climate and tropical breezes throughout most of the year. The possibility of extremely turbulent storms is, however, a concern.

The waterfront location brings to us images of seagoing vessels from distant ports and pleasure boats enjoying a calm afternoon. These contrasting images of "vessel" and "boat" help establish a dichotomy of function and form: a vessel in an independent, enduring, and enclosed instrument; a pleasure boat is restricted, vulnerable, and open.

These same images are expressed in the "house-vessel" on the north, which is rigid against harsh winds and stands tall to separate public from private domains. In contrast, the "house-boat" on the south is passive in form and solar qualities, expressed through the south glazing being echoed by the exploding out of the frame—a metaphor of its vulnerability.

Ideally, a house that's ready to sail; in reality, a summer home that mirrors its surroundings.

Daniel Grandy

Perspective

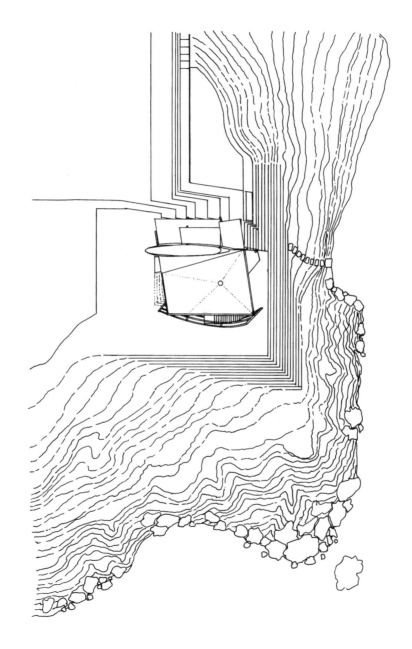

Site Plan

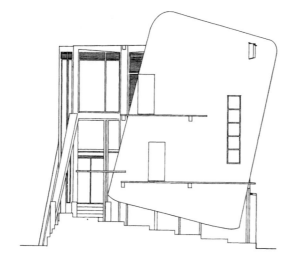

North Elevation

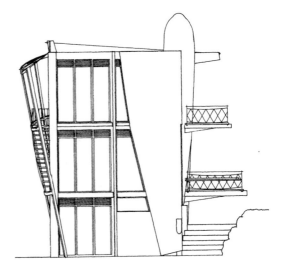

East Elevation

South Elevation

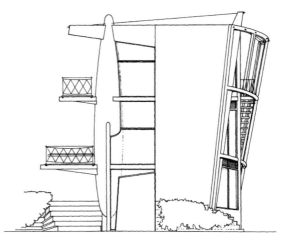

West Elevation

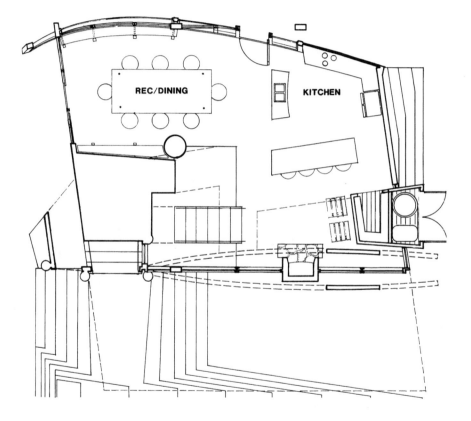

First Floor Plan

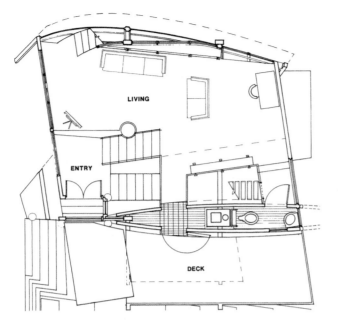

Second Floor Plan

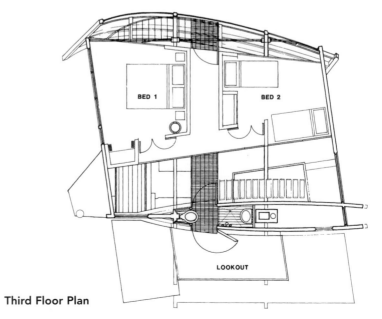

Third Floor Plan

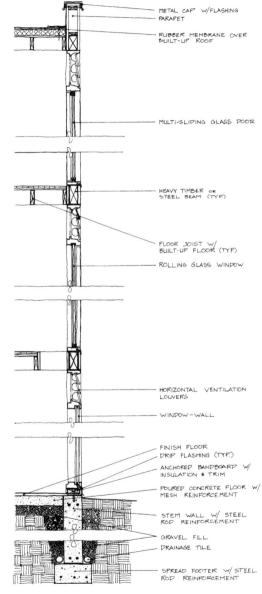

METAL CAP W/FLASHING

PARAPET

RUBBER MEMBRANE OVER
BUILT-UP ROOF

MULTI-SLIDING GLASS DOOR

HEAVY TIMBER OR
STEEL BEAM (TYP)

FLOOR JOIST W/
BUILT-UP FLOOR (TYP)

ROLLING GLASS WINDOW

HORIZONTAL VENTILATION
LOUVERS

WINDOW-WALL

FINISH FLOOR

DRIP FLASHING (TYP.)

ANCHORED BANDBOARD W/
INSULATION & TRIM

POURED CONCRETE FLOOR W/
MESH REINFORCEMENT

STEM WALL W/ STEEL
ROD REINFORCEMENT

GRAVEL FILL

DRAINAGE TILE

SPREAD FOOTER W/ STEEL
ROD REINFORCEMENT

South Wall Section

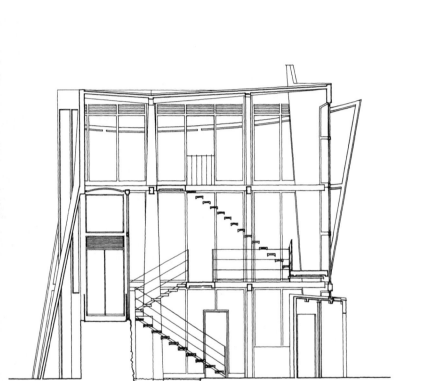

Section

Vertical Space

Bayview, Idaho
1,238 gross square feet (excluding decks)

The house is organized on a stacked nominal 12' x 12' x 10' nine-square grid. The architectural style and materials are indigenous to the coastal Northwest: expressive but simple forms and geometry, elements of whimsy, and openness to relieve "cabin fever" and increase natural light and a feeling of warmth in frequently overcast skies.

The central south-facing solarium/entry and spiral stair is the organizational and visual focal point of the plan and volume and provides a serving area for entertaining.

The upper glazing continues second-floor views to the south via louvered doors and frames to Goat Mountain and the National Forest and maximizes solar gain in winter. The side windows are placed for cross-ventilation and intimate views of landscape elements. Bedrooms on the second level have private decks, which also have southerly views and exposure. Corner forms house stove flues and create supports for light globes and pennants.

David A. Harris

**Perspective
(Axonometric)**

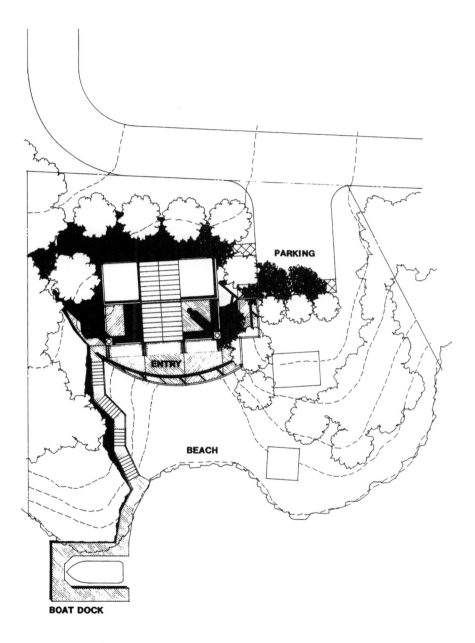

PARKING

ENTRY

BEACH

BOAT DOCK

Site Plan

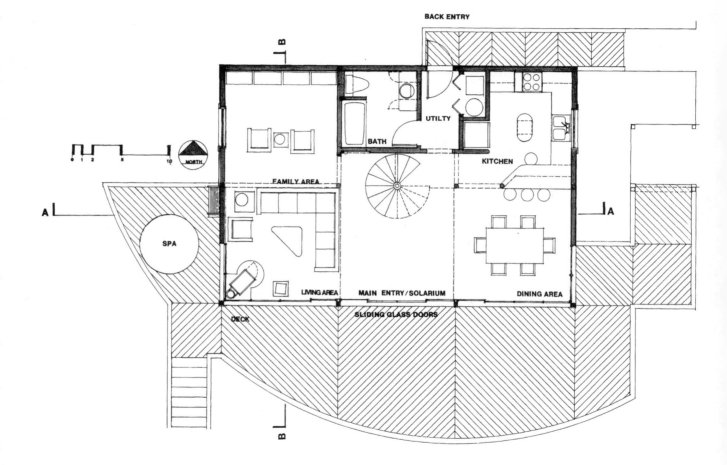

BACK ENTRY

B

NORTH

0 1 2   5   10

A

FAMILY AREA

BATH

UTILTY

KITCHEN

SPA

LIVING AREA

MAIN ENTRY / SOLARIUM

DINING AREA

A

DECK

SLIDING GLASS DOORS

B

First Floor Plan

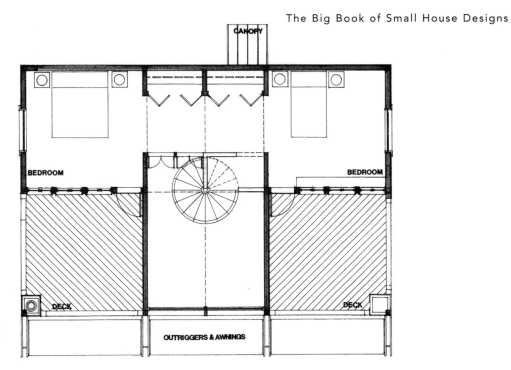

Second Floor Plan

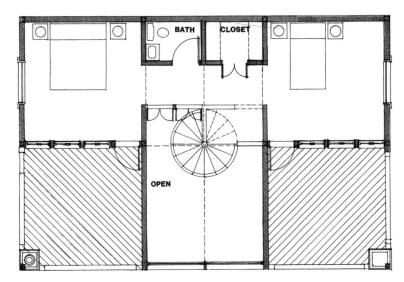

**Alternate
Second Floor Plan**

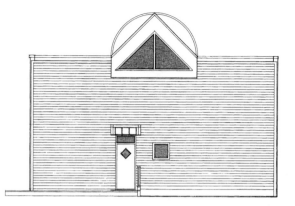

North Elevation

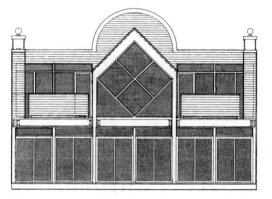

South Elevation

East Elevation

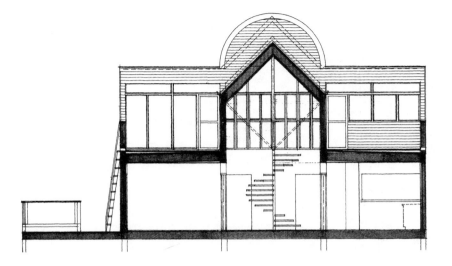

Section A-A

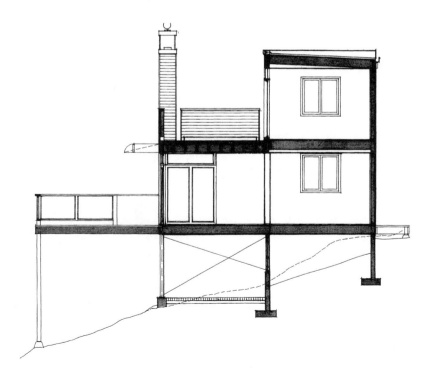

Section B-B

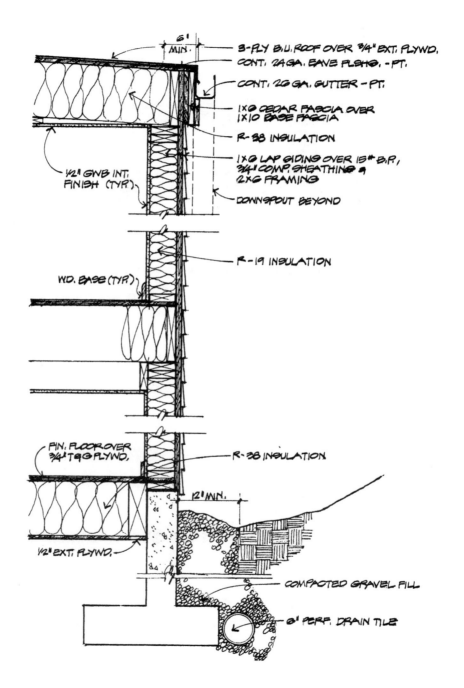

3-PLY B.U. ROOF OVER ¾" EXT. PLYWD.

CONT. 24 GA. EAVE FLSHG. - PT.

CONT. 26 GA. GUTTER - PT.

1X8 CEDAR FASCIA OVER
1X10 BASE FASCIA

R-38 INSULATION

1X8 LAP SIDING OVER 15# B.P.,
¾" COMP. SHEATHING &
2X6 FRAMING

DOWNSPOUT BEYOND

½" GWB INT.
FINISH (TYP.)

R-19 INSULATION

WD. BASE (TYP.)

FIN. FLOOR OVER
¾" T&G PLYWD.

R-38 INSULATION

12" MIN.

COMPACTED GRAVEL FILL

½" EXT. PLYWD.

8" PERF. DRAIN TILE

Wall Section

Victorian Barn

Non-specific Location
1,136 gross square feet

Although suitable for most regions of the United States, this house design is reminiscent of the farmhouses and barns which dot the New England countryside. A cruciform plan clusters functions around a compact service core. Rooms are clearly defined while maintaining a sense of spatial continuity. Circulation square footage is minimized. Living areas extend outside to trellised porches. An unfinished basement provides convenient expansion opportunities.

Windows are located to catch southern sun and promote cross-ventilation. A cupola introduces daylight to the center of the house. East and west facades are windowless to ensure privacy from neighboring dwellings or to facilitate connection as a multiple unit structure (with minor modification).

Thomas McClellan Haskell

Perspective

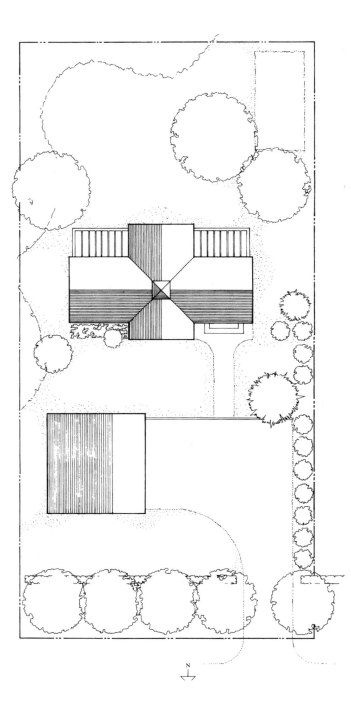

Site Plan

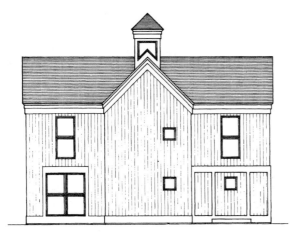

North Elevation

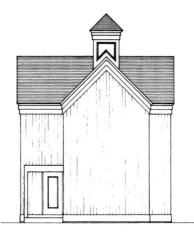

East Elevation

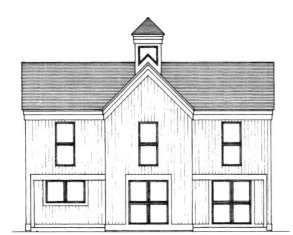

South Elevation

West Elevation

Victorian Barn

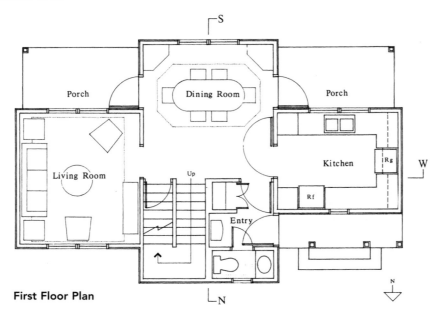

First Floor Plan

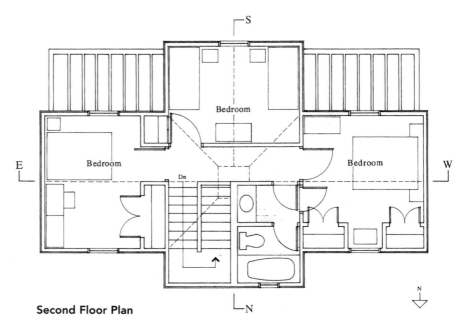

Second Floor Plan

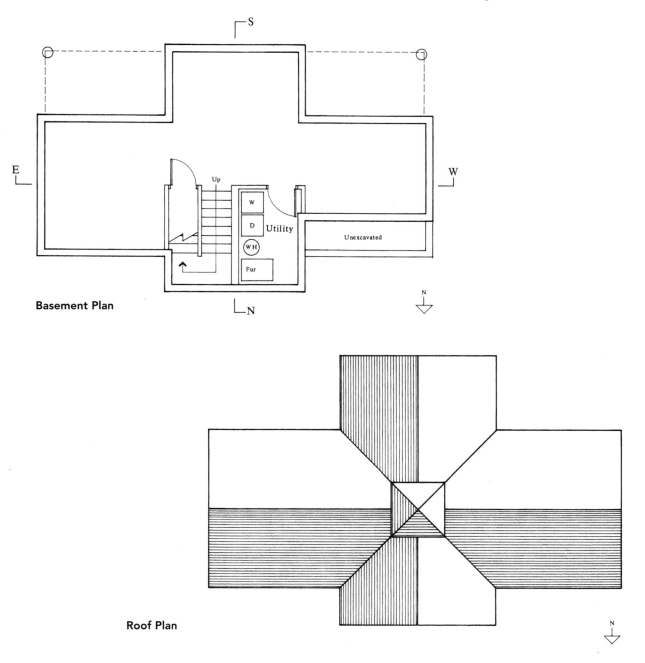

Basement Plan

Up

W

D Utility

W H

Fur

Unexcavated

Roof Plan

Victorian Barn

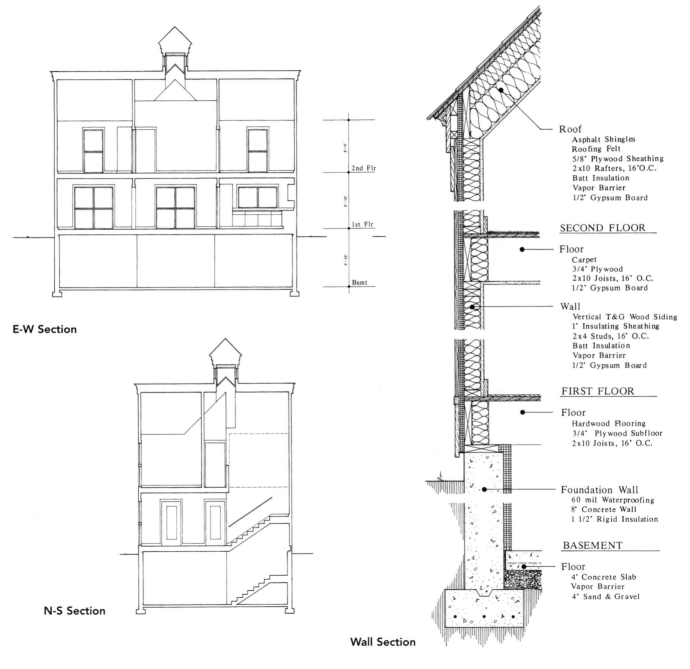

E-W Section

2nd Flr
1st Flr
Bsmt

N-S Section

Wall Section

Roof
    Asphalt Shingles
    Roofing Felt
    5/8" Plywood Sheathing
    2x10 Rafters, 16"O.C.
    Batt Insulation
    Vapor Barrier
    1/2" Gypsum Board

SECOND FLOOR

Floor
    Carpet
    3/4" Plywood
    2x10 Joists, 16" O.C.
    1/2" Gypsum Board

Wall
    Vertical T&G Wood Siding
    1" Insulating Sheathing
    2x4 Studs, 16" O.C.
    Batt Insulation
    Vapor Barrier
    1/2" Gypsum Board

FIRST FLOOR

Floor
    Hardwood Flooring
    3/4" Plywood Subfloor
    2x10 Joists, 16" O.C.

Foundation Wall
    60 mil Waterproofing
    8" Concrete Wall
    1 1/2" Rigid Insulation

BASEMENT

Floor
    4" Concrete Slab
    Vapor Barrier
    4" Sand & Gravel

Classic Rural Style

Mouth of the Connecticut River
1,250 gross square feet

The house is composed of a compact, two-level block of bedrooms and baths attached to a comparatively voluminous living/dining/kitchen room. The house entry is a contained, low-ceilinged space that opens to the upward and outward expansion of the living space — the effect is to diminish the feeling of smallness in the compact spaces of the house. The supporting truss spanning the living space implies a separation of living and dining spaces within the large room. The fireplace is a major focus of the living space that encourages a grouping of furniture around it. The exterior massing and detailing of the house has its roots in the Shingle-style beach cottages that are part of the history of this area of the Connecticut coast.

J. Whitney Huber

Perspective

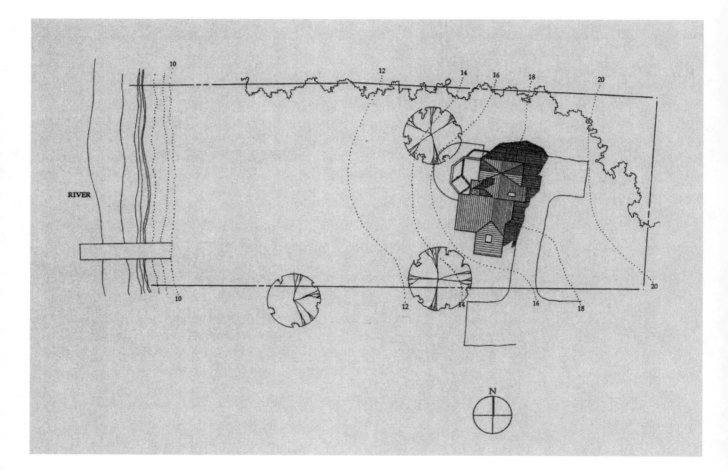

RIVER

10

12   14   16   18   20

10

12   14   16   18   20

N

Site Plan

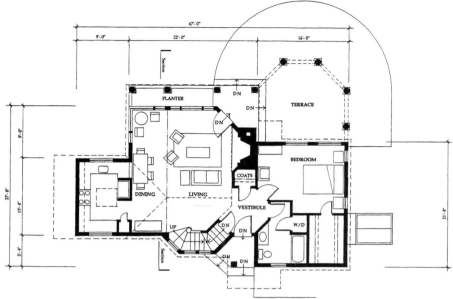

First Floor Plan

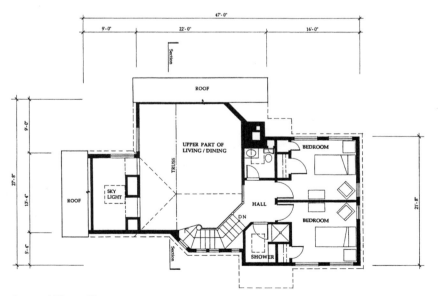

Second Floor Plan

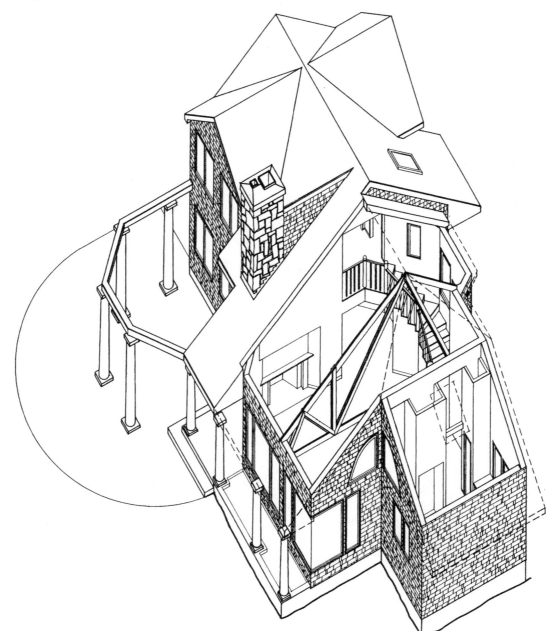

Axonometric

East Elevation

North Elevation

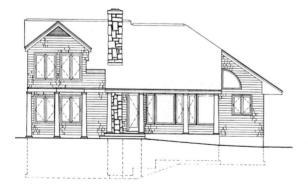

West Elevation

South Elevation

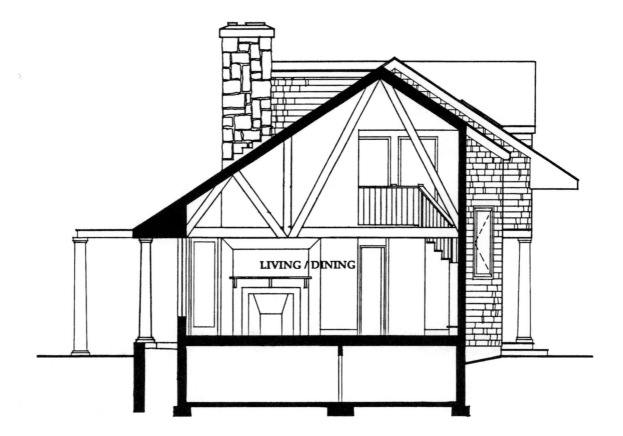

LIVING / DINING

Section

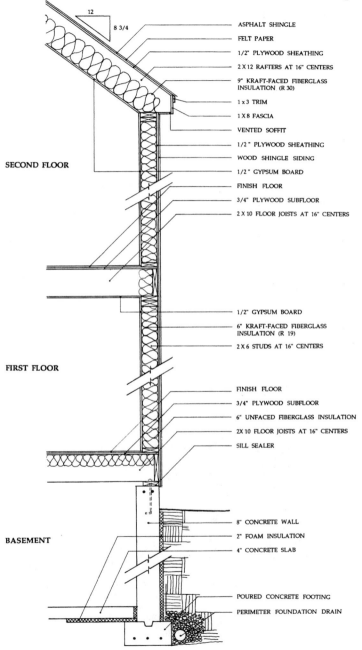

12
8 3/4

ASPHALT SHINGLE

FELT PAPER

1/2" PLYWOOD SHEATHING

2 X 12 RAFTERS AT 16" CENTERS

9" KRAFT-FACED FIBERGLASS
INSULATION (R 30)

1 x 3 TRIM

1 X 8 FASCIA

VENTED SOFFIT

1/2" PLYWOOD SHEATHING

WOOD SHINGLE SIDING

1/2" GYPSUM BOARD

FINISH FLOOR

3/4" PLYWOOD SUBFLOOR

2 X 10 FLOOR JOISTS AT 16" CENTERS

SECOND FLOOR

1/2" GYPSUM BOARD

6" KRAFT-FACED FIBERGLASS
INSULATION (R 19)

2 X 6 STUDS AT 16" CENTERS

FIRST FLOOR

FINISH FLOOR

3/4" PLYWOOD SUBFLOOR

6" UNFACED FIBERGLASS INSULATION

2 X 10 FLOOR JOISTS AT 16" CENTERS

SILL SEALER

8" CONCRETE WALL

2" FOAM INSULATION

4" CONCRETE SLAB

BASEMENT

POURED CONCRETE FOOTING

PERIMETER FOUNDATION DRAIN

Wall Section

Clean and Simple Living

Southern U.S. or Caribbean

1,248 gross square feet (house) and 448 gross square feet (terrace and entry)

This house is designed to provide exciting and comfortable living amenities within a small footprint.

The spaces are articulated into two zones defining the various activities of daily life. These zones are expressed as linked volumes containing public and private functions. The foyer, providing the circulation linkage between the two, also contains the mechanical core.

Separating the plan into two basic elements provides a protected central entry courtyard and a covered terrace. These exterior spaces expand the living space visually and literally and create private views inward from most rooms, minimizing exterior openings toward neighbors in close proximity.

The kitchen is central to both living and family room and is open for ease of service to both areas, and through patio doors to the terrace. Partitions are door height to allow the vaulted ceiling to flow uninterrupted. Roofs are steeply pitched to create interior volumes and promote air circulation.

Paul Robin John

Perspective

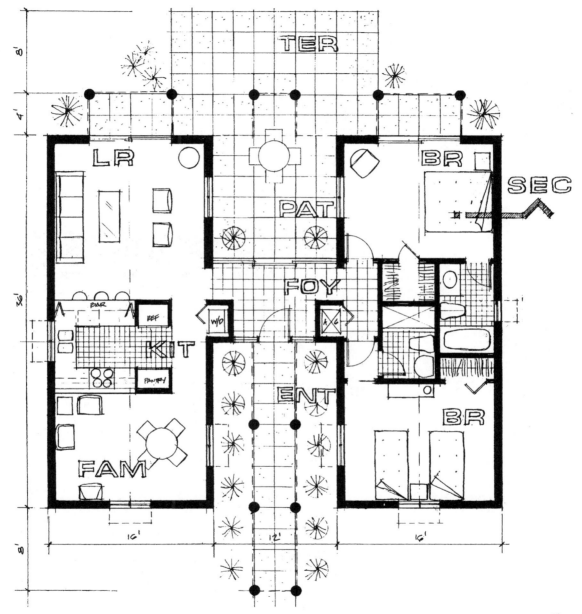

Floor Plan

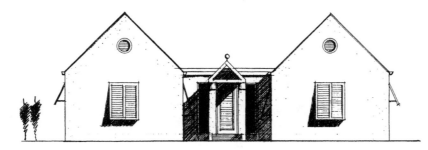

Front Elevation

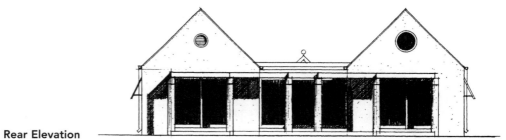

Rear Elevation

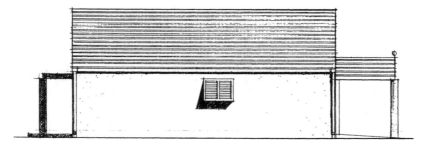

Side Elevation 1

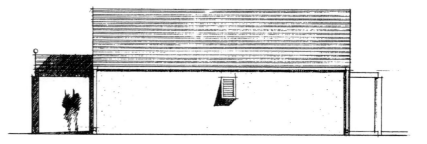

Side Elevation 2

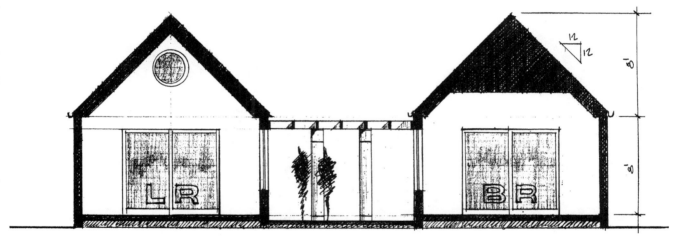

12
12

8'

8'

LR

BR

Section

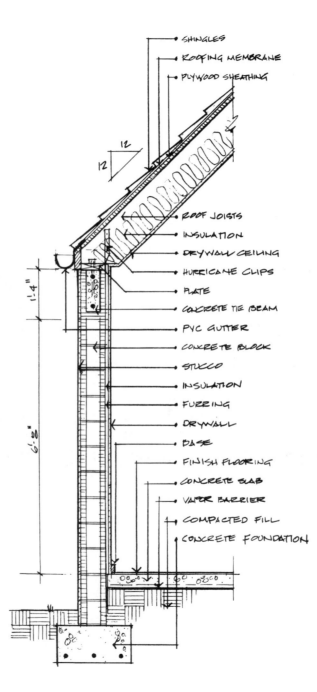

- SHINGLES
- ROOFING MEMBRANE
- PLYWOOD SHEATHING
- ROOF JOISTS
- INSULATION
- DRYWALL CEILING
- HURRICANE CLIPS
- PLATE
- CONCRETE TIE BEAM
- PVC GUTTER
- CONCRETE BLOCK
- STUCCO
- INSULATION
- FURRING
- DRYWALL
- BASE
- FINISH FLOORING
- CONCRETE SLAB
- VAPOR BARRIER
- COMPACTED FILL
- CONCRETE FOUNDATION

12
12

1'-4"

6'-8"

Wall Section

Classic Ranch

Black Forest, Colorado
1,248 gross square feet

A gabled roof and false beams were substituted for the flat roof and vigas of the conventional Santa Fe home due to the high snow loads in this area. Peeled ponderosa pine logs were used at the front and rear portals, however, as they grow in abundance on the property.

Window trim, shutters, doors, base, and casing will be shop-built by the owner in order to follow through on the Southwest style.

With a crawl space there is the option of various heating systems, such as a gas down draft forced-air furnace with metal ductwork, or a "plenwood" system. Another option would be an "in-floor" hot water radiant floor system using poured gyp-crete over plastic pipe.

A good part of the heating requirement will be provided by an efficient zero-clearance fireplace insert, which can be finished with tiles in the traditional manner.

Charles H. Ludeke

Perspective

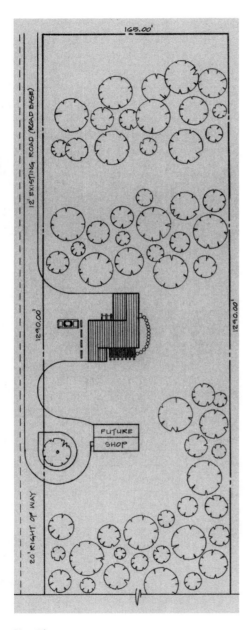

Site Plan

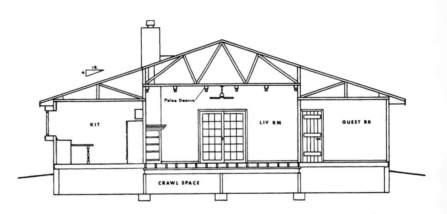

Section

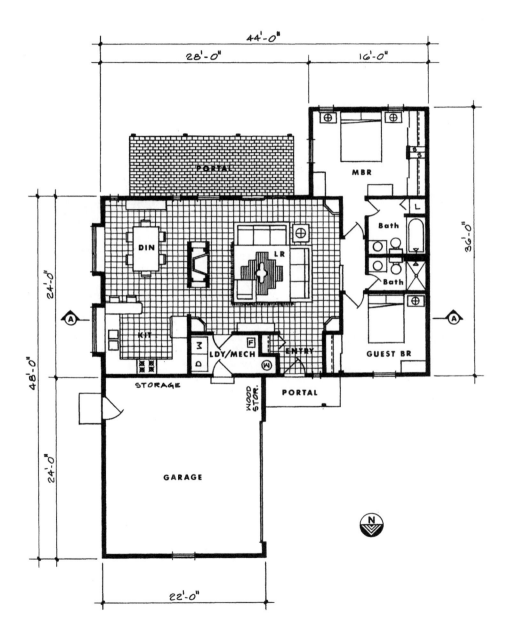

Floor Plan

Classic Ranch

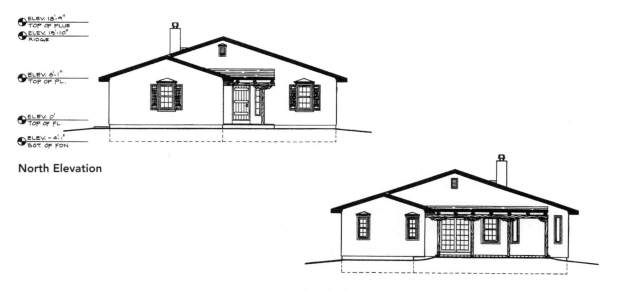

ELEV. 18'-9"
TOP OF FLUE

ELEV. 15'-10"
RIDGE

ELEV. 8'-1"
TOP OF PL.

ELEV. 0'
TOP OF FL.

ELEV. -4'.1"
BOT. OF FDN

North Elevation

South Elevation

East Elevation

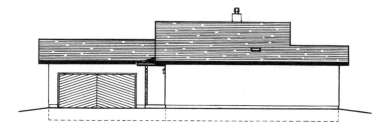

West Elevation

Wall Section

1 220# fiberglass/asphalt 3-tab shingles over 15# asphalt felt

2. $\frac{7}{16}$" waferboard roof sheathing

3 Double-thick 6" fiberglass batt. insulation, installed at 90° to each other for a total of R-38

4 Scarfed 2" x 4" trusses @ 24" o.c.

5 $\frac{1}{2}$" gypsum board, taped and "Spanish lace" textured

6 Double 2" x 4" top plates

7 1" x 4" #3 spruce continuous ledger

8 $\frac{3}{8}$" Cladwood textured soffit

9 8" x 16" G.I. soffit vents

10 1" x 8" primed pine, $\frac{3}{8}$" plowed fascia

11 4" x 3" OG galvanized iron gutters connected to 3" x 2" rectangular downspouts

12 2" x 4" 92$\frac{5}{8}$" S&B white wood studs at 16" o.c.

13 R-13 fiberglass batt. insulation

14 $\frac{1}{2}$" Styrofoam "blue board"

15 2 coat stucco

16 2" x 4" sole plate

17 2$\frac{1}{4}$" #0366 oak baseboard

18 $\frac{3}{4}$" T & G oriented strand board subfloor, glued in joints over joists and nailed; $\frac{1}{4}$" luan mahogany plywood underlayment stapled over it where tile or vinyl finish floor is used

19 2" x 8" H.F. #2 joists @ 16" o.c.

20 R-19 fiberglass batt insulation

21 1" x 8" #3 spruce rim joist

22 2" x 4" construction common redwood

23 $\frac{1}{2}$" diameter x 10" anchor bolts @ 6'0" o.c. (max.)

24 8" x 41" poured concrete stem wall

25 2 - #4 grade 60 rebar at top and bottom

26 3" x 8" cardboard voids or footers as per engineer

27 30# asphalt felt, lapped and sealed

28 Brown coat stucco

29 Finished grade

30 Compacted earth fill

31 Sand

32 36" - 6 mil. black visqueen mopped to wall and carried under drain

33 Pea gravel

34 4" perforated ADS pipe to daylight

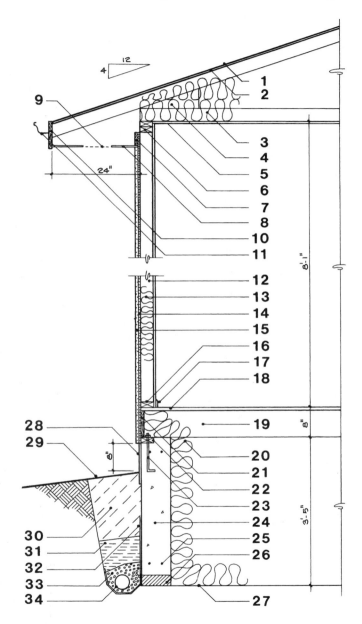

More Than a Cabin

Lake Champlain, New York
1,230 gross square feet

This camp building, located in New York State's Adirondack Park, was developed for a club that was founded in 1890. The building is one of several new prototype camps to be proposed for new development on 1- to 3-acre lots. Most existing buildings in the club were built between 1890 and 1930; some atypical structures/remodels were built in later years.

Sites are on a variable degree slope on the western shore of Lake Champlain, overlooking the lake and the mountains on the opposite shore. The site for the specific design shown is on the shoreline, with an average slope of 10 percent.

Interior Considerations
Interior functions are grouped in four quarters: entry; utility; food preparation; laundry, dining, living, and sleeping.

For summer use, "porch walls" fold away and screens are installed on first-floor porches. By opening all casement windows, combined spaces form one large "porch."

Two axis paths form a direct pattern of circulation, also providing alternate access and privacy, all at the discretion of the dweller.

The long paths, with framed views at each end, and the upper dormer lights, along with interior walls selectively terminating at 6 feet, 6 inches, allow awareness of nature, time, and light at all times of the day, perhaps giving an illusion of grandeur in a very small and humble building.

Nils Luderowski

Perspective

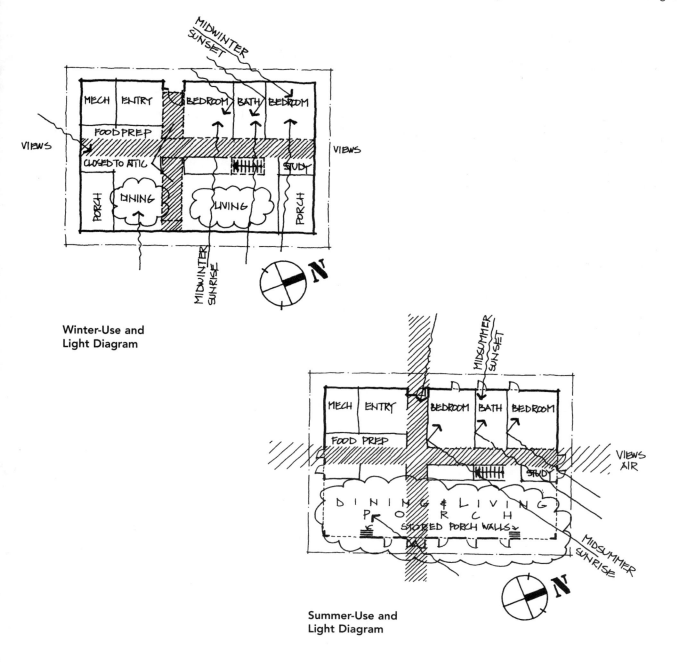

MIDWINTER SUNSET

MECH | ENTRY
FOOD PREP
VIEWS
CLOSED TO ATTIC
PORCH | DINING

BEDROOM | BATH | BEDROOM
VIEWS
STUDY
LIVING | PORCH

MIDWINTER SUNRISE

N

**Winter-Use and
Light Diagram**

MIDSUMMER SUNSET

MECH | ENTRY
FOOD PREP

BEDROOM | BATH | BEDROOM
VIEWS AIR
STUDY

D I N I N G & L I V I N G
P O R C H
STORED PORCH WALLS

MIDSUMMER SUNRISE

N

**Summer-Use and
Light Diagram**

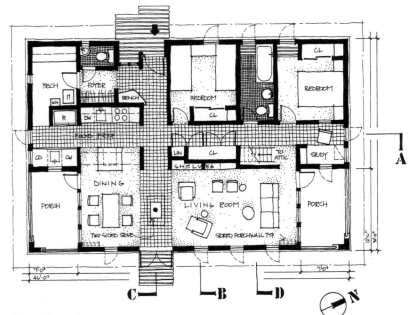

First Floor Plan

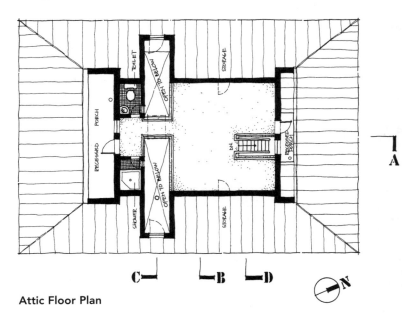

Attic Floor Plan

East Elevation

West Elevation

South Elevation

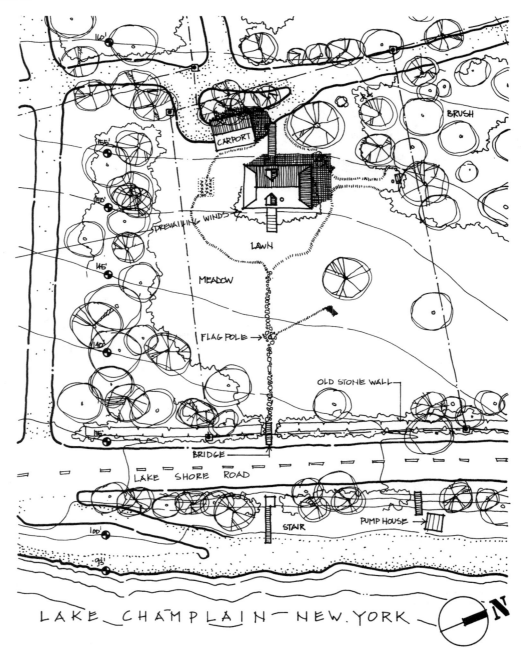

LAKE CHAMPLAIN · NEW · YORK

N

Site Plan

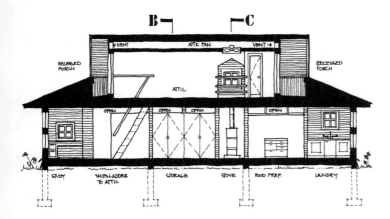

Section A-A

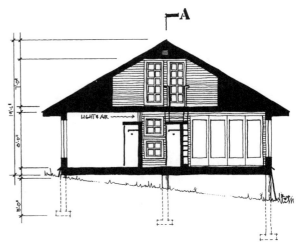

Section B-B

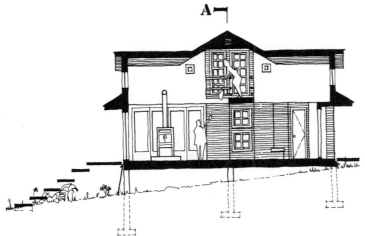

Section C-C

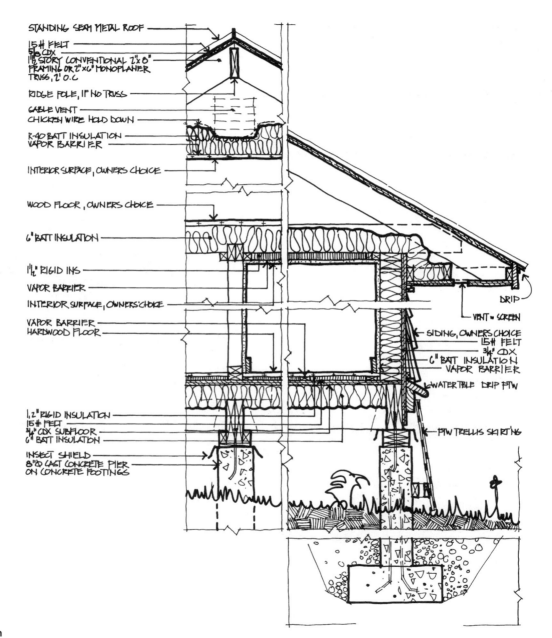

STANDING SEAM METAL ROOF

15# FELT
5⁄8 CDX
1½ STORY CONVENTIONAL 2"x 8" FRAMING OR 2"x 6" MONOPLANER TRUSS, 2' O.C.

RIDGE POLE, IF NO TRUSS
GABLE VENT
CHICKEN WIRE HOLD DOWN
R-40 BATT INSULATION
VAPOR BARRIER

INTERIOR SURFACE, OWNERS CHOICE

WOOD FLOOR, OWNERS CHOICE

6" BATT INSULATION

1½" RIGID INS
VAPOR BARRIER
INTERIOR SURFACE, OWNERS CHOICE

VAPOR BARRIER
HARDWOOD FLOOR

1,2" RIGID INSULATION
15# FELT
¾" CDX SUBFLOOR
6" BATT INSULATION

INSECT SHIELD
8" Ø CAST CONCRETE PIER ON CONCRETE FOOTINGS

DRIP

VENT w SCREEN

SIDING, OWNERS CHOICE
15# FELT
¾" CDX
6" BATT INSULATION
VAPOR BARRIER

WATERTABLE DRIP PTW

PTW TRELLIS SKIRTING

Wall Section

Urban Geometry

Dhaka, Bangladesh
1,050 gross square feet

This compact house is designed for a tropical climate, but it might be implemented with little modification anywhere in the world where justified by the site, access, orientation, etc.

The elevations are simple geometric forms: a rectangle with a vaulted roof, a cube with a pitched roof, square openings, terraces, and an external stair make for varied perspectives from different angles. The whole building is framed by a free-standing column with beam, which creates a homogeneous facade in the urban context.

The most important aspects of this design are the interior circulation, the definition of space (private, semiprivate, public, etc.), and the sequence of space according to its function. The flow of space, the openness of the design, and the different levels create a cozy, intimate home environment.

Atiqur Rahman

Perspective

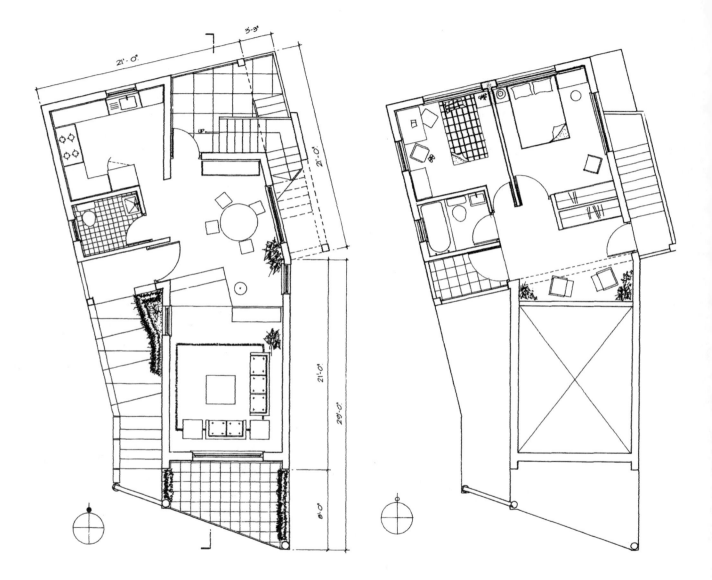

First Floor Plan

Second Floor Plan

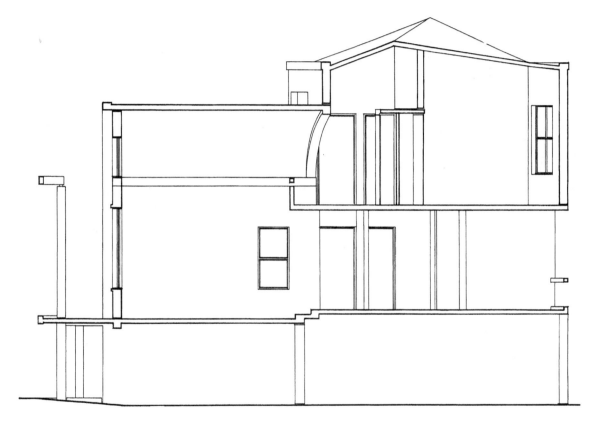

Section

Urban Geometry

South Elevation

East Elevation

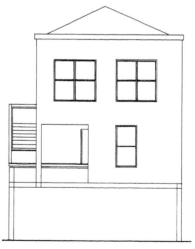

North Elevation

336

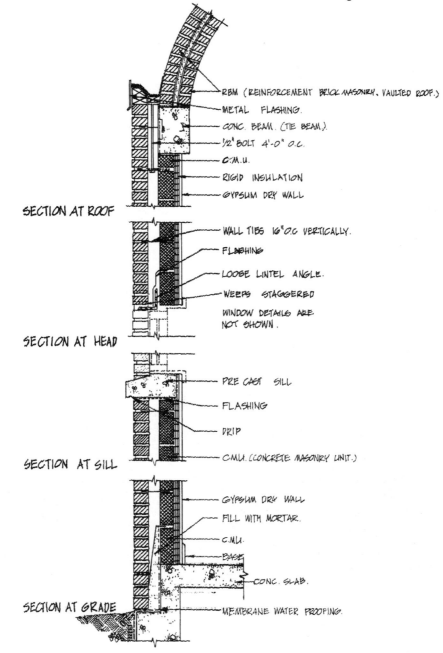

RBM (REINFORCEMENT BRICK MASONRY, VAULTED ROOF.)

METAL FLASHING.

CONC. BEAM. (TIE BEAM.)

½" BOLT 4'-0" O.C.

C.M.U.

RIGID INSULATION

GYPSUM DRY WALL

SECTION AT ROOF

WALL TIES 16" O.C VERTICALLY.

FLASHING

LOOSE LINTEL ANGLE.

WEEPS STAGGERED

WINDOW DETAILS ARE NOT SHOWN.

SECTION AT HEAD

PRE CAST SILL

FLASHING

DRIP

C.M.U. (CONCRETE MASONRY UNIT.)

SECTION AT SILL

GYPSUM DRY WALL

FILL WITH MORTAR.

C.M.U.

BASE

CONC. SLAB.

SECTION AT GRADE

MEMBRANE WATER PROOFING.

Wall Section

Pretty and Practical

Upper Peninsula, Michigan
1,250 (excluding basement and garage)

A pproaching this house from the east, the expansive, linear porch suggests, not a "compact" house, but a large home. This initial perception is carried through the inside of the house with the manipulation of form and space. Through this manipulation the "typical" compact house, often dominated (out of necessity) by function, becomes a creative integration of aesthetics with the functional, cost-saving requirements.

Lisa Raskin

Perspective

Alternate Perspective
(with Garage)

LAKE

ORCHARD

ROOF TERRACE
1250□'

GARAGE

DECIDUOUS TREES

EXISTING ROAD

Site Plan

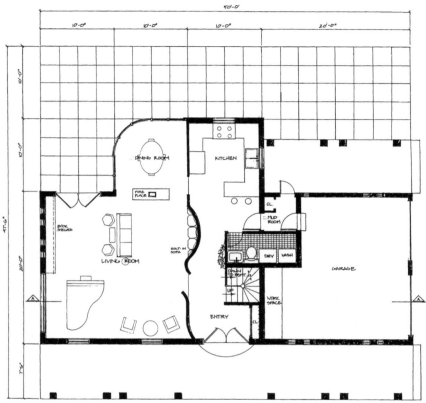

First Floor Plan

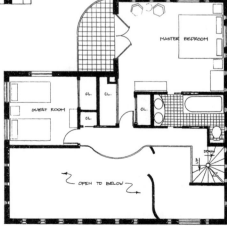

Second Floor Plan

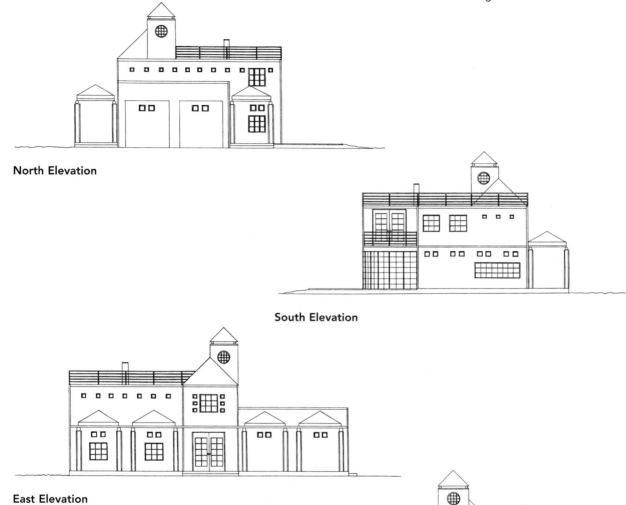

North Elevation

South Elevation

East Elevation

West Elevation

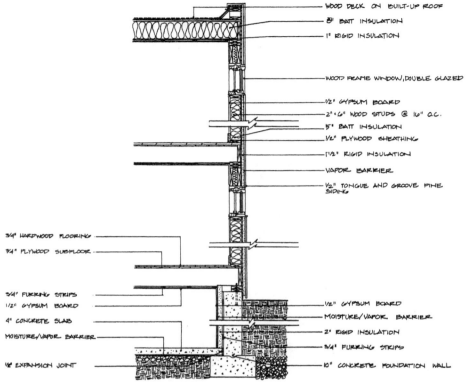

WOOD DECK ON BUILT-UP ROOF

8" BATT INSULATION

1" RIGID INSULATION

WOOD FRAME WINDOW, DOUBLE GLAZED

1/2" GYPSUM BOARD

2"×6" WOOD STUDS @ 16" O.C.

5" BATT INSULATION

1/2" PLYWOOD SHEATHING

1 1/2" RIGID INSULATION

VAPOR BARRIER

1/2" TONGUE AND GROOVE PINE SIDING

3/4" HARDWOOD FLOORING

3/4" PLYWOOD SUBFLOOR

3/4" FURRING STRIPS

1/2" GYPSUM BOARD

4" CONCRETE SLAB

MOISTURE/VAPOR BARRIER

1/2" EXPANSION JOINT

1/2" GYPSUM BOARD

MOISTURE/VAPOR BARRIER

2" RIGID INSULATION

3/4" FURRING STRIPS

10" CONCRETE FOUNDATION WALL

Wall Section

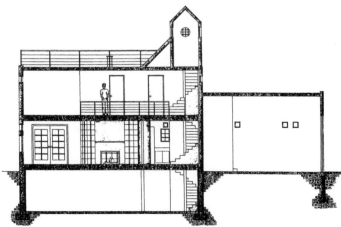

Section

Modern Tudor

Suburbia
1,250 gross square feet

This compact house was designed to be sensitive to contemporary living, yet maintain traditional elegance at the same time. Though cottage-like, there's an aura of stateliness to the exterior appearance. Traditional materials such as brick, wood, and stucco are combined to form a contemporary timber-framed house. Contrary to traditional Tudor-style homes, which use heavy, dark timbers, this design uses timbers that are lighter, both in weight and color.

In keeping with the sophistication of the exterior, the interior projects a formal sense combined with casual living capabilities. Upon entering the house, you're greeted by a stair hall with a cathedral ceiling and a balcony overlook. From here, a narrow passageway opens up into a large living area. The primary living space is comprised of the living room, dining room, and kitchen—all of which contribute to a spacious "great room" atmosphere since there are no partition walls.

Upstairs, a loft hallway looks down on the grand living room fireplace. The second-floor bedroom is cozy with clipped ceilings leading to an octagonal lookout cupola. The master bedroom and bath are richly proportioned with high ceilings, generous storage, and large floor space. The compact house offers the characteristics of a large home with the intimacy of a smaller one.

Thomas Rutkowski

Perspective

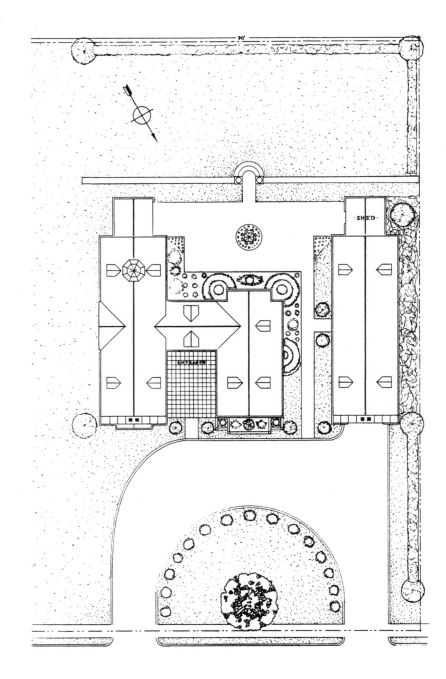

Site Plan

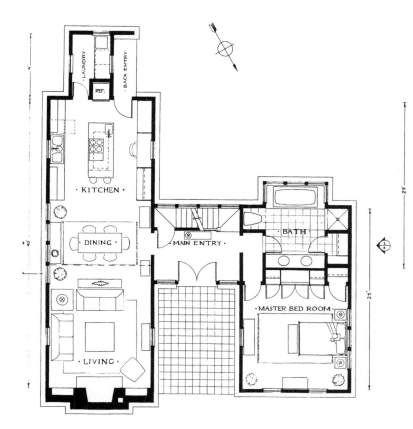

First Floor Plan

· LAUNDRY·

· BACK ENTRY·

REF.

· KITCHEN·

· DINING·

· MAIN ENTRY·

· BATH·

· LIVING·

· MASTER BED ROOM·

23'

25'

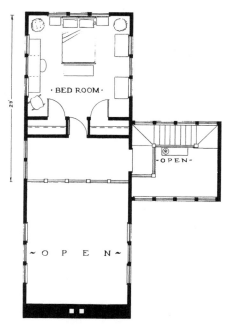

· BED ROOM·

~OPEN~

~ O P E N ~

Second Floor Plan

Modern Tudor

Side Elevation 1

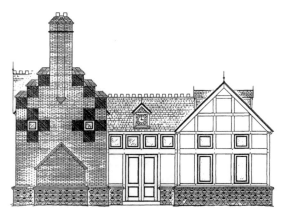

Front Elevation

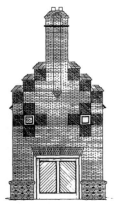

**Optional Garage
with Studio Above**

Rear Elevation

Side Elevation 2

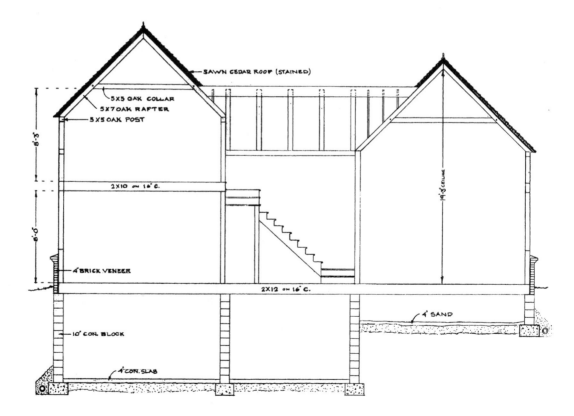

SAWN CEDAR ROOF (STAINED)

5X5 OAK COLLAR

5X7 OAK RAFTER

5X5 OAK POST

8'-3"

2X10 ON 16" C.

19'-3" CEILING

8'-0"

4" BRICK VENEER

2X12 ON 16" C.

4" SAND

10" CON. BLOCK

4" CON. SLAB

Section

Ecology House

North America
1,035 gross square feet (plus 162 sq. ft. greenhouse)

The Ecology House design is a plan designed in collaboration with the New Alchemy Institute of East Falmouth, Massachusetts, as an affordable "starter home" that is energy-efficient and environmentally wise.

The home is designed for maximum energy efficiency for North American temperate and cold climates (above 40° latitude). Energy-efficient specifications include high insulation standards, south-facing windows and greenhouse, and an optional solar hot water system. The double-height living room and open stair provide a simple means by which solar heat is distributed throughout the house. Clerestory windows allow winter sun to reach throughout the interior. The south-facing windows are shaded in summer.

The plan allows three options for arranging the living, dining, and kitchen areas, either as separate areas or combined as a "great room." The greenhouse option—also earth-bermed—provides space for an interior working garden or a sun room/family room. Outside the greenhouse is a wind-protected sun patio. The design is easily adapted to flat or sloped sites and can also be used with attached housing in duplex and triplex arrangements.

Donald Watson

Perspective

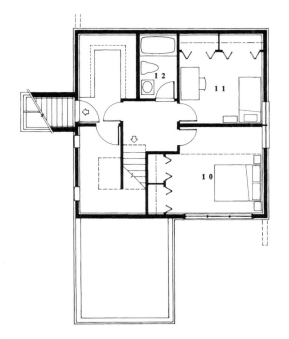

Basement Plan (Future Options)

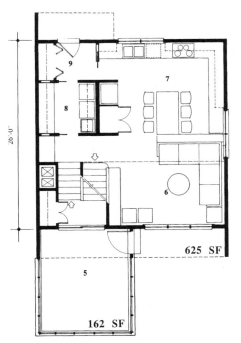

625 SF

162 SF

First Floor Plan

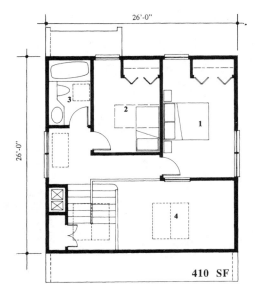

26'-0"

410 SF

Second Floor Plan

349

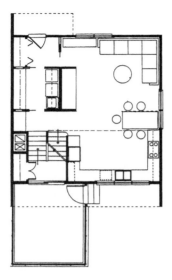

**Plan Option
(Kitchen on South)**

**Plan Option
(Kitchen and Dining)**

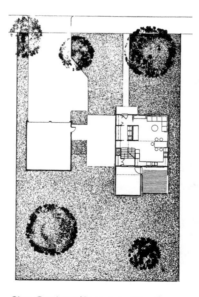

Site Options/Street to North

Site Options/Street to South

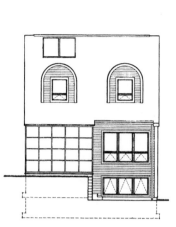

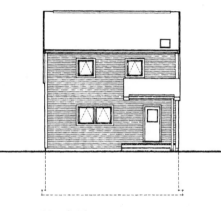

North Elevation

**South Elevation
(Various Options)**

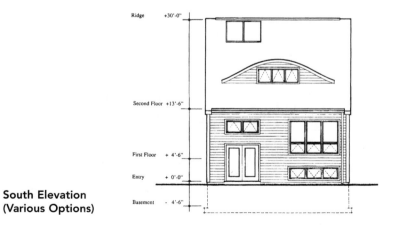

Ridge   +30'-0"

Second Floor +13'-6"

First Floor   + 4'-6"

Entry   + 0'-0"

Basement   - 4'-6"

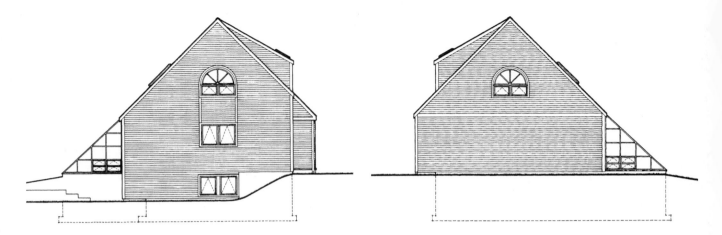

East Elevation

West Elevation

Multi-Family Option (Attached)

Section through Stairwell

Section through Living Room/Kitchen

Ecology House

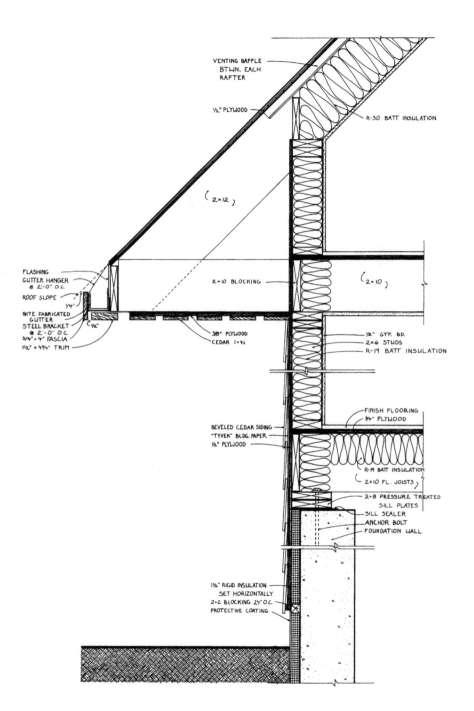

VENTING BAFFLE
BTWN. EACH
RAFTER

½" PLYWOOD

R-30 BATT INSULATION

(2×12)

2×10 BLOCKING

(2×10)

FLASHING
GUTTER HANGER
@ 2'-0" O.C.
ROOF SLOPE ¼"
SITE FABRICATED
GUTTER
STEEL BRACKET
@ 2'-0" O.C.
¾" × 4" FASCIA
1½" × 4¾" TRIM
½"

⅜" PLYWOOD
CEDAR 1×4½

½" GYP. BD.
2×6 STUDS
R-19 BATT INSULATION

FINISH FLOORING
¾" PLYWOOD

BEVELED CEDAR SIDING
"TYVEK" BLDG. PAPER
½" PLYWOOD

R-19 BATT INSULATION
(2×10 FL. JOISTS)
2-8 PRESSURE TREATED
SILL PLATES
SILL SEALER
ANCHOR BOLT
FOUNDATION WALL

1½" RIGID INSULATION
SET HORIZONTALLY
2×2 BLOCKING 24" O.C.
PROTECTIVE COATING

Wall Section

354

Key West Cottage

Key West, Florida
801 gross square feet

This was first inspired ten years ago when I was designing a series of cottages for a Bermuda development. Over the years various versions of this plan have sparked the interest of clients from all parts of North America. Full access front and rear, a bungalow styling, and open living areas make the cottage fit right into most landscapes. For a small building it has an interesting and functional layout.

In any project, my goal is to develop a plan to meet the cultural, personal, and financial requirements of the client. The same floor plan can have many different outcomes in the elevations. With this plan I've provided two alternate possible elevations.

Catherine Treadway,
adapted from her book *Dream Cottages:*
25 Plans for Retreats, Cabins, and Beach Houses

Front Elevation Features, Alternative "A"

- Palladian-style front porch
- Hip-style metal roof
- Nine-foot ceiling on main floor
- Generous glazing with transom windows

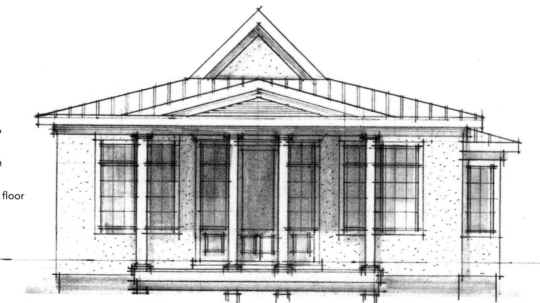

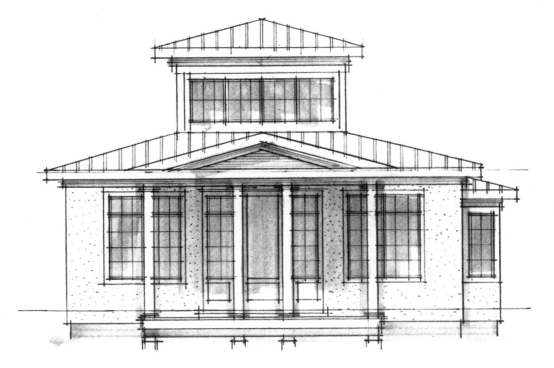

Front Elevation Features, Alternative "B"

- Lookout tower from second-floor loft
- Coastal detailing
- Square columns on optional screened porch
- Clapboard or stucco siding

General Features

356

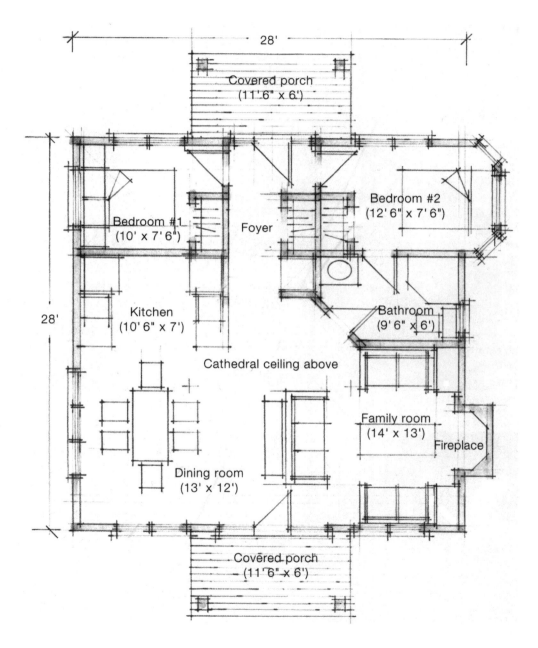

28'

Covered porch
(11'6" x 6')

Bedroom #1
(10' x 7'6")

Foyer

Bedroom #2
(12'6" x 7'6")

28'

Kitchen
(10'6" x 7')

Bathroom
(9'6" x 6')

Cathedral ceiling above

Family room
(14' x 13')

Fireplace

Dining room
(13' x 12')

Covered porch
(11'6" x 6')

Floor Plan

Desert Oasis

Taos, New Mexico
1,088 gross square feet

This cottage is a result of a trip I took to New Mexico a few years ago. I was taken with the purity of adobe structures. The buildings I saw—all set against the fleshy local sand, turquoise sky, and local brown barks—embodied a perfect marriage between built and natural things. Besides that, I just love homes where the inside spills to the outside with lush garden terraces, colorful pottery, and textiles hanging out to air.

This design is inspired by the adobe method, but it could easily be built with more conventional materials. The cottage breaks down distinctions between indoors and out with its multiple French doors, its porches, and its private garden terrace. A fireplace or kiva forms the centerpiece of the open living/dining areas.

I envision high ceilings with round, rough-hewn logs stained white. Saltillo tiles and sisal rugs would cover the floor for an earthy finish.

Catherine Treadway,
adapted from her book *Dream Cottages:
25 Plans for Retreats, Cabins, and Beach Houses*

Front Elevation Features

- Round log detailing
- Decorative upper feature windows
- Galvanized metal roofing on all porches
- Round log columns with bold brackets
- Decorative front entry

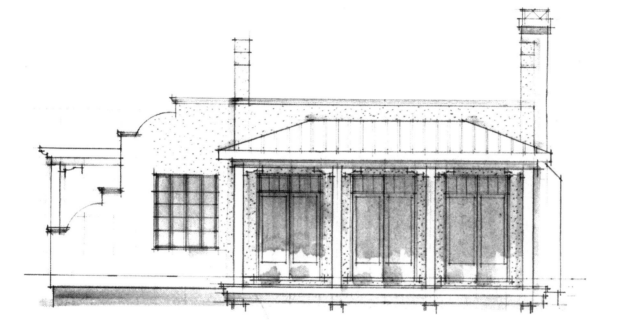

Left Elevation Features

- Full porches front and rear
- Rustic detailing with round raw columns and simple brackets
- Finely detailed transition in terrace area with matching pergola
- High ceilings for transoms above all windows
- Earth tone finishes in stucco or adobe
- Cedar decking

General Features

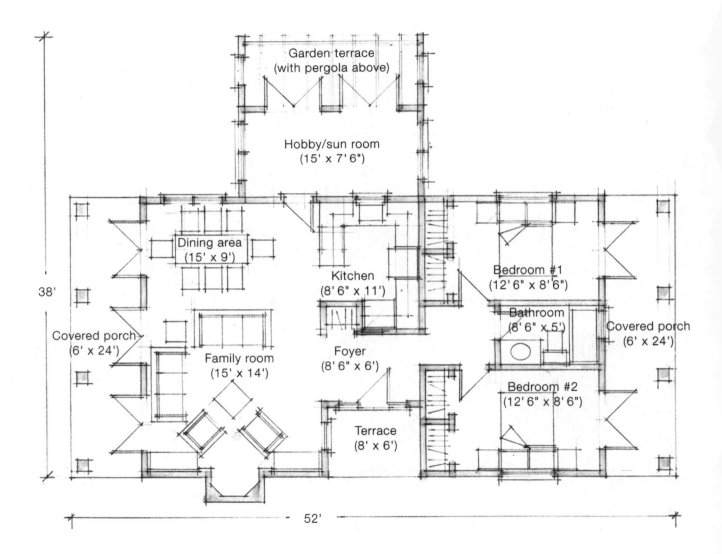

Garden terrace
(with pergola above)

Hobby/sun room
(15' x 7' 6")

Dining area
(15' x 9')

Kitchen
(8' 6" x 11')

Bedroom #1
(12' 6" x 8' 6")

Covered porch
(6' x 24')

Bathroom
(8' 6" x 5')

Covered porch
(6' x 24')

Family room
(15' x 14')

Foyer
(8' 6" x 6')

Bedroom #2
(12' 6" x 8' 6")

Terrace
(8' x 6')

38'

52'

Floor Plan

Contacts

Hasan Akkurt
Akkurt + Akkurt Design
1814 Duff Avenue
Ames, IA 50010

Reed M. Axelrod
Reed Axelrod Architects
2016 Walnut Street
Philadelphia, PA 19103

**Alain Berteau and
Patrick Verougstraete**
496K Chaussee de Waterloo
1060 Brussels
Belgium

Christopher Blake
CBDESIGN
50 Chester Street
Allston, MA 02134

William H. Boehm
369 Congress Street,
8th Floor
Boston, MA 02210

Gerard Bolsega
2832 Grand Boulevard
Highland, IN 46322

Don Buoen
1520 South Evanston
Tulsa, OK 74104

Jeffrey Burton
2251 Canal Street
Oviedo, FL 32765

Michael Clark Connor
28 Chaplin Street
Chaplin, CT 06235

James M. Corkill
3919 Waverly Drive
Norman, OK 73172

David B. DiCicco
School of Design
College of Architecture and
Environmental Design
Arizona State University
Tempe, AZ 85287-2105

Giulio Fabbri
Via Sammartina 12 —
44040 Chiesuol Del
Fosso Ferrera
Italy

Daniel L. Faoro
Department of Architecture
North Dakota State University
P.O. Box 5285
Fargo, ND 58105

Christophe Fayel
15, Rue de la Grande
Armee
13001 Marseille
France

Harvey Ferrero
774 W. Oakridge
Ferndale, MI 48220

Richard B. Ferrier
School of Architecture
Box 19108
University of Texas at Arlington
Arlington, TX 76019

James F. Finigan
Five Lewis Road 1
Winchester, MA 01890

Jeffrey Fleming
Ben Allers Architects
543 28th Street
Des Moines, IA 50312

Michael W. Folonis
Michael W. Folonis
and Associates
1731 Ocean Park Boulevard
Santa Monica, CA 90405

Michael J. Fritschij
2220 DeVries Avenue
Winnipeg, Manitoba
R2E 0E7 Canada

**Graham Smith
and Tina Dhillon**
Smith Architecture
1809 Fir Street
Vancouver, BC
Canada V6J 3A9

Carlo Giuliani
Studio Architetto Carlo
Giuliani
Dorsoduro 623 —
30123 Venezia
Italy

Antonio S. Gomes
Donald Gillespie Architects
325 Columbus Ave. #11A
Boston, MA 02116

Daniel Grandy
Department of Architecture
Ohio State University
189 Brown Hall
Columbus, OH 43210

Jawaid Haider
School of Architecture
Pennsylvania State University
178 W. Hamilton Avenue
State College, PA 16801

Frank Alfred Hamilton
50 Cambridge Ave.
Toronto, Ontario
Canada M4K 2L3

Hammond and Green
Hammond and Green PTY.
LTD.
87 George Street
East Fremantle
Western Australia 6158
Australia

De Petter Hans
Brusselsestraat, 290 Bus 22
3000 Leuven
Belgium

David A Harris
DHT² Architecture/Interiors
P.O. Box 483
Spokane, WA 99210

Thomas McClellan Haskell
26 Ralston Avenue
Hamden, CT 06517

Ulrik Hellum
Eidesten
3267 Larvik
Norway

Nigel A. Holloway
5 Forest Road
Paddock Wood
Kent TN12 6JU
UK

J. Whitney Huber
Box 441
Essex, CT 06426

Stephane Jacq
15, rue Larrey
31000 Toulouse
France

Paul Robin John
1335 2nd Street
Sarasota, FL 34236

Mark and Linda Keane
Studio 1032 Architecture
4200 Lake Drive
Shorewood, WI 53211

Craig King
Firm X
1628 Connally Terrace
Arlington, TX 76010

Kenneth E. King
K Architecture
568 Beatty Street
Vancouver, B.C.
Canada V6B 2L3

Contacts

Tom Leytham
TBLA
50 State Street
Montpelier, VT 05602

Charles H. Ludeke
7185 Shoup Road
Black Forest, CO 80908

Nils Luderowski
66 West Broadway
New York, NY 10007

Mark B. Luther
School of Architecture
and Building
Deakin University
Geelong
Victoria 3217
Australia

Dave Madigan
2970 N. Sheridan #1129
Chicago, IL 60657

Lillian Mei Ngan Mah
Mnemosyne Architecture
7688 Ontario Street
Vancouver, B.C.
Canada V5X 3C5

Olgierd Miloszewicz
Oldi Constructions
71-073 Szczecin
Ul. Ku Sloncu 23
Poland

**Radu Molnar and
Pascal Piccinato**
41, rue du Bon Pasteur
69001 Lyon
France

Geoff K. Nishi
95 Hickory Hill
Tappan, NY 10983

Michael Noble
125–1857 W. 4th Avenue
Vancouver, B.C.
Canada V6J 1M4

Nancy Nugent
11 West 11th St.
New York, NY 10011

Kenneth E. Overstreet, III
84108B N. Central Avenue
Phoenix, AZ 85020

**João Branco Pedro
and José Pinto Duarte**
Av. 1 de Mato, 22, 9D
2500 Caldas Da Rainha
Portugal

Frederick Phillips
53 West Jackson Boulevard
Chicago, IL 60604

Primitivo Emilio Conde
5933 SW 147 Place
Miami, FL 33193

Rammed Earth Works
P.O. Box 5006
Napa, CA 94581

Atiqur Rahman
902 44th Street, D-7
Brooklyn, NY 11219

Lisa Raskin
604 Lakewood Lane
Marquette, MI 49855

Thomas Rutkowski
431 Walnut Street
Spring City, PA 19475

Richard Sammons
111 Bank Street
New York, NY 10014

Madeleine Sanchez
270 Lafayette Street
New York, NY 10012

Todd Alan Sarantopulos
P.O. Box 151
Cascade, CO 80809
Sheng and Lesser Studio
729 Via De Monte
Palos Verdes, CA 90274

Bruce Shindelus
25487 Buckly Drive
Murrieta, CA 92563

W. I. Shipley
21 Zamia Road
Gooseberry Hill
Western Australia 6076
Australia

Tina Shum and Toby Wang
70 Santa Cruz Boulevard
Clear Island Waters
Queensland 4226
Australia

Jan Stipek
Petrska 10/1135
110 00 Praha 1
Czech Republic

Studio of Pacific Architecture
2nd Floor
Hibernian House
89 Willis Street
PO Box 11517
Wellington
New Zealand

Synthesis Architects
P.O. Box 383
Schenectady, NY 12301

Robert Takken
School of Architecture
Queensland Univ. of
Technology
2 George Street
Queensland 4005
Australia

Hideyuki Takita
Institute of Engineering—
Architecture
Kanto Gakuin University
4834 Mutsuura-chyo
Kanazawa-ku
Yokohama 236
Japan

Terra Firma
RR1 Box 371A
Randolph Center, VT
05061

Remus S. L. Tsang
33 Young Street East
Waterloo, Ontario
Canada N2J 2L4

Tim Utt
P.O. Box 153
Old Turnpike Road
South Strafford, VT 05070

Andy Verhiel
Architects Institute of BC
28-1376 Bute Street
Vancouver, B.C.
Canada V6E 2A6

Eric Wagner
27 63rd Street, 2nd Floor
West New York, NJ
07093

John B. Wald
RNL Design
1225 17th Street #1700
Denver, CO 80202

Donald Watson
2 Irving Place
Troy, NY 12180

**Anna Kemble Welch
and Martin Hanley**
Red Design
123 Daniell Street
Newtown, Wellington
New Zealand

Megan Williams
2 Grenville Road
London N19 4EH
UK

Claudia Zanirato
Via Belvedere 7
1-40069 Zolo Predosa
Bologna
Italy